LIGHTS, CAMERA, CANCER!

A FARM BOY'S JOURNEY FROM SOAP OPERA BAD BOY TO CANCER SURVIVOR

LIGHTS, CAMERA, CANCER!

A FARM BOY'S JOURNEY FROM SOAP OPERA BAD BOY TO CANCER SURVIVOR

BY ALAN DYSERT

Blue Isle Media

Lights, Camera, Cancer!

A Farm Boy's Journey From Soap Opera Bad Boy To Cancer Survivor

For speaking engagements or personal appearances, please contact Alan directly at: AlanDysert@ICloud.com

Hardcover ISBN: 978-1-0880-6574-7

Trade Paperback ISBN: 978-1-0880-3305-0

EBook ISBN: 978-1-0880-6587-7

Cover and Interior Book Design: CaligraphicsDesign
https://www.caligraphicsdesign.com/

Book Cover Photography by Herlihy Photography

DEDICATION:

To Michele,

I would not be here today if not for your unconditional love, strength, and determination to keep me alive.

INTRODUCTION

Several years ago, I formed a partnership with an ABC affiliate in Nashville. We intended to create exciting entertainment programming that would first air locally, and then be sold to other affiliates.

The first project (which I didn't really want to do) was Behind the Scenes of All My Children, which involved working with a talented producer named Jennifer. She and a videographer accompanied me to New York, where we shot interviews with the show's actors, producers, and the legendary soap creator, Agnes Nixon. About a month later, I needed some raw footage from the shoot in order to pitch the project to another ABC affiliate. So, I called the station and asked to speak with Jennifer. There was a long pause at the other end of the line.

"I have some bad news," began the station manager.

Jennifer was dead. A brain aneurysm. No warning. Just died one morning in her bathroom, holding a toothbrush. She was only twenty-seven. In an instant, her story ended.

None of us know the day our story ends. But those of us with more years behind us than ahead know that time is not our friend. Whatever we do needs to be done with some sense of urgency. Especially if we want to be the author of our own story.

"I have some bad news" is a refrain I've heard more times than I care to recite. So before I hear any more bad news, I'd like to share my story with you.

* * *

No one knows the life I've lived and nearly lost better than me. And no one appreciates the wild and circuitous ride more than I do. I'm among the lucky ones.

I have no complaints for a farm boy from Illinois. I've had a very full and exciting life. I'm one of the lucky ones and probably didn't appreciate how much so until I was forced to slow down and come to terms with the fact that I'm on the last two days of my vacation on planet earth. It's been a great ride and I am grateful for every bit of it. There was a time when I wasn't—but I am now.

I decided to write this book because I'm the only person in the world who knows more than twenty percent of my journey. I remember most of it and will relate what I would want my children, grandchildren, family and friends to know, so they can celebrate my life when I'm gone, rather than mourn my passing.

My grown sons, now in their early 30s, have heard bits and pieces from me, in addition to what they lived through with me. They've heard many stories that are only partially accurate or exaggerated.

I've found, in my thirty years of teaching young actors, that most kids and teens don't really know, or care, what their parents do for a living. Sad but true. I don't know if my sons are interested in reading the highlights of my life but at least it will be there for them if they are curious.

I do want my grandchildren, who probably won't know me well before I leave the planet, to be able to read about their grandpa, if they so desire. I wish my grandparents had written books about their lives.

I have concerns that the effects of chemotherapy, 29 CT-scans, 2 PET scans, many MRIs, X-rays, and anesthesia from nine surgeries have already damaged my brain and will take a greater toll in the future. So, no better time than now to write the book. I took advantage of the spring COVID-19 lockdown to start the book. For me, it's the one positive that came out of an unbelievably bizarre and horrifying 2020.

But it's all good. I'm here now and I plan to enjoy it.

Chapter 1—No Complaints

I have chased rainbows and tornados and never caught either.

I have lived through one hurricane and had my home devastated by another.

I grew up in a world with fire station fish fries, street dances, school dances, sock hops, homemade ice cream, taffy pulls, drag racing, drive-in movies, county fairs, and Friday night football games.

I was there for the very beginning of rock & roll and Motown Records (the best music ever made).

We sought out places to dance until we were spent from our joyous physical expression. We would dance until we were forced to leave. Parties were pizza, soda, and a record player in a basement. Everyone brought their favorite 45s and we took turns changing them.

I remember the very day The Beatles' music was introduced to America. We went to S.S. Kresge, our local five & dime, where Mom and Dad would allow us to buy our favorite new single record almost every Saturday. The record department of the store was no more than fifteen feet by fifteen feet. Albums were not big in our world, but as I was paying for my newest favorite single, I looked up and saw the Beatles' debut album.

We immediately made fun of their stupid haircuts and laughed about the fact that they spelled "beetle" wrong. Within two weeks, I owned a Beatle wig, Beatle boots, my first guitar, and that album we had made fun of at the five & dime.

My parents enrolled my brother, Terry, and me in voice, piano, and dance lessons at a very early age. Terry was two-and-a-half years older, but Mom put us in the same classes, even if it didn't make sense. She also often dressed us alike: cute but weird. The dance lessons were actually to make us better athletes; they thought Terry was a little clumsy. I wasn't sure why they wanted us to take voice and piano, but I learned later in life that Mom and Dad had both played the violin, loved music and dancing. In his seventies, Dad had Eric Clapton tapes in his El Camino pickup.

I've had some amazing cars in my life. Not because I was rich, but because I saved for them. That was the way I was brought up. We started saving for our first cars when we were young boys. We worked hard because we dreamed of having a "cool car." If I had lived in the 1800s, I would have had an amazing horse, not some old nag.

I went to schools so small I knew every student, their brothers and sisters, and where they lived. I knew who had indoor plumbing and who had an outhouse. It was easier to stand out and feel like you could do big things with your life in an environment like that.

I know what it's like to walk into a grocery store and see my face on the cover of *People* Magazine.

I've been picked up in a limo and driven to a private jet, where I was flown to a private airport, then helicoptered to a mall parking lot where they had taken the glass entrance out so they could drive my limo into the mall and up to the stage, where 3,000 crazed fans sang "Happy Birthday" to me as they unveiled a cake made from 1,500 eggs with a picture of my face on it.

I know what it's like to have The Grateful Dead pick me up at my apartment to ride with them to their gig at Madison Square Garden. Once there, I was on stage but out of the lights, hanging out with Phil Lesh and his wife, Jerry Garcia, and Bruce Hornsby, who was playing keyboards with The Dead at that time. It was a trip. After the gig, we all went to The Plaza Hotel, where they were staying, and had drinks with Robert Palmer.

Late in life, I learned that I'm a descendent of the great Shawnee Chief, Tecumseh, on my mother's side, and John Endecott, the longest serving governor of the Massachusetts Bay Colony, on my dad's side. My grandmother was an Endicott. My brother, Terry, and I are the only two people on earth where these two bloodlines come together. I think this means we're supposed to do something very special—but I haven't figured out what that is yet.

I've driven across the United States six times. I learned something every time. One thing I learned was to turn the radio off and just be with myself.

I have lived in Los Angeles, San Francisco, New York City, Connecticut, Nashville, The University of Illinois, on a farm in Illinois, and I have a home in Perdido Key, Florida.

I was a VIP guest at one of the earliest Space Shuttle landings with my songwriter friend, Thom Bishop, and TV producer Alan Rosen (*Head of The Class* and *Archie Bunker's Place*).

I spent a day and an evening with one of my all-time favorite English music superstars, Peter Noone of Herman's Hermits. Fellow soap star Jensen Buchanan (of *One Life to Live*) and I spent hours hanging out and having drinks with Peter, when Jensen, Peter and I had all been hired to appear at a giant food convention in Orlando. Most people don't know Peter had more #1 hits than The Beatles. Peter then invited us to a special concert he was doing, where he gave us the best seats in the house.

Alan Dysert and Reba McEntire

I know what it's like to have a crazy night with Jimmy Buffett and Hunter Thompson, work with Cheech and Chong, spend three days with Diana Ross and crew, and hang with Gladys Knight. I've consulted and had dinner with Garth Brooks, sang a duet with Reba, shared two bottles of champagne at the Beverly Hills Hotel with John Denver before the Grammys, wrote a song with the legendary Carl Perkins ("Blue Suede Shoes"), taught Miley Cyrus in private sessions, and MC'd a concert with Taylor Swift.

I've taught the craft of personal communications and acting to more than 4,000 people over the past 30 years, more than any coach east of the Mississippi. I've taught in Nashville, Chicago, Indianapolis, St. Louis, Tampa, Naples, Orlando, Memphis, Miami, Atlanta and many other cities.

I built the largest training center for actors, singers, voice-over artists and public speakers in the South.

I've appeared on prime-time television, in movies, and in national commercials.

I've chased whales in Cabo and kayaked in Cancun's alligator alley.

I served as an executive producer on six feature films and recently completed a comedy film I wrote, directed, produced and starred in called *The Senator*. I also have multiple film and TV projects in development that had to be put on hold due to COVID-19.

I have two very smart and fine sons in their thirties who work hard, are entrepreneurial, are good to their mother, have never been nasty to me, and never got into trouble.

I never thought I would live long enough to know my grandchildren, but thanks to my oldest son, Cody, and his wife, Brianna, I am blessed to know my amazing grandson, Jack. In October we welcomed our granddaughter, Camille, into the Dysert family. She is the first girl born into the Dysert family in over 110 years.

I will brag much more about my wife, Michele, later in the book; but if it weren't for her love, support, dedication to keeping me alive, I would not be here today.

I never dreamed I would have such a full and colorful life. I have NO COMPLAINTS.

Chapter 2—Cancer Taught Me How To Dream

My cancer is a very rare one and it has no cure. It can come back at any time—and has come back once already. I've had 29 CT scans and will have them frequently for the rest of my life. I would worry about the radiation, but what am I supposed to do? If I hadn't had regular CT scans in the past, I would be dead from the last recurrence.

Cancer taught me to have dreams: to breath fresh air again, to have no pain without pain medicine, to be allowed to eat food again or drink water (even just a few ice chips), to pee without a catheter, to be able to get out of the hospital bed without help, to get out of the hospital, to be able to walk ten steps, to have a cup of coffee, to not have people feel sorry for me when they looked at me, to be able to sleep in the same bed as my beautiful wife, to go to the gym, to not have neuropathy, to never have chemo or another major surgery again, to play my guitar, to sing again, to teach my students and not have them wonder if I was sick or dying, and to not have my mother find out I had cancer.

I never had a "real dream" like most people. I take that back: I did dream of having a horse when I was a boy. That doesn't count though because I'm talking about big picture dream stuff. But I tried to force many things to be my dream.

I never dreamed of going to college, being a Realtor, a comedian, an actor, a musician, an acting teacher, a corporate trainer, a movie producer, a songwriter, a live concert producer/creator, director, or an art director. These were all opportunities that just came my way and I went with them, or somebody said, "A Guy Like You Should Do This." This has been a major theme—and sometimes problem—in my life.

I've been searching for my purpose on this planet my entire life. One entertainment magazine psychic wrote I was the oldest soul in television, having lived 104 past lives. The next closest was nine: a 95 past-life gap. I found that incredibly weird. To me, it meant I had never managed to get it right, so I had to keep coming back. Maybe I've tried all these different career options in this lifetime as a last-ditch effort to figure out who I really am before I'm allowed to rest.

The day my *All My Children* cast mates brought that magazine with the psychic's article into the makeup room is still fresh in my memory. My fellow cast members were all standing around laughing as they read the stories about actors we knew that supposedly were queens or princes and all kinds of wonderful things in their past lives.

What I read wasn't funny because it all resonated so strongly with me. According to the psychic, I was never a king, prince, or historical figure in any of my past lives. I was a courtier during a particular dynasty in China, an unrecognized poet, a priest in Romanville, France, and a devout pacifist in the early part of the 20th century.

What the psychic had written about me rang true: I had taken all the Chinese history classes I could find at the University of Illinois; I am a songwriter who, at that time, would never show my work to or play for anyone; I had an unusual thing about Catholic churches and would often sit in older Catholic churches by myself when no one was there. I wore a St. Christopher's medal, even though I wasn't Catholic, and I married a Catholic. I have always been a pacifist and I don't shoot animals for food or sport.

As a child, I had negative thoughts and nightmares about living "forever and ever in heaven with God." At church it was presented as a good thing, but I wanted to know if there was an end, when I could rest. That's odd for a child to think about. It seems like the thought process of an elderly person.

What if the psychic was right? Could it be that I didn't get life right in 103 attempts, and this is my last go around? In that case, I'd better get busy and learn all the lessons I can.

Chapter 3— Ten Lessons Learned & Things I Didn't Know Before

Lesson #1: Someone always has it worse…

I was unhappily sitting on a bench in front of the Apple Store waiting for an appointment at the Genius Bar to resolve an aggravating issue with my MacBook. I was feeling sorry for myself and pissed off that I needed another surgery and the neuropathy pain from chemo was driving me crazy. Then I looked up and I saw a young man rolling out of the store operating his wheelchair by blowing into a tube, with no ability to use his hands or legs. He had the biggest smile on his face; he was so incredibly happy and excited about the new computer sitting on his lap. He smiled at me as I watched him roll by me blowing into the tube that commanded his wheelchair. I watched him until he was out of sight. Then I slapped myself in the face and swore right then and there I would never ever feel sorry for myself again. Someone always has it worse.

Lesson #2: Being the guy no one wants to be…

I know what it's like to be the guy trying to walk down the hall of the hospital with his ass hanging out with nine tubes coming out of his body, hanging on to an IV tower, with people looking at him like he's the most pitiful looking person they've ever seen.

Lesson #3: Stuff means nothing…

As I was projectile vomiting in my hospital bed, and the frantic nurses were explaining to me I might die if they didn't immediately insert an NG tube into my nose, down my throat, through my esophagus, and into my stomach without any pain medication or anesthesia, I realized stuff means nothing. If I died right then and there, I was leaving the planet alone, wearing a hideous hospital gown, with nobody to say "I love you and goodbye" other than total strangers.

Lesson #4: I'm very hard to kill...

Between cancer, car wrecks, motorcycle wrecks, childhood diseases, stupid stunts, tornadoes, a storm at sea, and lack of respect for my body/temple, I should have been dead by now. But I'm not.

Lesson #5: When death is a real possibility...

You learn what means nothing and what means everything.

Lesson #6: Fighting for your life makes everything else seem dull...

I believe I made that up; there is a possibility I read it somewhere or heard it on TV. I wrote it in the notes app of my phone when I was going through some bad health stuff and possibly on pain meds.

Lesson #7: It's not about money...

I watched my mother slowly going through the dying process in the nursing home. Never once did it matter to her that she was richer than 99.9% of the people on the planet.

Lesson #8: I'm living proof...

I am living proof of the possibilities and the marvels of modern medicine in the hands of very gifted and dedicated men and women. They saved me as God guided their hands.

Lesson #9: A "God Thing" is a real thing...

I will never be convinced that "luck" caused me to jump on the abdominal machine that I had never used in three years, that led me to discover the large tumor in my abdomen. I remember the voice in my head saying, "Why haven't you ever used that oblique machine? You should try it out, Alan."

I will never be convinced it was luck that I just happened to have a pathologist from Johns Hopkins Hospital who took acting classes from me, who had the ability to set me up with the best cancer and oncological/reconstructive surgeons at Johns Hopkins to save my life.

And I will never be convinced that God didn't have a hand in bringing my wife, Michele, into my life to love me, nurse me, be my health advocate when I was not able, travel with me, feed me, make sure I took my supplements, held my hand, changed my bandages, and all kinds of other gross stuff. No one could have done more. She truly stood by her man and refused to let go of me. She refused to let me see her cry. That's why I'm here today to write this book.

Lesson #10: First Class Won't Save Your Ass When The Plane's Going Down...

I don't think this one needs any explanation.

CHAPTER 4—THE PEOPLE WHO MADE ME

My mother was a very fast driver. Ninety was not unusual. No seat belts, metal dashboards, and we still lived through it. Even with the distractions of Terry and I fighting in the back seat, she still managed to maintain her speed as she tried to swat us to get us to stop. Cars were big in those days, so it was hard for a 5'2," 120 pound woman to reach two boys in the back seat trying to dodge her swats.

The only thing that would stop us were her frequent threats like, "I will stop this car, pull your pants down alongside the road, and spank you where everyone can see." It never happened because we actually stopped fighting, realizing she was mad enough to possibly do it. Mom often said, "I will wash your mouth out with soap." That one I did experience. Soap does not taste good, even if it is 99 and 44/100 percent pure and floats.

This was an era when spanking was not just allowed, it was expected. It was the main instrument of discipline, even in schools. I could always tell my parents hated doing it, but it was considered their duty. For Mom, the device of choice was a wooden yardstick. For Dad, it was the plastic belt. Just so you know, a plastic belt stings much more than a leather belt. "Go get the plastic belt," were words that struck fear in us. It only happened a few times that I can remember because the memory of the last time was enough to keep us in line. It was obvious that Dad hated doing it. They seemed to experience guilt after we were punished. We were spanked (given a whoopin' as they used to say) but not brutally by any means. Just enough to make us not want it to happen again.

Mom started making scrapbooks to chronicle our lives from the time we were very young. I thought it was strange back then, but now I'm amazed at the detail and love she put into the amazing scrapbooks that document the first 40 years of my life. She assembled six very large books about my life including: photos, report cards, newspaper articles about sports achievements, and any and every important event in my life. You can see and feel the love she put into those six volumes that chronicle my life.

Mom had a great sense of humor and loved to laugh. She was also very creative but really didn't have an outlet for it. She was a very kind woman and was extremely protective of her two sons. You had better not say anything bad about her sons, or hurt them in any way, or you would see the lioness come out in my mother. We could do no wrong outside our family home environment as far as she was concerned. She loved her sons and her husband with all her heart.

Caffeine was her only drug of choice, even though she was very caffeine sensitive. It really wasn't good for her, but she loved the buzz. She could out clean any human on earth after she drank a half-pot of percolated Maxwell House. Our house was always spotless and tidy. She didn't want us to pick up or put our clothes away because nothing was worn twice. She would tell us to drop it on the floor where we took it off. This was a tough habit to break in my twenties when there was no one there to pick my clothes up or wash them for me. I guess we were spoiled. But I have learned.

Mom didn't just wash our clothes; she starched and ironed everything. Underwear, sheets, socks, jeans—everything. Starched jeans and sheets are really rough for the first few hours. I would always be bummed out when I realized Mom had changed the sheets.

If you threw a Kleenex in the bathroom trash can, and then came back ten minutes later, that Kleenex would have magically disappeared. Mom thought that was normal.

She didn't just clean the windows of our house; she waxed them with a product called Glasswax. It was like car wax for windows and just as hard to rub off. It was a major undertaking because our house had lots of windows. She would enlist the help of a wonderful woman, Violet Cunningham, to help her with this twice per year project. Violet was also a world class cleaner. She helped Mom until the day Mom died at age 91 in 2018.

Somehow, Mom managed to always "have her face on" when we got up. It was magic. It was like the Merle Norman genie came by at 4:00 A.M. and "did her face." I don't think I ever saw her putting her makeup on.

She was very pretty and had a twinkle in her eye until the day she died. She really didn't need much in the way of makeup, but that's what they did in her era: lots of foundation, powder, rouge, lipstick—the works. Dad liked the way mom "did her face" and always said that no matter how broke we were, Mom had a blank check for the Merle Norman store.

Mom weighed in at 120 pounds and always looked fit, even though I never saw her exercise in my life. She was probably able to achieve this by doing lots of housework, gardening, canning in the early years, cooking three full meals each day, and washing tons and tons of laundry in the basement that meant lots of stair climbing. Of course, there were the ironing binges to keep her arms in shape.

* * *

Our farm, which I now manage and co-own with my brother, Terry, was about 220 acres of some of the richest soil in the Midwest. Dad also leased about 400 acres that was owned by local folks that weren't farmers or had aged out of farming.

We also had a very nice wooded valley with a big creek/small river, artesian well, and Indian burial grounds.

Dad didn't become a farmer because he was following in his father's footsteps. His father was a coal mine manager in Southern Indiana. But after living the life of a soldier in WWII, he didn't want people telling him what to do all the time. He felt that working on his grandfather's farm would give him the freedom and independence he needed after four years of serving in the Army during the war. Dad wasn't big on authority figures: maybe that's where I inherited that trait.

As a child, Dad spent his summers on his Grandpa Endicott's farm in Central Illinois. From the stories I heard, his mother didn't want him around all summer, so she shipped him off to the farm. He loved everything about the farm and of course his grandparents spoiled him. He had a pony he could ride whenever he wanted, and he loved being around the sheep and other farm animals. Grandpa Endicott's house was big and had a large porch where they would often spend the evenings in rocking chairs, enjoying doing nothing, smelling freshly cut grass or hay, feeling the breeze, hearing the sheep baaing, and eating his Grandma Nettie's cookies with milk before re-tiring for the evening.

Dad and Grandpa Endicott had put together a plan, long before Dad got back from the Philippines, for Dad and Mom to move to Illinois and manage the farm. This also meant he would be doing much of the actual farm work.

Dad and Mom, like so many young wartime couples, eloped two weeks before Dad was shipped off to boot camp. Mom was only 17 and Dad was 18. She had just graduated from high school and was working in an insurance office. Dad had been working in a wartime plant in Evansville, Indiana, that built tank landing ships, called LSTs. LSTs were used for amphibious operations by carrying tanks, vehicles, cargo and landing troops directly onto shore where there were no docks or piers.

When they eloped, they needed two people to stand up for them, so her sister, Lorene, who was just one year older than Mom, and her husband, Nolan, went with them across the Indiana state line into Kentucky where they were married by a justice of the peace. Lorene and Nolan had also eloped not long before; Mom and Dad had stood up for them in Kentucky as well. Nolan, who was dad's friend, was also being shipped off to war.

It was a very different time. It was a romantic idea to get married and see your man go off to war just like they had seen in so many movies. I believe it was often a way for the men to keep their girlfriends from dating while they were gone, and to have someone to write to and dream about coming home to after the war. I understand this idea, but it was selfish. Sometimes the men were up to "mischief" overseas while the women worked for the war effort back home and weren't allowed to go anywhere there would be other men. At least that was the experience for Mom and Lorene. They were living with their parents, who made sure their married daughters weren't out gallivanting around town.

Mom actually moved to the farm in Illinois months before Dad came home from the war. She hated being there without Dad. She waited in a little house in the country writing letters and waiting for her man to come home to her so they could get on with the future they had planned together.

He surprised her once by coming home much earlier than she had thought: He managed to get a thirty-day leave. That was the good news. The bad news was that he had signed up for another two-year hitch and would be going back to the Philippines. He told Mom the Army offered him a month at home to be with his wife, if he signed up for another hitch. If he didn't, he might not get home for a year-and-a-half anyway, since there were so many soldiers to ship back at the end of the war. He would also get a big raise in pay and a bonus. It all seemed a little fishy to me, but I will never know the facts.

Dad was military police, an MP. His job was to guard American prisoners who had committed major crimes in the Philippines. Dad did contract malaria in the Philippines and had health issues from it for many years after the war. He had nightmares about things that happened while he was there, but he wouldn't talk about them. He also had back problems caused when his tank crashed and rolled over during training exercises. I never heard him complain about the malaria attacks or the pain in his back. He considered himself very lucky never to have been in combat.

Chapter 5—Shepherds For Over 100 Years

Dad never wanted or encouraged us to be farmers. He wanted us to go to college and be whatever we wanted to be, just like he had done.

He didn't make us work in the fields unless he paid us. He didn't believe in having children to supply your farm operation with free labor. Many of the local farmers would have their kids on tractors by eight or nine years of age. We had a family friend whose son fell off of a tractor and ran over himself. He lived, but another boy in the community wasn't so lucky. He fell off the tractor in the field and died when he was run over by the plow attached to the tractor.

At that time, tractors were much more dangerous than they are now. They didn't have fancy seats, air conditioned cabs, radios and TVs like they do now. They also didn't cost upward of $400,000. There were no safety belts or safety guards. You had to hang on to the wheel for dear life. Another common hazard was getting an arm or leg caught in a piece of equipment. If you got a piece of clothing caught in a rotating machine, it had devastating results. Many farmers have lost an arm, hand, or leg in farm machinery.

Alan (left) and Terry at the Illinois State Fair

Dad hired seasoned men who had worked around farms and farm equipment for years. This way he protected his children and his equipment.

I did drive the grain truck during harvest time when Dad needed me. He would load the truck from the combine with corn or soybeans. Then I would drive it into town to the grain elevator where they weighed it, tested it for moisture, and then I would dump it in the bin to be sold or stored. I really enjoyed being a part of the harvest like that.

The local farm women thought Terry and I were always sick because Mom kept us too clean. They said, "Those Dysert boys are always sick because Faye (my mother) didn't let 'em eat enough dirt." Mom probably was too concerned about us getting dirty.

Maybe we should have eaten more dirt.

The real problem was that we were allergic to just about every plant, grass and tree on the farm. Dust was another big factor as well as all the toxic chemicals that we now know are extremely harmful to humans, not to mention carcinogenic.

Sometimes a couple of the boys would tease us about not being trusted to do the plowing or harvesting. But they couldn't push it too far, since we were bigger and stronger than they were. There was only so much crap we would take.

Dad didn't pay us for the work we did with our flock of sheep, since that business was ours. He supervised everything, but we were the ones that got up early in all kinds of weather to do the feeding and tending of our registered show flock of English Suffolks.

We were in 4-H, and part of the program was to keep herd records and do the bookkeeping for our sheep business. It was great training for us at such a young age. We learned "you can't spend it if you don't have it without going into debt." If we bought an expensive ram or ewe for breeding, we needed to have a plan to make it pay off on the breeding side of our business. I'm sure Dad secretly supplemented our business's income at times, but he always let us feel like we were real businessmen.

We made quite a bit of money (for kids) showing our sheep at county, regional, and state fairs during the summers. This taught us a lot about competition, showmanship, and being prepared for the big moment. We had special clothes we wore that had the name of our business printed on them, "Dysert Bros. Registered Suffolks."

We were gypsies during the summers. We lived at the fairgrounds during the fair season. Dad had the local tent and awning company make a tent that fit the back of his large grain truck. It had electricity, two cots, room for our hanging clothes, and a large trunk for other clothes and grooming supplies. I felt like a big boy since I was probably only nine- years-old at the time we started living at the fairgrounds during fair season.

I wanted to be a rancher and have horses or at least cattle, but our family had been in the sheep business for generations. My brother and I were the fourth generation of shepherds. Even though I never knew a day in my early life when we didn't raise sheep, I never knew or asked why we did it. It was just something we did. One day, when I was about eight, Dad asked me if I wanted to ride to the "sale barn" to take a load of lambs to market. I jumped at the chance because I had never been to the sale barn. I never really understood what "the market" was, even though I had heard Dad talk about it many times.

We loaded up a truck load of lambs that were sale weight (110 to 120 pounds) and drove to the sale barn where sheep and other livestock were sold based on their weight and quality. It was very exciting to see all the farmers unloading their livestock. The livestock were auctioned in the auction pit, which was like a small arena.

After the auction, Dad said we should get something to eat, since it was lunchtime. There was a small diner in the auction barn, so we headed in and sat at the counter. I remember looking up at the menu that was posted on the wall behind the counter; and one of the choices was a "lamb sandwich."

That hit me like a sledgehammer. At that moment, I realized why we were raising lambs and what was going to happen to that load of lambs we just unloaded. I had never thought of it before. Suddenly, it all made sense: we raised sheep so they would have lambs, and so we could fatten them up and then sell the lambs to people who would eat them.

I did not order a lamb sandwich that day. To this day, I do not eat lamb.

CHAPTER 6—SPORTS WERE A BIG DEAL

Sports were a big deal in our family. Dad never missed one of our basketball, football or baseball games. He was always the loudest fan there and a couple of times was threatened to be kicked out of the gymnasium. He would get very agitated and scream at certain basketball referees. I'm sure they didn't look forward to having him in the stands. He was pretty over-the-top, but it was nice to know that he cared and was having a great time. I think it was an escape from the pressures of farming and politics.

He didn't come to our track meets, but he had great excuses since our meets were always in the afternoons during the busiest part of the year for farming and meetings for the county. I don't think he was very big on track and field, but he never expressed it. He was always there to congratulate us after a meet. He was proud that I set shot-put records for the county, conference, and my high school.

I was a shot put and discus guy. I started throwing the shot put and discus while in elementary school after watching the Olympics on television. It was one of those things Terry and I could do for hours in our expansive front yard until our arms would feel like they were going to fall off.

I continued to throw the discus in high school, but the shot put was my thing. For some reason I started throwing the shot put in the fourth grade. I believe it was a Zen or Taoist sort of thing for me. Something I could do by myself and just focus mind and body on this one thing for less than three seconds. I would sometimes throw for a couple of hours at a time. Fortunately, it did not do any damage to my right shoulder. However, my left shoulder was blown out in football.

I have held my high school shot put record for 50 years. It is actually one of the oldest records in Central Illinois sports. Not that anyone cares, but it means something to me.

Baseball was the one sport I believe I could have played pro. I was the league's "Home Run King." I was a pitcher my last two years of little league. I'd played second base up until then, but as I got older, I was a pitcher. I was very fast, but very wild at times. I never really had anyone to coach me on my pitching, so I was just throwing fast balls all the time.

But once I hit a batter, I started to lose control of my pitches, fearing I would hit another kid. Once I hit eight kids in one game. The mothers of the opposing team were booing and screaming for my coach to take me out because I was killing their kids. But my coach wouldn't take me out. In the end, his approach worked; the kids were so scared they were going to get hit by one of my fast balls, they backed up and never swung at the ball. That fear helped us win the league tournament.

* * *

Alan's 8th Grade Basketball Photo

I, like my dad, was basketball obsessed. We had an outdoor court and an indoor half court. Dad had a concrete floor poured in one of our equipment sheds big enough to play half court basketball, complete with a drop-down fiberglass backboard and rim. We played all the time. When there was no one to play one-on-one, 21, or horse with me, I shot by myself for hours. During one obsessive period, I wouldn't come in until I made twenty free throws in a row.

All the practice paid off because I ended up being a very good elementary school player. I scored more points than any other player in our conference during my 6th, 7th and 8th grade years, and I averaged 74% from the free throw line. I have the trophy to prove that. I don't think of this as bragging. I think of it as proof that practice makes perfect. I practiced so much that muscle memory just kicked in and did the work. I suppose it didn't hurt that I was almost six-feet tall by the time I was a 7th grader, which was considered pretty tall in the 60s.

As a tall, high scoring, good rebounding team leader every year since the 5th grade, the high school coaches scouted me during my 7th and 8th grade years. This meant the high school coaches were waiting for me when I got there.

Unfortunately, my first high school basketball season started out with me on crutches from a knee injury sustained during the last week of football. Luckily, I didn't have to try out for the team since they had seen me play a lot in elementary school. They just put me on the team and waited for me to heal.

I did continue to play basketball my junior year, but by then I had years of football behind me. Playing football had made me extremely aggressive and too physical on the basketball court. I actually fouled out once in six minutes of play. That may be a record.

* * *

At our school, athletes were not allowed to sit out a season. If you wanted to play basketball, you had to either play football or run cross- country. In the 1960s, the word "jog" didn't even exist. Nobody I knew ran for fun or sport. The idea of running over three miles every practice and meet sounded like torture to me. I decided to play football so I'd be allowed to play basketball. They probably established that rule because our school was so small they needed anyone that was athletic to participate in as many sports as possible to fill the rosters of all sports.

I started high school at 6'2" and 170 pounds. By the end of my sophomore year they had me up to 210. Even though I had never planned to play football, I guess my competitive nature and desire to please the coaches kicked in. I became a serious football player.

I actually started enjoying football during my freshman year, but the very last week of the season I sustained a bad knee injury in practice. One of the older linemen taunted me by saying, "Let's see how far you get if I don't block my man." I thought he was kidding, but it turned out he wasn't. The defensive player hit my left knee from the side at full speed. That was it for my football season and it didn't look good for basketball. The doctor put me on crutches and told me to stay off that leg for weeks and hope it healed without surgery.

I played fullback on offense and middle linebacker on defense. Playing both ways is exhausting because you never come off the field unless you're knocked out of the game with an injury, or you're taken out of the game for making a big mistake.

Coaches didn't worry much about our injuries. We were expected to stay in the game unless we couldn't get up. I was knocked out once and they just brought out the smelling salts, cracked them open, and waived it under my nose until I regained consciousness. Then they got me back on my feet and shoved me back on the field. We had never even heard of a concussion.

By the time I was a senior I was a solid 218 pounds. I was co-captain of the team and expected to do anything possible to help our team win. I wanted to win, but I also wanted a football scholarship to a good college. To achieve this I needed to make sure my statistics were great. But our coach asked me to play defensive and offensive tackle for two games because our big tackle was injured. We didn't have a good backup for him. We did have a good backup for me. The coach asked me to take one for the team as co-captain, knowing it would seriously damage my statistics and my chances for consideration for state honors.

In the end, however, I decided not to play college football at all. I wasn't excited about the smaller colleges that made offers for me to play running back; and the big schools wanted to take me up to 250-260 pounds and make me a guard. I wasn't fast enough for a Big Ten running back but I had very good speed for a guard. There was also the fact that I had shoulder, ankle, and knee injuries the colleges didn't know about.

I started questioning why I even wanted to play football in college. I had to admit I really wasn't passionate about it and realized I might be doing it because it sounded cool.

Not playing college football was one of the most honest and wise decisions I made in my life. I had enough injuries: I still suffer from them today. I can't imagine if I had played four years of college football.

Chapter 7—Politics Were Big In Our Family

Dad was a serial joke teller who was kind and friendly to everyone; it didn't matter who they were, their ethnicity, what they did, Republican or Democrat. He said hello to everyone he passed on the street and gave everyone the "finger wave" when he passed them in his car or truck. I would often ask him, "Who was that?" and he would respond, "I don't know."

Dad started his political life when I was around seven or eight. The first office he ran for was Township Supervisor. He held this position for many years and ended up being the Chairman of the Vermilion County Board of Supervisors for many years. Later he was elected County Treasurer for two terms.

The local Republican party had planned for him to run for the United States House of Representatives from Illinois's 15th Congressional District, when Leslie Arends, the House Republican Whip, decided to retire. Unfortunately, Dad had a heart attack and a triple bypass operation the year before Leslie retired. Dad was only forty-six at the time. At that point, Mom and Dad decided he would live a lot longer if he stayed in local politics and gave up any aspirations of being part of the national political scene.

* * *

In 1973, Dad was in the hospital for an intense month after having his triple bypass operation. Dad was only 48 at the time. At that time, bypass surgery was very new and risky. Now, open heart patients are often in the hospital for only three to five days.

His surgery was late in the summer, so it was nearing time to harvest the soybean and corn crops. Without being asked, local farmers showed up at our farm and harvested all our crops with their combines and trucks, using their fuel, and never wanting a penny for it.

That's the way it is there to this day. I can still call people I've known for 60 years and ask them to check on something at the farm or go into the homestead, where nobody has lived for the last eight years, and check on the furnace or water heater. They just do it because they know they can call on me if they need help.

Decades later, I got a call from a man back home asking if I could donate something to be auctioned at a benefit for a guy I'd known my whole life, Marvin Duden. I remembered watching Marvin play basketball when he was in high school. He was a star, and I was in awe of him when I was in elementary school. I, like the people I grew up with, wanted to do all I could to help out. Through my clients and contacts, I managed to put together thirty-eight auction items from many of the biggest stars in country and Christian music, as well as from the soap opera world.

The auction was held at the local volunteer fire station and a considerable amount of money was raised with the auction. They had me help the auctioneer since I knew everything about the items I had brought, as well as who had donated them.

When you're known from television, a lot of people think you will forget where you came from. But I will never forget the community that helped shape who I am today and who I will be until the day I die.

My parents were sitting in the front row at the auction. I will never forget the look of pride on Dad's face when he saw what I had done for Marvin and the community I grew up in. He was beaming.

That was the last time I ever saw my dad. He passed away shortly after that. I think it's such a blessing that I was able to make my dad so proud of me the last time I saw him.

Chapter 8—Classmates, Community And Church

Our community was as stable as they come. I have photos of me with Kevin Green and Judith Brothers, two of my classmates from first grade through high school graduation, napping in cribs together. Our mothers were friends from the time we were born until they died. They were in "G and B Club" together for years. For some reason, I never asked what "G and B Club" stood for until fifty years later; Mom was shocked that I didn't know it stood for "Girls and Babies Club," as if everyone in the world knew that. I still see Kevin and Judy sometimes when I'm back home, usually at a class reunion or a funeral.

As I mentioned before, most of my original nine first grade classmates went all the way through grade school (we didn't call it elementary school) and high school together. That's stable.

I had my first girlfriend, Mary Jo Hendricks, in the second grade. She was a year older, which made me very cool. Her parents owned the little grocery store in our tiny town of less than one hundred. I still see Mary Jo at funerals. She would often visit Mom when she was in the assisted living facility.

We had a milk break in the morning. This was a big deal, especially if it was your turn to go to the cafeteria for the milk run. Everyone had their regular order. Mine was two chocolate milks. To this day, I can remember who drank chocolate milk and who drank white milk. Kevin and Judith were the only ones to order white milk every day. I wondered, "What kind of weirdo would choose to drink white milk when they could have chocolate milk," especially since we never had chocolate milk at home. Maybe Kevin and Judith were ahead of their time and realized the chocolate milk was loaded with sugar.

Another big deal was getting to raise or take down the flag on the giant flagpole in front of the school. It was the small things that felt big back then. Folding the flag had to be done perfectly or you never got a second chance. I wasn't the greatest flag folder but I was never fired from the job.

* * *

Some of my earliest memories are of going to church in the small town of Oakwood, Illinois. Oakwood was two miles from our farm, and had a population of about 700, until the trailer park was developed. The trailer park contributed to the town's population as well as the increase in crime; but nothing one part-time police officer couldn't handle.

Our little Methodist church was very small, and on a summer Sunday, we might only have twenty to twenty-five churchgoers in attendance. Of course, on Easter, Christmas, and Mother's Day they would need to open the annex to fit all the "sometime Christians."

We didn't get the best of pastors. We were like one of the "farm teams" of the Methodist Church. They would send us all the new, inexperienced, weird, or soon to be excommunicated preachers. If they turned out to be really good, they were moved up to the major leagues of the Methodist Church and we were left waiting for the next new recruit.

Sometimes, they would send us an older preacher that had serious "problems" at another church. I'm sure the church board never got the whole story, but sometimes those "problem" preachers would have the same "problem" at our church. Usually, this would have something to do with the wife of a church member that needed special spiritual guidance.

My great-grandfather, Frederick Lincoln Endicott, and a few others built our church over 100 years ago. It's the kind of church where everyone knows which pew is theirs. The hymnals in our pew had our names embossed on them because we donated them to the church.

The large gold cross at the front of the church was in memory of my Grandpa George Dysert, who died before I was born. Grandpa George was the manager of a coal mine in Southern Indiana and dropped dead on an Indianapolis street at age forty. I think he may have been a heavy smoker and maybe a fairly big drinker, although that was only suggested in my later life. I always felt like there was much more to that story than we were told.

* * *

I called my great-grandfather, Fred Endicott, Grandpa since Dad's father died before I was born. He was a real salt-of-the-earth kind of man; he once traveled to Wyoming to bring back a full trainload of lambs to Illinois to raise to slaughter weight.

He was very respected in the area as a farmer and a former politician. I remember men, who were running for different state and local offices, coming to visit him with hopes that he would endorse their candidacy. As a kid it made no sense to me. To me, he was just Grandpa. But all these men would come out to the farm and suck up to him, hoping he would give them his blessing.

There are many stories of his frugality and his estate planning; he wanted to save everything he could for his four children. Sad as it was, all four thought they got cheated in some way when the farm and assets were divided into four parts. Some of them never spoke to each other after that.

Grandpa Endicott would pull and save old, rusty, bent nails and keep them for future use; and he kept a pile of old lumber that most people would have thrown out. I painted for him a lot: fences, barns, corn cribs, and even a house. His paint brushes were the worst and he would make me mix a new gallon of paint with a 1/4 can of old curdled paint to make sure every drop was used. Grandpa's chair was held together with wire and a metal plate. The idea of getting a new piece of furniture was not a consideration at all. He would order a new basic Pontiac Catalina with no A/C or even a radio. He was definitely a no-frills guy.

He used to babysit me pretty often, but I thought we were just hanging out. I learned a lot from that old, wise man. He taught me about the weather; how to smell a storm; and sense the changes that indicated a tornado was brewing. He never missed the evening news with Walter Cronkite; but that was it for television, other than the weather. He talked of truth and honesty in a man and could see a lie or fib coming from a mile away; I knew better than to try to sneak a fib past him. He always wanted Old Spice for his birthday and Christmas. Not sure I ever saw him laugh though.

Grandpa E. had a 12-gauge shotgun that was not in great condition, but, like all other things he owned, was good enough for his purposes. The stock of the gun was partially wired together.

One day, when I was hanging out with Grandpa, we heard several dogs barking wildly. This was always a bad sign because their barks were different when they were attacking sheep. They would attack in packs made up of an indigenous wild dog or two (coyote/dog mix or coyote/wolf hybrid) and some local dogs that had been corrupted by the wild dogs. The local dogs were often the farm dogs of some of our friends and neighbors. Once these dogs tasted fresh blood, there was no turning back; they were primal and dangerous from that point on.

Grandpa grabbed his 12-gauge and yelled, "Come on, son!" as he ran out the door to the field where the pack of wild dogs was taunting and biting at the hind legs of some of our flock.

When we reached the field, we yelled at the dogs. Two of the wild dogs turned and came running at us side-by-side. Grandpa aimed his old, wired together, double-barrel, 12 gauge between the two dogs and pulled both triggers. I will never forget the sight of the two dogs falling, one to the right and one to the left. It was like something you would see in a cartoon. I was so impressed, and relieved, to see the dogs go down. When we walked up to the two downed dogs, I realized one of the dogs belonged to a farm family we knew very well. They had to be told the bad news, but everyone in the community knew their dogs would be shot if they were found attacking livestock. Still, I knew there would be some strange vibes at school the next day, since it was the dog of the farmer's son.

* * *

Story has it that Grandma Esther wanted to be an actress but turned up pregnant (with my dad); she and Grandpa George were forced to marry by their families. Neither one of them had really planned on getting married that young, but it was the "honorable thing to do" in that era.

Grandma Esther, supposedly, had a tumultuous relationship with Grandpa George. There was a lot of screaming and fighting, partially due to Grandma's sometimes explosive and nasty personality. I think she blamed George for ruining her chances of being an actress. One family member suggested, as the baby of four children, she was spoiled rotten and would not accept the fact that she was as much to blame for the pregnancy as George.

After George died at age forty, Great-Grandpa Fred got Grandma Esther, his daughter, a job at the State Capital working for the Secretary of State. Not sure what happened with that job, but story has it she ran off to Miami with a rich older man. After that didn't work out, she came back home to her parents, because she had no place else to go.

Her mother, Nettie, was alive at the time, and Grandma ended up being their housekeeper and cook. When Nettie died, Grandma Esther did everything for Great-Grandpa Fred. They yelled at each other a lot; they were both hotheads, but he usually won since he held all the cards. She was given a home, food, and a small monthly stipend.

Mom, who was not the biggest fan of Grandma Esther, told me that

Grandpa George was very sweet and easy going. She also, for some reason, would often tell me how beautiful his feet were. I always found that odd.

Mom told me Grandma Esther rarely showed much love for Dad because she looked at him as the reason her life didn't turn out the way she had planned. When he was a child, she would put a harness on him and tie him to the clothes line in the yard. He could run back and forth along the metal clothes line, but could not go any further. Grandma said it was because he kept running away. Dad always thought it was because she wanted him outside and out of her hair.

As an older child, he was expected to stay out of the house until dinner time. His bicycle gave him freedom from the turmoil at home and allowed him to explore his small hometown of Oakland City, Indiana. He used to follow the fire engine for entertainment. Once, much to his surprise, he followed the fire engine right to his own burning house.

Until I was two years old, we lived in a converted chicken barn next to Grandpa's house. In 1953, Mom and Dad started building the new house on two acres on U.S. Route 150, across and down the road a piece. They used a veteran's loan to build it. Dad did most of the grunt work on the house, but they hired an actual house builder to do the big stuff, and a German stucco specialist to do the interior walls.

Mom and my Grandma Esther didn't get along that well. I think Grandma was jealous of my mother because she was pretty, had a good figure, was happy in her marriage, and seemed to have more money to spend. Grandma often said nasty things to Mom and yelled at Dad a lot. There was always tension, especially when she moved out of the main house when Grandpa Endicott died and into the small rental house right next door to us, a mere two hundred feet from our front door.

Grandma Esther was always very nice to me. She is also the one who felt the need to tell me late in her life that my other grandfather, Earl Miller (Mom's father), was a bootlegger when he was young. She told me that was why Mom's family was so freaky in their denial and hatred of all things related to alcohol. It explained everything. I never asked Mom about it because it was so deeply imbedded in the image that her family had created. That image was that no one in their family would ever let alcohol touch their lips.

CHAPTER 9—TEETOTALERS
OR BOOTLEGGERS?

Alcohol played a huge part in the story of my family for three gener-ations, and even into a fourth. This was not the role we usually hear alcohol playing in the lives of families all over the world. There were no alcoholics in our family. In fact, if you listened to any of the women on Mom's side of the family, alcohol had no place in our family, and never had. No one in the family ever drank alcohol, and alcohol would never touch the lips of her sons, her husband, her grandsons, her sisters, her mother, her father, her nieces and nephews, or even their children. It was a big deal and we never asked Mom why she and her family were so obsessed with making it known to the world that no one in the family would ever drink.

Mom was a wonderful mother, but when it came down to being anti-alcohol, she was hardcore. It was over-the-top.

I can honestly say I never tasted alcohol until I was in college. I wasn't around it because no one in my little bubble was drinking. We were busy going to school and playing sports, so it was easy to stay away from alcohol. The idea of drinking never crossed my mind, and even if it had, I wouldn't have known where to get it. I never saw a bar at any friend's house. We had parties, but I never once saw any alcohol. It was all about girls, pizza, sodas, and lots of music. That was all we needed.

When I was a young boy, we would occasionally attend reunions for Dad's side of the family, where I would see some drinking among the adults. Mom hated that we would see Dad's relatives drinking. She made me think they were fallen and weak people because they "needed" alcohol in their lives.

When I moved straight from my parent's house into the fraternity house, I realized the world I had been living in was not the real world at all. Most of the guys I was living with had been drinking in high school, even some of the athletes. I may have been the only one, other than two football players, that didn't drink. Our campus had over 30,000 students and the cam-pus bars were very much open for business and ready to provide alcohol to anyone with a thirst for it. I don't know who the bar owners were paying off, but all you needed to get in these very nice clubs and bars on campus was your student ID, even though the drinking age in Illinois was 21. They were packed and rockin'. I was blown away.

Going to the bars after studying was almost a nightly event for many of the brothers, so I would often go with them to meet girls. I would have a Coke. I was intrigued by this whole scene where everyone was "breaking the law" and nobody cared or worried about "getting busted." This sounds so stupid now, but I was especially surprised that the girls were drinking almost as much as the guys. In my farm boy brain, I thought, "Does this make them bad girls?" I never knew any girls that drank.

When I first got on campus, I decided that I wouldn't start drinking because of peer pressure; it would be because I wanted to do it. Once I tried it, I realized it wasn't the evil potion that I thought it was, as long as I did it socially and not habitually. I was having fun with it and it felt like a new adventure. But Terry and I still kept up the charade for Mom. At one point, I told Terry I was tired of all the pretense. I told him I was going to tell Mom that I have a drink once in a while. Terry said, "If you tell her, I will kill you! If she knows you drink, she'll know I drink. That's not happening." This was a turning point. I should have gone ahead and told her, but instead we kept up the ridiculous show for Mom until the day she died at 91 years of age.

There was no alcohol at my wedding because my in-laws didn't want to offend my mother. People had to sneak around with flasks and go to their cars to have a drink. All my friends from my entire life had to be instructed on what not to say around my mom. Everyone in the community, who had known us our whole lives, knew not to ask us if we wanted a drink or mention seeing us anywhere having a drink. It became a joke later in our lives. Mom really had no idea how much her obsession affected so many people.

I'm not saying everyone should drink alcohol. I applaud those that don't do it for health reasons, religious reasons, or lack of interest. I just believe it's wrong when people get overly judgmental either way. Personally, I think alcohol consumption is out of control and it's become far too popular due to the endless promotion of the thousands of new alcohol products that are heavily targeting young people. But Mom went too far in one direction.

* * *

When I was in my late 30s, during a casual visit with Grandma Esther, something prompted me to ask her why she thought Mom's family was so weird about alcohol. I thought she might have some insight since she lived in Oakland City when Dad was growing up, and it was the kind of town where people knew a little something about everybody.

First, I should explain that Mom and Grandma never got along all that well, and Grandma thought Mom and her family were too pretentious.

Grandma said, "I never would have said anything, but now that you ask…your Grandpa Miller was a bootlegger when he was a young man. At least that was the story around Oakland City."

I was speechless. She continued, "So your Grandma Miller and her entire family have denied anything and everything that might associate them with alcohol ever since."

OMG! All the lies that had been told, and the guilt that had been felt over so many years, were all because of something Grandpa Miller did as a young man? Who cares? He was a great guy and an amazing father to his three daughters. It is so tragic. I could go on and on about how much this affected me and the people around me over the years. I would've never told this story when my mother was alive, but it feels good to tell the story now.

Chapter 10—High School

My high school, Oakwood Township High School, had fewer than 400 students. My graduating class totaled 69 students, and we were the "Class of '69." Even though there were fewer than 400 students, it took the consolidation of five elementary schools to come up with that number. All the elementary schools were small like mine. My class from Muncie Grade School contributed only around twelve students to the freshman class.

Our high school was not in a town: it was a mile east of Muncie (population 100-ish) and two miles west of Oakwood (population 700-ish). It was in the middle of nowhere. The school and our home were located on State Highway 150, but it was still very rural.

The school was within 150 yards of our house because my great-grandfather, Grandpa Endicott, sold the school district the land for the high school around 1920. It was there from the day I was born. We could see the football games and the scoreboard from our backyard. In a way, Oakwood High School was always in my world. All the buses and cars would be slowing down in front of our house to make the turn into the school. So, when it was time to go to high school, it was just a matter of putting on my clothes, eating breakfast, and walking next door. The transition was very easy and not foreign at all.

I'm not sure how it happened, but somehow I ended up being voted president of my class even though I didn't know eighty percent of my classmates when I started my freshman year. It may have been the fact that many of the boys and girls from the other schools knew me from playing their schools in basketball.

I ended up being president of my class all four years. I also ended up being valedictorian of my class, co-captain of the football team, shot put record holder, student athlete of the year, Mr. OTHS, and in my senior year I was elected to lead the student councils of 74 high schools in Central Illinois as President of the Champaign District Association of Student Councils.

I understand it may sound like I'm bragging, but that was my high school experience and I have to own up to it. I can't even say I'm proud of it and sometimes I even laugh about how ridiculous it all sounds. I feel a little

34

guilty about trying to be Mr. Everything, because it looks like I was trying to impress people. But I don't think I was trying to impress anyone. When presented with a possibility, I would think, "Why not?"

I don't even know who that guy is anymore.

Now, I'm shocked that I put that much stress on myself. Maybe I was shooting for perfection for some reason? I have always been a "people pleaser," so maybe I didn't want to let down those people who thought I had the ability to achieve in many areas. Now, I realize there's no such thing as perfection, other than in nature, and most people hate someone who even gets close to it.

I mention the high school "achievements" because, sadly, I don't think I really wanted to do most of that stuff in the first place. I was easily influenced and sometimes manipulated by teachers, guidance counselors, coaches, friends, and in a subtle way, my parents. My parents never pushed, but they did expect me to do my best at whatever I was doing. That's what they did, and they were my example. It was a way of life in our family: "If you're going to do it, do it right."

I was listening to all the people who said, "A Guy Like You Should...," whether it was run for class president, be on the football team, try to graduate with a 5.0 average, date the cheerleader, or go to West Point. It was a pattern.

At the time, it all sounded interesting and fun. Wow! There were so many cool choices I had never thought were available to a farm boy. Possibly, I looked at it as a one big game that I was supposed to win. I do admit I was very competitive back then.

It seems odd for a guy who wasn't sure if he even wanted to finish high school, who just wanted to be a ranch hand, and loved basketball not football. It was obvious when I went to college that I was fed up with trying to be "Mr. Everything." I decided to simply be a student and have some fun. It felt so good to take all that pressure off. It was such a relief to be anonymous on campus. No one expected anything from me.

Chapter 11—College

I went to college at a very interesting time in American history. The Vietnam War was going full blast and luckily I decided not to take the appointment to West Point, something my guidance counselor had pushed for me to do. I would've ended up as a 2nd lieutenant in the Army headed for Vietnam.

Second lieutenants dropped into a hot war zone in Vietnam in 1968 usually didn't live very long. They were easy targets getting off and on a helicopter because they looked eager, neat, and fresh; and they usually came off the chopper early. The enemy could immediately spot them as a young officer and loved to pick them off.

This was one time I didn't fall for the "A Guy Like You Should…" that I had fallen for so many times in my early life. Instead, I went to the University of Illinois and joined a fraternity.

Joining a fraternity was far from being a freshman at West Point, but being a pledge often felt like we were in the military with the older brothers yelling at us, giving us orders, punishing us for minor infractions, and often for crimes we didn't even commit. It was bad. I often wonder how or why we put up with all of it. I guess it was all about showing them they couldn't break us. There was also the desire to stay in one of the top two fraternity houses on campus.

Some of the guys in my pledge class, who said they would make sure no one ever went through the same cruel and brutal hazing we did, were the first ones in line to torture the pledges the next year.

When I started at the University of Illinois, my brother, Terry, had already been at the University of Illinois for two years, where he played football and was a member of Beta Theta Pi. He and his best buddy, Rich, who was an ATO (Alpha Tau Omega), thought I would be a much better fit for ATO than Beta Theta Pi. ATO was a jock house whose members were also good students with good GPAs. Several of the ATOs were on the University of Illinois varsity teams, but almost everyone had excelled at one or more sports in high school. Each had chosen, as I had, not to play sports in college.

I had scholarship offers to play football at smaller colleges but had decided to play as a walk-on at Illinois instead, like Terry. But when they sent my summer training materials and told me they wanted to put another 40-50 pounds on me and make me a guard, I decided to end my football career. I was a 215-pound fullback and middle linebacker in high school, with no desire to be a 260-pound lineman.

It was a huge relief once I decided not to play college football. I realized I never really wanted to play football in the first place. My passion was basketball.

* * *

In the '70s, fraternities and sororities were extremely popular on college campuses. At the University of Illinois, every fraternity and sorority that existed in the country was represented on campus, totaling over 50.

Intramural sports were huge at the University of Illinois. The fraternities and the dorms lived and breathed intramural sports. The football games were big events, and the playoffs and championships drew large crowds. They were very serious about it. If a fraternity won the "All Points Trophy" for all intramural sports, it was a big deal. That's what our house was always shooting for with their recruits—smart athletes that would insure great intramural teams, whether it was football, basketball, swimming, or other sports. We often won that coveted trophy. These trophies were prominently displayed in the stately first floor trophy cases to impress all visitors, especially the most desirable candidates for future membership— and, of course, the women.

I don't think any of this would matter much to most college students today, but it was a very big deal in the '60s and '70s. There were a lot of khaki pants, polo shirts, penny loafers, and windbreakers back then. No one carried a backpack; I don't know if they even made them for students back then. They were probably just for hikers and adventurers. Students carried a stack of books and notebooks under their arms. The engineering students were the only ones that dared to carry a briefcase. I tried carrying a briefcase once, because it was a gift from my parents; I caught so much abuse from my fraternity brothers that I tucked it away in my closet and never carried it again.

ATO also wanted their members to excel academically. This would keep the house GPA high, which had its advantages with the university, the national ATO organization, and the Illinois ATO alumni. The alums would more likely help support the house financially if the house was excelling on all levels.

This was all part of building the reputation of the house; and the reputation of a fraternity or sorority was extremely important when recruiting pledges each year. If a house wanted to recruit the most desirable candidates, it was necessary to impress them with the accomplishment of the fraternity and its members on all levels.

In my case, they came after me when I was in high school, and even invited me to spend a weekend before I entered college. It was very common for fraternities to "rush" high achieving high school seniors that had been recommended to a member because they thought the individual would fit in well and help perpetuate or improve the reputation of the house on one or more levels. Some of these young men ended up being my pledge brothers. I think there were eight or ten of us that moved straight from our parents' homes into the ATO fraternity house with 80 men ages 18 to 24.

Sometimes, an individual would be pledged only because they were a "legacy," meaning a family member had been an ATO in the past. Rarely did members vote against the legacy even if they weren't excited about the candidate. It was a tradition but sometimes it caused problems because they really weren't a good fit for the house.

Our pledge class bonded quickly because the "actives" forced us to do so by torturing us with extreme amounts of hazing. Hazing was not illegal at the time by any means. It was a daily event. The weekends were the worst. Some of our "pledge trainers" were actually in ROTC and truly enjoyed inflicting mental and physical torture on us. We had to lean on each other to get through it. I'm sure it must be similar to young recruits in the military going through boot camp or going to war together. Often guys would reach the breaking point, but we would all rally around them to help get them through it. One of our pledge brothers was smart enough to call bullshit on all of it and quit. He became a famous Chicago folksinger.

I hate to say it because it sounds very snooty, elitist, and obnoxious, but it was very important to be one of the top fraternities on campus if you wanted to have "social events" with the top sororities. The top sororities had reputations for high achievement on many levels for decades, as did the fraternities. Both looked for members that would fit in because they had common interests, talents, and experiences. The top sororities were also where one often found some of the most fun, smart, and attractive women on campus. Sorry, we were young men and that was important to us, although I know it sounds shallow now.

In the end, I learned a lot about living with others and working together as a group to achieve common goals. Living with a large group of men can be challenging and it requires a great deal of compromise. This was very different from living with my parents.

For anyone, starting college on a campus of 36,000 students can be a lonely and overwhelming experience, but for someone coming from an independent farm background and a high school of less than 400, it would have been much harder to have made that transition without my pledge brothers. We were all in it together and could help each other with classwork, curriculum choices, relationships, and personal problems. We were not alone. I'm still friends or in touch with several of my pledge brothers and roommates, even though it's been 50 years since we pledged ATO. That says a lot. I often go back for the homecoming football game to meet up with the guys at the fraternity house for a pre-game brunch, and to meet the young brothers that live at the house now. It feels like a large family or club where you are still a member.

But once again, pledging a fraternity wasn't my idea. I was told by my brother and his friend, Rich, I should do it. I'm not saying it was a bad idea, but it was another time where I did something because others said, "A Guy Like You Should" do something. Maybe that's the way life works. Choices are put in front of us, we weigh the choices, and then we decide which path looks best for us. I just feel like I have often made choices based on what other people thought. Maybe I was afraid I would make the wrong choice, so I picked what others thought. Guess I will never know.

CHAPTER 12—VIETNAM OR... NOT VIETNAM

The Vietnam War was escalating when I entered college. All young men worried about being drafted and being shipped off to Vietnam. Some of my high school classmates had already been drafted straight out of high school because they weren't going to college. None of them came back the same.

It wasn't a fair world: if you were entering college, you received a deferment as long as you were in college. Some people only went to college to stay out of the military. Other high school classmates enlisted before they were drafted so they could choose which branch of the military they entered. It was a mess, and the war was extremely unpopular. Most people had no idea why we were even in Vietnam. They would just say, "We gotta stop the commies."

There weren't enough young men enlisting, so the government came up with a way to supply the military with the bodies they needed to escalate our participation in the war in Vietnam: The Draft Lottery. It was the first time a lottery system had been used to select men for military service since 1942.

The United States became more and more involved in the conflict in Vietnam. President Johnson had sent 82,000 troops to Vietnam by the end of 1965, but his military advisors wanted another 175,000. Due to the heavy demand for military personnel, the United States increased the number of men the draft provided each month. In 1967, the number of U.S. military personnel in Vietnam was around 500,000.

December 1, 1969 was the very first Draft Lottery for men born between 1944 and 1950. The lottery included every date of the year. The dates were drawn one at a time until everyone's birthdate had been drawn. I missed that first lottery, since I was born in 1951; but they had a second drawing on July 1, 1970, which included me, my friends and classmates. We were all very anxious about the day they were to draw our numbers. Even though we were in college, we would be drafted as soon as we graduated if we drew a bad number. If we dropped out, or flunked out, we would immediately be drafted.

The winners that year were anyone that drew a number above 210. Anyone with a number 210 or lower would be drafted: luck of the draw. Draftees usually ended up being shipped off to Vietnam, which was a terrifying thought because every day on the news they would tell the new body count for soldiers that would be coming home in a coffin.

I will never forget that extremely hot July day that would determine my draft number, and seriously affect my life no matter how it played out. I was working for a small construction company that was putting in sewer lines for a new mobile home development, basically digging ditches. We had planned to take a long lunch break and listen to the draft lottery on the company truck's radio. There were three of us sitting in that pickup glued to the radio.

I was a loser: My birthdate, June 12th, was drawn #51. It wasn't a puking situation, but close to it. There was no question about whether I would be drafted when the time came. Some of my friends drew very safe numbers, so they partied. My brother had drawn a number in the 300s in the first lottery, so he was safe. He was also allergic to wool clothing (uniforms) and most green plants, so he never had to worry about it.

I never planned to drop out, and I was nearly a straight A student, so I had some time to think about my options. Somewhere between 50,000 and 100,000 young Americans went to Canada to escape the draft. I knew I would never do that; it seemed too un-American, considering my conservative farm boy background with a Republican politician father. I also couldn't imagine leaving all my family and friends behind. The term draft dodger had a very negative connotation at the time, but many years later, I respected what many of them had done. They didn't believe in the war and they didn't want to be sent there to kill people or be killed.

I started my sophomore year as a much different person. The draft lottery forced me to wake up and pay attention to what was going on in my country. I realized that I had been sheltered. Life got very real during the Vietnam War. I had an awakening of sorts. I was starting to take a more liberal stance as I learned the truth about the war and the lies that were being told to the American public by the government and the politicians. I realized I had been very unaware and naive: I had trusted that everyone was telling me the truth and the government was doing what was best for all of us.

I started going to hear speakers with other points of view. I went to rallies and protests as an observer. I was a watcher who wanted to know the truth about what was going on in his world. Before this, I was caught up in my own little world; but now my little world was starting to be less important to me.

I remember going to hear Jessie Jackson speak at our auditorium. He was the most dynamic speaker I had ever witnessed in my life. He was masterful in his ability to get the audience to respond to what he had to say.

I also heard Senator George McGovern speak when he was running for President in 1972. I believed everything he said was true, and he had a great sense of humor. I felt like I had listened to a man who was a true public servant. He ran on an anti-war platform that advocated withdrawal from the Vietnam War in exchange for the return of American prisoners of war and amnesty for draft evaders who had left the United States. McGovern was defeated by incumbent President Richard Nixon by a landslide. Nixon later resigned in the face of almost certain impeachment and removal from office due to the Watergate scandal.

President Richard Nixon's decision to invade Cambodia sparked many protests around the country. Many of those protests were highly volatile and many turned violent. The Ohio National Guard fired on students during a rally at Kent State University, killing four students and wounding nine others.

The University of Illinois students reacted to the Kent State killings by calling a three-day strike on May 6, 1970. The Illinois National Guard were called in while ninety percent of all classes were shut down.

The University of Illinois, along with University of Wisconsin-Madison, became hotbeds of radical activity. Who would think this would be happening at a university sitting in the middle of corn and soybean fields?

We were under curfew, but that did not stop the protesters or me, the observer. Radical protesters fire-bombed the ROTC lounge and one of the main campus buildings. They protested the presence of General Electric recruiters on campus, as well as those of other corporations that manufactured war materials and reaped massive profits from the war effort in Vietnam. There was quite a bit of vandalism of stores and other buildings that led to many arrests.

I was very curious about the events that I had heard were going on after dark on campus. I was compelled to witness them for myself, so I would dress in all black and stealthily make my way to where all the action was taking place. I got a serious adrenaline rush from knowing I could be arrested if caught out past curfew, but I was pretty confident they had bigger fish to fry.

It was the wildest thing I had ever witnessed. There were a few hundred of us standing back from the violence as protesters set fire to a building and broke windows out of others. The destruction of property struck me as being very wrong. I had never seen such passion and anger before, other than on television. It was very surreal.

One night during the student strike, I snuck out because I had heard there was going to be a large gathering on the lawn in front of the Student Union Building to protest the killing of the four students and the wounding of nine others at Kent State University by National Guard troops.

The Student Union lawn is a very large area and approximately a thousand energized students were gathered there. I was one of them, even though I considered myself an observer rather than a protester. There was a vast array of protest signs and lots of loud chanting as protest leaders with bullhorns tried to rally the group to take action. There was a tremendous amount of tension in the air and it was building.

Then the National Guard arrived with helmets, shields and batons. They surrounded the crowd on the west and north sides. The Student Union Building was on the south side, leaving only the east side for escape. Over their bullhorns, the National Guard commander warned the students to leave "NOW!"

The students didn't move.

The order to move came again, and once again the students didn't budge. Then came the order, "CHARGE!" They came with their helmets and their shields, swinging batons and hitting students as they tried to get away. I, along with most, ran to the eastern escape route and got away unharmed. I didn't hang around long before I headed back to the safety of the fraternity house, which was quite the contrast from where I had just left.

There was conflict in our fraternity as well during this time. We had members that had turned very anti-war, and then there were those that were in ROTC and very supportive of the war effort. Sometimes, it seemed like there was going to be a little war in our fraternity between the two different factions, but it never got too far out of hand.

Two years later, things heated up again when it was learned we had invaded Cambodia and were conducting a secret war there. There were more marches and protests. The protests led to a student strike that caused the

University of Illinois to tell students they could leave campus and take the grade they had at the time, or they could stay and finish out the semester. A large percentage of the student population left. I decided to stay because I liked learning and going to class. I also felt that being on campus was a lot more fun than going home. The campus was a ghost town.

That war impacted so many lives. Like me, many guys my age experienced survivor guilt over getting out of the Vietnam War. Even though it was totally legitimate, it bothers me to this day that I wasn't drafted, simply because I was in college. If I hadn't been in college, I would have found myself in Vietnam. This might explain why I've watched *Apocalypse Now* over twenty times. Thousands didn't make it back, and most that did were changed physically or emotionally, just because they weren't going to college.

It's not a fair world.

Chapter 13—Biggest Defining Moment Of My Young Adult Life (Maybe My Entire Life)

My freshman year had dramatically affected the way I looked at life: the war, living with a bunch of men, new freedoms, new music, exposure to new lifestyles, the hippie movement, free love, people from different cultures. It was mind blowing. I started to think more about what I really wanted to do with my life.

I started my sophomore year as a finance major, having changed from a curriculum headed in a pre-med direction. I had passed on the pre-med idea while sitting in a microbiology class. I decided it was going to be a very long and difficult journey, especially since I wasn't even sure if I would be happy with the end result.

Then one day in the second semester of my sophomore year, I found myself staring at a formula on the board in my business calculus class. I was getting an "A" in the class, so it wasn't a matter of not understanding it: it was more a matter of "why."

"Why am I doing this?" I couldn't come up with an answer. I thought to myself, "If this has anything to do with the rest of my life, I'm going to shoot myself right now." It meant nothing to me.

After class, I went straight to my room at the fraternity house and pulled out the University of Illinois Course Catalog. I was determined to find a new curriculum that made sense to me, not anyone else. I literally ran my finger down the pages until I came across The College of Communications. There I found "Television, Film & Radio." Bingo! That's it!

I immediately applied to the College of Communications for my junior year. That department was one of the tougher to get into because very few students were accepted each year. You had to be a junior with at least a 4.5 GPA (we were on a 5 point system at that time). I had a 4.9+ so I was accepted. I was very happy with my new choice. I could actually visualize how it would turn into something I would like to do with my life.

Two of my fellow classmates in the Film and Television curriculum went on to make a real mark in the world of film and television, both of whom I worked with on student productions: Film director, Chuck Russell (*The Mask* with Jim Carrey, *Collateral* with Tom Cruise, *Eraser* with Arnold Schwarzenegger, *The Scorpion King* and others); and Linda Brill, broadcaster at KING 5 TV in Seattle for 37 years. There have since been others like Nick Offerman from *Parks and Recreation* and two-time Academy Award-winning director Ang Lee (*Life of Pi, Brokeback Mountain*).

From that day on, life would never be the same.

CHAPTER 14—EUROPE ON $5.00 A DAY

The draft was ended one month before I graduated. What does a young guy do in the early '70s after finishing college, luckily escaping the draft that would have landed him in the Army at the tail end of the Vietnam War? He decides to avoid making a lifetime decision by going to Europe for the summer. Why not?

After reading a James Michener book titled *The Drifters,* I became obsessed with the idea of experiencing Europe as a young man. *The Drifters* was a novel that follows six young characters from various countries that met along the way and traveled together through parts of Spain, Portugal, Morocco and Mozambique with very little money.

I wanted to be one of those free, adventurous, and fearless characters, not an employee of some faceless corporation.

I always wanted to consider myself an artist of some kind. I didn't realize that search would go on my entire life. I thought I wanted to make movies with a small tight-knit crew, and have no one to tell me what I could and couldn't do with my little movies, unlike the way things were done in Hollywood.

I was referred to a popular book for travelers titled *Europe on $5 a Day* by Arthur Frommer. This was in the early '70s, so it would probably be $50-$100 per day now. This book was a godsend to me and all young Bohemians. It was my bible for the summer. It had great suggestions on inexpensive hotels and restaurants.

My girlfriend at the time, Sara, who was by no means bohemian (pretty preppy, actually), asked me in the late spring what I was going to do for the summer. I told her I thought I was going to bum around Europe like the kids in *The Drifters.* This was news to her and she was in no way excited about me taking off for the summer. I had figured this would be the case, but I wanted that *"Drifters"* experience once in my life. I feared I would never do it if I went straight into the working world.

That was the experience of all of my friends that immediately took jobs straight out of college. Many of them became very successful, but none of them have gone to Europe for a whole summer, winging it every day with just a backpack and a copy of *Europe on $5 a Day*. It isn't the same if you're staying in five-star hotels and traveling first class all the way. You can't go bohemian after you're successful: you would be a poseur.

There's a rush you get when one minute you don't have any idea where you're going to sleep that night, and the next minute, you end up scoring a great little room in a quaint boutique hotel for $5, just like the book said. On another day, you meet some young locals that say, "Would you like to stay in our family's cabin in the mountains for a few days?"

Sara's parents were very conservative, so I was 100% sure there was no way they would ever let her go to Europe with a mere boyfriend, especially since her brother and sister-in-law were going to be in Europe at the same time on their honeymoon. That would not look good. So, I felt it was safe to tell her she could go with me if she wanted. This way, she couldn't be mad at me for going. I don't mean to sound cruel, but I just knew it would change everything if she went. Also, her parents had money and I didn't think she would be very good at bumming around Europe on $5 a day.

Well, her parents totally shocked me by telling her it was okay for her to go. What am I going to say at that point? I won't go deep into how this changed everything because she was a great person and I did care about her. Just let me say, she wasn't a big fan of going the cheap route, and she had a hard time not being able to communicate in foreign countries. She pretty much shut down on me for the first two weeks.

The relationship ended within 30 days after we got back.

I did the whole European trip, including airfare and a Eurail pass, for about $900. The Eurail pass allowed me to jump on a train anytime, anywhere I wanted. I wouldn't stay in those one to five dollar hotels today, but when I was young, I didn't care. I wasn't spoiled yet. If the room had a mattress, and no visible rodents or bugs, it was probably OK. The idea was not to enjoy the room anyway, but rather to get out and experience the towns with all their character.

Europe was so amazing in the '70s and unlike anything I had experienced in the United States. The great majority of Europeans embraced the hundreds of years of their extremely rich history, whether it was their museums, architecture, cuisine, or their culture in general. Everything tasted better, whether it was a tomato, a slice of cheese, or a bottle of wine.

Everything had more texture and the colors seemed more vibrant.

They didn't feel the need to tear down the old and build something shiny and new. Everything didn't have to have a fresh coat of paint. They let the aging of things add color and texture. They also had an appreciation for older people.

Many of the problems they face now did not exist then. For example, Paris in the '70s was very much like what you saw in the movies. It didn't feel dangerous and there really was romance in the air. Paris was what I had hoped it would be.

Today it's a mess, as are so many of the wonderful but dangerous cities in Europe that must find a way to assimilate millions of refugees, and deal with very difficult economic and healthcare problems. I wish everyone could experience Europe the way I did, but time marches on and everything changes.

* * *

When Sara and I were in Europe, I told her I really wanted to go to Berlin and see what it was like, since the city was divided into free West Berlin and communist East Berlin. I was especially interested knowing our train would have to go through communist East Germany to get there. I wanted to know what it was like. She wasn't very comfortable with the idea, but I have to give her credit for going anyway.

We took a train 342 miles from Frankfurt, in West Germany, to Berlin, in communist East Germany. So our train had to travel through East Germany to get to West Berlin, which was occupied by Western Allies.

When we crossed into East Germany, the train stopped and armed guards from the East German military boarded the train. The mood immediately changed. The men had machine guns and intimidating uniforms just like in the movies. They went through every passenger car asking each passenger for identification and looked for anything suspicious. It was intimidating. There were no smiles or "Welcome to communist East Germany" from the guards. I had never seen a machine gun.

Once in Berlin, I was determined to go into East Berlin to see what communism looked like with my own eyes. This meant going through the infamous **Checkpoint Charlie** to get there. Everyone had to show passports and answer questions before they were allowed to pass to the other side. The guards were heavily armed and very intimidating. There was tension at the checkpoint that day for a reason we soon learned.

Once we had crossed into East Berlin, we learned there was a huge, multi-day International Communist Youth Festival going on. There were young communists from all over the world participating in parades and events through the banner covered buildings and streets.

At first, I was a little uneasy since I was not a communist. I wondered if they would be hostile toward us once they realized we were Americans. But they really didn't care and no one even stopped me from taking lots of photos. It was shocking to see the difference between East and West Berlin. West Berlin was vibrant and colorful and people seemed happy and more like what I was familiar with in America. It was obvious that East Berlin, without the parades and the banners, was very gloomy and drab, much like what I assumed it looked like after WWII. It was ugly and the people were very serious even though there was a festive atmosphere due to the festival.

Once I ran out of film, we crossed back through Checkpoint Charlie into West Berlin. We had experienced all the young communism we could take in one day. It was a relief to get out of East Berlin with my camera before the chanting crowd turned on us.

It hit me as we were passing through the checkpoint that we had gone down on government records as Americans who had crossed into East Berlin during the International Communist Youth Festival. I've always wondered if I'm on a watchlist of some kind as a communist.

For the record, I am not a communist.

CHAPTER 15—BACK FROM EUROPE/ TIME TO GET SERIOUS

I came back from Europe ready to sell out to corporate America.

Before I left for Europe, I had received offers from companies like Proctor & Gamble and Xerox that followed an amazing sales training program that I was hired for between my junior and senior years.

I had interviewed for the summer training program with Vicks Chemical (Vicks Formula 44, NyQuil, VapoRub and 49 other products) because it paid very well, gave me a generous expense account, a great wardrobe allowance and a new car to travel my three-state territory. It was the most amazing summer job and sales training a twenty-one-year old college student could imagine. When I took the job, I had no idea that Fortune 500 companies would try to recruit me and the other twenty-three young men hired from Ivy League, Big Ten, and Pac-12 universities.

But I just couldn't do it.

So I borrowed $200.00 from Bob the Banker, packed my car, and left for Nashville with my guitar, thinking surely there would be something there for a smart graduate in the field of film and television.

Mom was worried about me heading to Nashville without knowing where I would be staying. I reminded her that I had traveled all over Europe with no reservations and everything went just fine. She begged me to head straight for the biggest Methodist Church in Nashville and tell them that our family was one of the founding families of the Methodist Church in Oakwood, Illinois. I didn't want her to worry, so that was exactly what I did.

The Methodist Church on Hillsboro Road was the biggest church I had ever seen in America. I drove around the back of the church and found what appeared to be the parsonage, where I assumed the pastor lived. I knocked on the door and waited. After several attempts, a gruff man, who I assumed was the preacher, came to the door and said, "Whaddya want?" This was not the friendly welcome my mother had told me I should expect.

I told him about my family and our church in Oakwood. He said nothing. I continued with how I had just arrived in Nashville and my mother had suggested I go to the biggest Methodist Church and ask for a suggestion for where I might find a nice, clean, reasonably priced place to stay while I was in Nashville.

He snapped back with, "We don't do that. Goodbye," and slammed the door in my face.

I thought to myself, "Well, that's not very Methodist of him."

I did need a place to stay so I bought a newspaper and looked in the want ads. I found a motel room advertised for only eight dollars. I was very excited about my money saver motel room until I arrived and realized it was a duplex trailer.

There were several of these duplex trailers that made up a makeshift motel that could be moved at a moment's notice. It wasn't a regular trailer: it was actually built to be a mobile motel, but it was too creepy to stay more than one night. The next day I set out to find a better place at a better price.

Bingo! I found a room for rent behind a man's house. He had built a structure with three rooms that could be rented. There was one room on the lower level and two on the second floor. My room was on the second floor and I shared a bathroom with another guy that I never saw. I was very happy with my room that was only going to cost me $30 per week. It was all I needed to start my new life in Nashville.

As I was driving to check out the room that day, I saw a "Now Hiring" sign outside the neighborhood Pizza Hut. After I secured the room, I stopped at the Pizza Hut and applied for the job. Boom! I had a job and a place to live all in just two hours. I could look for a job in the entertainment business by day and toss pizzas at night. Nashville was my bitch!

Just a note about Pizza Hut: I was surprised and somewhat disillusioned when I was taught how to make a Supreme Pie. Every time we dressed a pizza, there was always stuff that fell off of the pizza and onto the preparation table. We would take that extra stuff and scrape it up into the corner of the prep table. When somebody ordered a Supreme, we would take all the stuff from the corner and throw it on the pie. We would add a few other items to make it pretty if needed, and *VOILA*! You have a Supreme. I assume they don't do it that way now, but that's how we did it in Nashville in 1974.

Nashville was a very, very different place in the '70s, nothing like it is today. There was only one tall building: no GM, Nissan, Mitsubishi, NFL, NHL, Dell Computers, Amazon, Virgin Hotel, JW Marriott, or Hilton. Now, the city is teeming with major corporations that have relocated to the area.

Nashville is the healthcare capital of the world, and book publishing is huge. In fact, music is the 6th biggest industry in Nashville, where most people probably think it's number one. Number one is actually automotive manufacturing.

I had one Nashville contact that was given to me by Mrs. Robeson, the family that owned Robeson's Men's Store, where I had worked in Champaign, Illinois. She had a friend from college that was the head of WSM, the classic radio station that also owned a television station. It was the only real game in town. The man was very kind and showed me around the facility. Just for fun, he even had me tape some radio commercials.

After the tour, he said, "I'm gonna to be very honest with you. What you're looking for is not in Nashville. I could give you a job here, but it won't lead anywhere you want to go. We have one live TV show that I produce, and if I could, I'd give you my job. Hell, I don't even want it."

It wasn't what I had hoped to hear, but it was exactly what I needed to hear. He was telling me I needed to get the hell out of Nashville before I got stuck.

Since I was in Nashville, I thought I should play some of the songs I'd been writing for somebody. Pat Dennis, my college roommate, said his mother had a friend that was a very successful singer in Nashville. He was sure his mother would be willing to arrange a meeting with her.

Her name was Dottie Dillard and she was one of the Anita Kerr singers. They were very popular on their own, but they also sang backup on the recordings of hundreds of the most famous country artists. Dottie had done extremely well for herself and knew everyone in town. She was gracious enough to invite me to her lovely condo for a bite to eat and a cocktail. She filled the evening with great stories as we ate a little—and drank a lot.

After we had been drinking for a while, Dottie got very sad and started to cry. I felt very bad for her, but I didn't think it was a good idea to comfort her too much. She was so upset and vulnerable that I was worried it might get weird. She was an attractive woman, but she was thirty years my senior.

She told me she never accomplished what she had set out to do. Although she was successful, she had never achieved her dream of having a successful solo career. She felt like she had failed. She was telling me the same thing I had heard from the man at WSM: Get out while you can.

My head was swimming at that point. I wasn't sure where to go next.

Dottie pointed out that all the male country artists were older men. There were no young recording artists on the radio. She said I needed to lead a more self-destructive life of drinking, smoking, womanizing, playing music for years in small bars and clubs, and then come back to Nashville. Then, I would be a legitimate country artist. In a very nice way, Dottie was saying I wasn't a real country artist. She was 100 percent right about that: I was grabbing for straws.

After work the next night, I partied late with two girls and one guy that I worked with at Pizza Hut. I got back to my room around 3:00 A.M. A few hours later, there was a knock on my door. It was my landlord and he didn't look happy.

"I don't know what you're up to comin' in at all hours of the night," he said. "…and drivin' that fancy sports car. I think you're up to no good and I want you out of here by tomorrow."

Wow! I'd never been kicked out of anywhere in my life: not a bar, a club, a skating rink, a restaurant, or my parents' house. I hadn't even done anything wrong. I was a suspicious character for the first time in my life. I'd just been kicked out of a $30 a week rooming house. Maybe I had the makings of a country artist after all. Maybe this was the beginning of my downward spiral into heavy drinking and smoking.

Needing to find a new place to live, I picked up a newspaper again. I was drawn to an ad in the "Help Wanted" section that said, "Real Estate Sales." I read the ad and called the number. The man told me what it would take for me to be a real estate salesman in Nashville. It required a lot more than an interview for the job and showing him my college resume. He told me I would need to take a real estate course, pass the real estate exam, and then network to find people that wanted to buy or sell homes. I would definitely be starting at ground zero.

Chapter 16—Real Estate Mogul
In The Making

I thought, "Why would I do that in Nashville when I could go back to Illinois where I had hundreds of contacts of my own, not to mention those of my parents?" I knew it wouldn't hurt that Dad was a politician as well as a farmer. I had a knowledge of land ownership and farming that I could put to use in Illinois. In Tennessee, I knew nobody except the people I worked with at Pizza Hut and Dottie Dillard.

This time it was me who thought, "*A Guy Like Me* could make a killing in the Illinois real estate market."

The decision was made even before I moved out of the room I'd been kicked out of for being an unsavory character. I decided to celebrate my decision by getting a room in a "real motel" for two nights before leaving Nashville. I also needed to quit my job and tie up some loose ends with a very short-term relationship I had developed with a young woman at Pizza Hut.

My first call was to my old boss, Bob Kelsey, at Robeson's Men's Store, where I had worked part-time all through college. Bob was much more than a boss: he was a friend, a mentor, and a confidant. I told Bob almost everything: things I would never tell my father. He kept me from doing a lot of stupid things and gave me some great business and life advice. Sometimes I even listened.

Bob was at least twenty years older, but we had a great time joking around at work.

Bob also taught me a lot about the art of dressing, style, the clothing business, and customer relations. We worked hard and played hard. Bob and his wife, Nancy, were close friends that I would make sure I visited anytime I was back in town, even during and after the *All My Children* days.

My time in the Champaign-Urbana real estate market went very well. It didn't take long to get started because several people jumped in to help. Bob set up a meeting with the owners of Hunt & Associates, the top real estate company in the area. They were eager to take on a young go-getter who dressed well and had great sales training and experience.

After a year of selling residential real estate, the owners of the company, Roger and Pat, pulled me in for a secret meeting. They told me they wanted me to take over a new commercial real estate division they were starting. Up to that point, Roger had handled most of the commercial deals. They wanted to go bigger on the commercial side and thought someone young and aggressive would be what was needed for the new expansion of the commercial department. They were only in their 50s at the time but felt they had worked very hard building the business and deserved to enjoy their lives more by being less involved in the day-to-day operations.

I told them that I was flattered, but I needed a few days to think about it. They told me not to mention it to anyone in the company because it would not go over well with some of the older guys that would think they should be heading up the new commercial operation, especially since two of them had been involved in some commercial deals. I had not been involved with any.

This came at the wrong time for me. Dad was recovering from a triple bypass operation at age 48. It hit me very hard and made me realize life is very short. Plus, Dad's father had died at age 40 of a heart attack, and Mom's father died at age 54 of a heart attack.

I went back to Roger and Pat and told them I had to pass on their generous offer. They were disappointed. Then I told them the rest of the story: I was going to leave the real estate business and move to California to pick back up on my original plans to have a career in the entertainment business.

I told them Dad's near-death situation made me realize I needed to pursue something that was fun and meant something to me, not just something that "A Guy Like Me" could do to make lots of money.

They weren't mad at me, but they were shocked and very disappointed. They felt they had an investment in me. I appreciated all they had done for me, but I didn't feel guilty since I had also made money for them. In the end, they understood my degree was in Film and TV, not real estate. Roger had some heart issues himself, so they understood the "life is short" idea.

I had never shut down my creative juices. The whole time I was selling real estate I was writing comedy material for a possible stand-up act. I was into political satire and had been listening to a lot of Lenny Bruce. I was also writing a comedy play. It was apparent that I really needed to express myself and I wasn't going to be able to achieve that through a career in real estate.

I rented my condo that I bought for a mere $13,000, after I got the kickback in commission. Our company handled the condo conversion of the property, so I got a true insider price and the choice of condos that were available. My mortgage was about $120 per month. I remember wondering if that commitment was a big mistake considering I had only been paying $75 monthly for a two-bedroom in a fairly new apartment complex with a pool. Quite the scary leap.

A few years later, I sold the condo for a big profit and used the money for the down payment on our first house in Inglewood, California. Inglewood is home to the Forum and the new Sofi Stadium, home of the Los Angeles Rams and Los Angeles Chargers.

* * *

I didn't waste a lot of time getting out of town. I sold my "real estate car," a 4-door Ford Galaxy, and kept my MGB-GT sports car. I sold or gave away what little furniture I had and stashed a few things at the farm. I really was a minimalist in those days. I was able to get everything I needed, or meant anything to me, in that little MGB-GT. That included my black and white Sony television with a 9-inch screen, my guitar, camera, and my clothes. What else did I need? I had traveled all over Europe with only what I could stuff in a backpack. I did have a luggage rack on top of the car that held one medium-size suitcase.

A few days before leaving town, I was going around to say my goodbyes to friends I knew I might not see for a long time. One of those people was my ex-girlfriend Liz's mother, Francie Dobbles. Francie was a huge sports fan so I and other guys would often stop by to talk sports. She would also catch me up on Liz and the rest of the family I had known since I was fourteen. When I told Francie I was headed to Los Angeles, she insisted I visit Liz and her first cousin, Teresa, in San Francisco, where they had moved a few months earlier. She said they were homesick and would love to see me. I reminded Francie that San Francisco was four hundred miles from Los Angeles, but she insisted we call Liz and Teresa to catch up and tell them I was moving to California. I should have realized that Francie had an agenda: she always wanted Liz and I to get back together. Neither of us were interested in that happening.

We called Liz and Teresa and they were very excited to hear that I was moving to California. They said they were homesick and begged me to come visit them. They tempted me by saying I could stay with them for two weeks, do some sightseeing, and then head down to Los Angeles. I'd never been to San Francisco and I wasn't on a schedule, so I decided I would be an idiot not to take a two-week vacation in San Francisco with a free place to stay.

I don't think I've ever felt freer than when I left my parents' driveway in my MGB-GT that day. I had enough money to last me for at least a year or two and zero responsibilities. I felt bad for my mother for a few miles, but like a typical guy, I very quickly focused on my super exciting journey.

After having my own children, I understand how much parents worry about their kids when they're far away, but at the time I was selfish enough to think they were excited for me. They thought I had come back to Illinois for good to have a real estate career and possibly follow my father's political path. Instead, I took off for a place over 2,000 miles away. The things we children do to torture our parents.

I had never driven west before, so the trip to San Francisco was very exciting for me. I decided to make the drive in four days. I stopped the first night somewhere unexciting in Nebraska and the second night in the Salt Lake City area. I remember thinking The Great Salt Lake and the Salt Flats were a disappointment and a waste of the time to get there. However, I was very excited about going to Reno. I'd never been to a gambling town in the

U.S. I had been to casinos in Nassau and Monaco, but I barely had enough money for food then, let alone gambling.

I had purchased a special blue suit, with no lapels, and red and white accents to wear at the casinos. Of course, I had a big-collared red, white and blue polyester shirt for the finishing touch. I thought I was pretty darn cool walking into the casinos. I realized very quickly that a person could lose a lot of money very fast. After I had lost my allotted gambling budget in twenty minutes, I decided I enjoyed watching other people lose their money much more than losing my own. Reno is where I realized I still wasn't a gambler.

The next morning, I had a good breakfast and hit the road for the final 218 miles to San Fran.

* * *

Liz and Teresa were very happy to see a familiar face. They had a nice two-bedroom apartment in San Bruno, 12 miles south of downtown San

Francisco and close to the airport. Their complex had a pool and other amenities, so it was a nice place to land—for free.

The three of us were having a blast hanging out and experiencing the city, so the girls offered me a deal: if I bought them a sofa bed, I could live there for two months. The sofa bed would be my rent, and where I would sleep. I decided San Francisco was a very cool town and I could test out my stand-up material there as easily as Los Angeles. My new plan was to stay for a few months, get my comedy act together, and then head to Los Angeles.

Only problem was I've always hated spending money that I've saved. I think it's the farmer in me. So after a month of watching my savings go down, Liz and Teresa suggested I make some quick cash waiting tables.

So I started looking. My first target was to be The Hungry Hunter, one restaurant in a chain that specialized in prime rib. We had enjoyed a meal there before, it was close to the apartment, and the crew seemed to be having fun. Much to my surprise, the manager hired me on the spot and wanted me to start training the next day.

There were dead animals, canoes, bear traps, and snowshoes all over the walls of this giant log cabin of a restaurant. The dark, no windows, wilderness theme was big in the West Coast restaurant chain world at that time. It was all about the meat.

Waiters, waitresses, cocktail waitresses, and bartenders all wore outfits to make us look like people from the wilderness. What we were supposed to represent was vague. Some of us thought we were supposed to be Native American, and we were wearing some designer's very bad interpretation of what a real Native American would have worn in the wilderness: fake suede, rawhide drawstrings, fringe on the sleeves, and brown jeans.

Most of us were wearing Earth Shoes. Look them up. They were big at the time in San Francisco, but almost as ugly as "Le Shoe" from SNL. The good news was the wardrobe was easy to wash and didn't wrinkle.

Things were different in the restaurant business then. We were paid full minimum wage, didn't have to declare our tips, and we had health insurance. Sometimes we would declare 10% of what we actually made, sometimes zero. And we were given good employee meals at no cost.

We had a surprising number of upscale patrons because our food was very good, not overly expensive, and close to the airport and several corporate headquarters. Quite a few of our customers were Asian businessmen. They went for the prime rib in a big way.

* * *

The Hungry Hunter restaurant had a lounge with a small stage where a solo artist would perform five nights a week. Once they heard I was trying to do the standup thing, the manager and the bar manager suggested I try it out there in the lounge.

A lot of my act was short, funny songs. They went over very well at the Hungry Hunter. Maybe because half of my audience was people I worked with and the other half were drunk by the time I went on stage. No matter what, it gave me confidence and inspired me to write more material and look for other venues.

Since the restaurant was a chain, they had other restaurants in the Bay Area that had different meat eating, mountain man-type names that were so popular in the '70s. Performing at another restaurant lounge other than ours gave me the last confidence boost I needed before approaching a club made famous by Robin Williams and Gabe Kaplan, The Holy City Zoo.

* * *

Once I was far enough away from Illinois that Mom wouldn't know, I went absolutely crazy and bought a motorcycle. In my family, riding a motorcycle was considered extremely wild, reckless, rebellious, dangerous, and taboo. Therefore, I didn't tell my parents that I was racing around the Bay Area on a motorcycle. I was in love with my motorcycle. I rode it everywhere. One of my favorite rides, that I took at least once a week, was along the coast. I would start at The Cliff House Restaurant and then on to the very curvy Devil's Slide, Pacifica, and ending up at Half Moon Bay.

I was going to try skydiving but I decided I was already doing enough crazy stuff. Instead, I took flying lessons at a cool little airport close to the ocean at Half Moon Bay. My instructor told me I had excellent instincts and touch for a newcomer to flying.

Curious as to how I would react, and without telling me what he was doing, he had me climb and climb until the engine stalled. I had no idea what was happening other than the fact the propeller stopped turning and the engine had stalled. We started to free fall. The instructor let me sweat it out. Finally, he explained what was happening and told me how to address the free fall. It totally freaked me out. He shouldn't have done that to me. He totally ruined the flying experience for me. I should've gotten back on the horse and rode again. I really did love it, but I have never flown a plane since then.

Chapter 17—San Francisco In The '70s— Apocalypse Not

The mid-'70s were a crazy time in San Francisco and I was a somewhat sheltered farm boy from Illinois. I thought college was wild and crazy, but San Francisco was a totally different ballgame.

This was a time when AIDS wasn't even a thing. The gay bathhouses were going full throttle. Some of the waiters that I worked with were gay and the stories they told totally blew my farm boy mind.

There were drugs that I had never heard of before; and it seemed like everyone was doing them, even though they were very illegal. I was too paranoid to do anything that might cause me to end up in jail, so I was an observer, not a participant.

Haight-Ashbury, the birthplace of the 1960s counterculture movement, was still rocking. Even though the original hippies were no longer there, the hippie vibe was still going strong. I would go to Golden Gate Park, which bordered "The Haight," and listen to the music that was ever-present. Bands like Jefferson Airplane could be experienced at Golden Gate Park concerts.

I always found the hippie world intriguing, but never felt like I fit in. I thought some of the men in the hippie movement looked a little too dangerous to be authentic "peace and love" people. I suspected they were there for the sex, drugs, and rock and roll.

I felt freer in California. I didn't feel like everyone was watching me and reporting back to Mom and Dad. I was convinced I wanted to be in the entertainment business and I was experimenting to see where I fit in.

One brave day, I decided to trot myself into Francis Ford Coppola's production company, American Zoetrope, present my resume and request an interview. I had decided on Zoetrope because I was a huge fan of Coppola's *The Godfather*, and it was the only serious film production company based in San Francisco.

It was a very relaxed and unassuming office in the historic Columbus Tower. I was surprised to find only one person there. Much to my surprise, the pleasant young lady seemed very interested to hear more about me and my film and television degree. She said she would pass my resume on to someone else she thought would want to speak with me and get back to me. I was excited and surprised to receive such a positive reception since Coppola and his company were at the top of the heap in the movie biz after their massive success with *The Godfather*.

Two days later, I got a call from a man at Zoetrope asking me if I could come in for a meeting with him the next day. I jumped at the invitation and could barely sleep thinking about the possibility of working for American Zoetrope.

After five minutes of getting to know more about me, the man got right to the point: He wanted to know if I would be willing to go to the Philippines to work as a production assistant on a new movie they were shooting about the Vietnam War. He told me I would probably be there for the better part of six months. I asked him when they would need me to start.

He said, "You would leave for the Philippines in seven days."

I was shocked and didn't know how to respond at first. Once I pulled myself together, I told him I was very interested but needed to discuss it with my girlfriend, since we had recently moved to San Francisco and rented a house together. That was an excuse to buy a day to think about it. It really was my decision.

Liz and I discussed it and she was definitely not excited about me flying off to the Philippines for six months to work with a bunch of bohemian filmmakers. I wasn't sure I wanted to either; it wasn't what I had come to California to do. I worried that I might never get back to my performance career if I took the production job. It would be too hard to break away from working with companies like American Zoetrope. But it sure sounded cool. I was flattered and very torn.

Turning down that opportunity to work with American Zoetrope was one of the hardest things I ever had to do professionally. At the time, I had no idea that movie would turn out to be the historic *Apocalypse Now*. OMG! *Apocalypse Now* began shooting March 20, 1976. Initially set to be a five-month shoot, the film ended up taking over a year to film and was not released until 1979. The production was plagued with problems, including: sets being destroyed in a typhoon that shut down production; Marlon Brando showing up very overweight and unprepared; Martin Sheen having a breakdown and near-fatal heart attack while filming; and Coppola needing to edit over a million feet of film.

Apocalypse Now was nominated for eight Oscars and won two. It is considered to be one of the greatest films ever made.

The decision to pass on working on the American Zoetrope film haunted me for several months. In fact, I still wonder what would have happened had I made that trip to the Philippines. It did make me realize that if I was going to pass on that opportunity, I needed to put up or shut up on the comedy front by pushing harder and faster.

I was still writing material and planning the debut of my comedy act and I enrolled in acting classes at San Francisco State University. I had taken a couple of acting classes at the University of Illinois, but the ones at SFSU were better. I had a great teacher and some very cool classmates, one of whom I dated. I always liked school, so it felt great being back in a classroom and working in the small theatre there. It felt right. I gained a lot of confidence in my acting classes and it made me realize I might be able to add acting to the mix later, once I got the comedy thing going.

The acting classes helped me gain the confidence I needed to test out my comedy act at the famous Holy City Zoo on their open mic night. It was nerve-racking but went well enough that I was invited to come back again.

* * *

It became more and more apparent that I was in the wrong city to take my performance career to the next level. I needed to go to Los Angeles where there were more comedy clubs and some comedians were getting their own TV series. Rather than move full-time, my plan was to go to Los Angeles during the week and come back to San Francisco on the weekends. My plan didn't go over well with Liz or, for that matter, with Teresa.

Liz and I had stopped seeing other people and had been together exclusively for several months. Liz and Teresa both thought the plan would never work. They asked why I thought I would come back on weekends when most bookings as a stand-up comedian would be on weekends.

There was a multi-hour powwow with the three us to look at all options. Liz and Teresa convinced me that my plan would fail: it would work for a short time and then I would stop coming back to San Francisco. Their strong opinion was that my plan would eventually ruin our relationship.

The idea of Liz and I getting married was proposed instead. Why not go home, get married, and then move to LA together? After drinking a lot of wine, all three of us agreed that was the best plan.

* * *

The three of us decided to rent a car and drive home for Christmas. The plan was to go home and tell the families that we were going to get married in April.

A little before Christmas, Liz's dad had a heart attack. He was doing OK, but while we were home, the doctor said he needed heart bypass surgery. At that point, it made no sense for Liz to go back to San Francisco with Teresa and me when she really needed to be with her family. In the 1970s, a heart bypass operation was very serious and the recovery took at least a month or more. There was also the wedding to plan.

The decision was made for Teresa and I to drive the rental car back and tie things up in San Francisco. We still needed to work because there were bills and rent to pay until our lease was up. I also had to move everything into storage until Liz and I came back to California. Teresa and I would head back to Illinois late March for the wedding.

Liz and I would be moving to Los Angeles after our honeymoon, so we would need to go back to San Francisco to get our stuff out of storage once we were settled in LA. We decided to sell both of our cars before we left. I really loved my MGB-GT, but it was time to say goodbye to the expensive car repairs. I did keep my motorcycle. I wanted to retain my rebel reputation.

CHAPTER 18—GETTING MARRIED: THE MAIN EVENT

Our wedding was at St. Patrick's Catholic Church in Danville, Illinois, on April 2nd (not April 1st), 1977. Everything went off without a hitch. However, looking back at the wedding photos, the mustache was a mistake. The cream tuxedo with the longest crotch you've ever seen on trousers was another change I should have considered; but it was springtime and black is so typical. It's hard to laugh at old wedding photos if everyone is wearing classy black tuxedos. Where is the fun in that?

The reception was a little strange in that there was no booze at all. Liz's parents were afraid they would offend my family if there was a drop of alcohol anywhere near the reception, so we had to tell our friends to bring their own and sneak out to their cars to get their alcohol fixes. Ours may have been the only dry Catholic wedding ever in the history of Danville Catholicism. I'm sure even the priest was wondering where to get a drink at our wedding reception.

Liz's family was able to hold down the cost of the wedding reception by having it at The Harrison Park Golf Course and Clubhouse. Sounds fancy, but it's not. It's an old public golf course and the rental fee for the clubhouse was less than $100. Liz's family made all the food and appetizer items, many of which were traditional favorites of her family like "egg cheese." Don't ask what egg cheese is because it's very hard to explain and it might gross you out.

In the end, the clubhouse cleaned up nicely, people enjoyed the band, there was plenty to eat, the egg cheese went over well, and our friends were still able to quietly get drunk if they wished. I don't think anyone shared their liquor with the priest.

* * *

We did the Icelandic Airways route from Chicago to Iceland, and then Iceland to Luxembourg, just like I had done in the summer of '73. We decided not to use the Eurail passes until later in the trip because the passes were good for only one month of unlimited travel.

We arrived in Paris on Easter. If you have never been in Paris on Easter, you would not know how crazed that city is with people coming in from all over France for the holiday. We didn't know this at the time and once we arrived at the Paris train station, we were told we would never find a hotel room. The hotel reservation center at the train station was packed with desperate travelers needing a place to stay for the night.

The reservation center was a large room and we were far from the reservation counter. When the agents had a room available, they would yell out where the hotel was and the cost of the room. We were sure we would never get a room and may even have to get back on a train and sleep there overnight.

Like a miracle, one of the reservationists called out a hotel and none of the people in front of us reacted right away. So, I yelled out, "YES!" The price was right, the location was good, and the continental breakfast was included. To this day, I have no idea how it happened the way it did. After the woman made the reservation for us, everyone looked at us wondering what just transpired as we walked out. To this day, I feel it was one of my greatest coups.

The sister of my fraternity brother/ex-roommate, Steve Stratton, was living in London with her husband, Dennis. Susan, a brilliant woman, was an editor and script reader; Dennis was working for the BBC. They offered to let us stay with them for a few days.

We tried to have a good time in London, but it was raining every day. It was totally depressing, so we decided to head back to France with the plan of ending up in Nice, on the French Riviera. The plan was to stay there for a month. Just twenty miles from Nice, the Cannes Film Festival would be going on during that month. I definitely wanted to experience that.

I convinced Liz we should buy two "mopeds" and ride them to France. We walked into a motorcycle shop, picked out two mopeds and two helmets, and paid for them with a credit card. The plan was to sell them to other traveling Americans when we were done with them later in the summer. It would have been a great plan if it had worked out that way.

We literally asked someone at the cycle shop, *Which way to France?*

We had a map, but there was no way to tell from the map which was the best route to get out of London. After riding around in circles in the rain for an hour, we realized it was going to be quite a challenge just to get out of London.

It was a crazy thing to do, especially since Liz had never ridden a moped or motorcycle before. I didn't even give her time to practice. I just assumed, if you could ride a bicycle, you could ride a moped. Of course, the moped is going 30-40 miles per hour, and a bike is not. I also didn't realize that Liz's instincts were to turn the handlebars when she wanted to turn, instead of leaning into the turn. It took a few crashes for me to realize why she kept crashing as we desperately tried to get the hell out of London. She crashed when turning from one city street to another if she was going too fast. She wasn't hurt, except for her pride.

After stopping several times to ask for directions, we found ourselves on what appeared to be a multiple lane, interstate-type road headed to France. Our plan was to spend the night in Dover, and then take the Hovercraft across the English Channel to Calais the next day.

The rain was coming down hard and the wind was strong. We were way behind schedule and it was starting to get dark. We were wearing backpacks and long ponchos that were blowing like sails on a schooner. We noticed there were only commercial trucks on the highway: no cars or motorcycles. After we had traveled many miles, we stopped to get gas. We asked a friendly face why there were no cars and they explained we were on a commercial motorway for trucks. They couldn't believe we hadn't been run over yet. But it was too late to change now, so we finished the journey.

By the time we got to Dover, we were cold, soaking wet, and tired. We found a cheap room to spend the night where the only heat came from a coin operated floor heater. We had to put ten pence coins in it to get any heat. Not having the correct coinage to operate the heater, we went across the street to a bar to have a beer, warm up, and get change. We were completely worn out, so we came back quickly to heat up the room and get some sleep.

The next day, we made our way to the Hoverport to catch the Hovercraft. We loaded up the mopeds and enjoyed the 45-minute ride across to Calais.

It was mid-afternoon when we arrived in Calais. We weren't on a schedule so we decided to ride the 22 miles to Boulogne, get a room, and rest up for the long haul to Paris the next day.

The next morning, we had a great continental breakfast at our Boulogne hotel and headed out. I was determined, and maybe a little cocky, with my plan to ride all the way to Paris, a total of about 133 miles. As a note to anyone that hasn't ridden a moped: that's a long ride on a moped.

It was a very windy day and we were not getting a lot of respect from the other vehicles on the winding, two-lane, rural road. We had only gone about fifteen miles when a large truck flew past us at a high rate of speed. The rush of air, combined with the wind, blew Liz off the road. It doesn't matter what you're riding; hitting the ground at thirty plus miles per hour hurts. I ran to her, checked her for injuries, and helped her get her wits about her. Luckily, she had landed in grass, so there were only minor scrapes. The moped suffered no real damage. But Liz was not in good shape emotionally. The crash totally freaked her out.

I looked around and saw three or four houses a short distance down a side road (I have Superman vision). I asked Liz if she was able to ride to the small enclave. She said she could make it, so we rode what was less than a mile to find a Band-Aid or two, cool out for a little while, and figure out our next move.

As we got close, I realized one of the buildings was actually a tiny bar/cafe. When I say small, I mean small. It was obviously just for locals. We walked in and there was only room enough for about eight to ten people total in the place. The bar was only big enough for two people. The men in the room, who all looked like local farmers, were drinking wine and espresso. I could tell they were farmers because they were dressed like so many farmers I knew from home, and they all had on rubber boots with dried mud or pig shit on them. They looked at us like we were Martians. The only woman there was the keeper of the bar. No one spoke English, so my eight years of French came in handy to ask them if there was a hotel nearby. The proprietor told me about a bigger small town less than five miles away that had a nice little inn.

After having a glass of wine (or two), I convinced Liz that riding the five miles to the inn was our best option. I told her we could stay until she felt like she was ready to travel again. The inn turned out to be very nice, peaceful, and not too expensive. It was a good place for Liz to get her courage back and make sure she was physically ready to travel again.

While we were at the inn, we decided riding the mopeds 132 miles to Paris, and then riding another 580 miles to Nice on the French Riviera, would be insanity and possibly deadly. After doing some research, we made plans to go back to Boulogne where we could ship our mopeds straight through to Nice by train. Instead of heading straight to Nice ourselves, we took a train to Paris for a few days of museums and sightseeing before heading south to Nice. That worked out well since it was going to take a week for our mopeds to arrive in Nice.

Paris was "Paris" in the 1970s. The Paris we would like it to be now, but isn't. It was very much like it was when I had been there in 1973; brimming over with charm and character. I won't do a travelogue here, but we packed in a record amount of sightseeing in those few days before leaving Paris for the beaches of the Riviera.

When we arrived in Nice, our first mission was to find a place to stay for at least a month. I don't remember how we found it, but somehow we came upon a rustic one-bedroom apartment very near the famous outdoor flower and food markets.

When the lady showed us the apartment on the 4th floor, she told us that Napoleon actually had an office in the building when he was First Consul of France, before he declared himself emperor. She also told us the elevator wasn't working at the time but would be fixed. That turned out not to be true, so one might question the story about Napoleon; but there was a plaque on the building. It was two streets north of the beach, and you could buy fresh produce, flowers, and wine all within three blocks of the apartment. It was a wonderful place to stay and it was "so French." I was inspired to write a lot there.

The local red wine was excellent and sold at the nearby open-air market for fifty cents when you brought your own bottle. They kept the wine in a monster-sized wooden barrel from which they filled our bottles. The wine was so good (and cheap) we often drank two or three bottles per day. It was red wine at lunch, dinner, and for fun at night. We definitely overdid it and finally curtailed the red wine drinking when we noticed our tongues were permanently purple.

One day we rode our mopeds twenty miles to Cannes where the Cannes Film Festival was in full swing. It was very exciting for a farm boy from Illinois with a degree in Film and TV to be in Cannes while the festival was going on. I still have the poster from the festival that I peeled off a pole. It hangs proudly in my acting studio. We thought it was so cool when a man came up to us and asked if we would like to have tickets to view one of the movies. We jumped at the chance. The movie was not a good one. Now, after serving as an executive producer on six films, I understand the film was a second or third-tier movie looking for distribution. They gave us the tickets because they wanted to make sure the theatre was as full as possible for a better image.

We also rode our mopeds fourteen miles along the coast to Monte Carlo to spend some time, and very little money, at the famous casino there. The people watching was great: gamblers were there from all over the world. It wasn't like a *James Bond* movie with everyone in tuxedos and evening gowns, but it still seemed glamorous. Today, casinos are filled with people in t-shirts and shorts that don't understand the fun in dressing for the occasion. I hope casino-goers still try to show a little class in Monte Carlo.

One night as we were tooling around on our mopeds, Liz, once again, wiped out while turning a corner. She and her moped went flying and landed on an old woman. I stopped to help Liz as several people came to the aid of the older woman.

After making sure the old woman was not hurt badly, I said to Liz, "If there is any way you can get on that moped, we need to get the hell out of here before the police arrive. It could get messy."

I picked up Liz's moped, she got on it, and we sped away with her in a daze. I know that may sound like a hit and run, but it wasn't. Liz hit the woman with her body, not the moped. When we got back to our apartment, we backed the mopeds up to a wall so the license plates couldn't be seen just in case the police came looking for us.

The next day we had a serious discussion about the moped situation. We decided we had exhausted our fun with the mopeds; it was time to get rid of them and start the month of travel with our Eurail passes. Easier said than done.

We checked into shipping the mopeds back home, but the cost to ship was more than we had paid for them. I also thought about throwing them off a cliff and collecting the insurance, but I had always been a pretty law-abiding person and insurance fraud was out of my league.

We made "A Vendre" (For Sale) signs and hung them on the bikes. We spent time looking for buyers at the American Express office, a mecca for American travelers, and especially for young tourists trying to sell stuff before they left Europe.

We didn't find any takers, but we did get busted by the police. They explained that we were not allowed to have an "A Vendre" sign on our mopeds. We thought that was a stupid law, so we went to other areas of town to look for buyers. We were busted again by the police. I explained our situation to the cop, but he was not sympathetic. We asked him how we were supposed to sell the mopeds and he told us about a shop that rented mopeds. He was sure they would be interested at the right price.

The moped guy knew he had us by the balls. We had to sell the bikes and he was the only guy around that could legally buy them. We started out asking for $200 per moped. He laughed and said he would give us $20. We laughed and said no way. He would not budge—not for $100, or even $50. Our negotiations were a complete failure. We had to cave and take the $20 each. To add insult to injury, he would only give us one dollar for each helmet. Of course, Liz's helmet had some damage on it. We walked out the door with $42. But we were free now and we could go wherever we wanted and not be concerned with the mopeds. We headed out for Rome.

Chapter 19—Free at Last-No Mo' Moped

Once again, I was very impressed by the European train system. We made a huge mistake in America when we let the auto industry destroy our train system. Our rail system sucks except in the Northeast. We need to do something about this, since we are supposed to be the richest, smartest, and most advanced nation in the world.

Just sayin'.

* * *

In Rome, we went to the Vatican where we had an audience with Pope Paul VI in the Pope's Audience Hall. Liz's family was very Catholic; she was raised Catholic, went to all Catholic schools and our wedding was a Catholic ceremony. I can't remember who set up the audience, but I think it was a monsignor from her parents' church that I had bonded with during our Pre-Cana course.

The audience at the Pope's Audience Hall was a much more intimate setting than the general audience with the Pope that is held in Saint Peter's Square where there may be as many as 80,000 in attendance.

The second most notable thing about Rome was how rude and aggressive the young men were toward women. They were so disrespectful: they acted like I wasn't even there. It was uncomfortable with them following closely and making suggestive gestures. I was ready to get out of Rome.

Florence was the next stop. It is such a beautiful city with an abundance of beautiful museums, churches, and palazzos. Unfortunately, I was dealing with an issue there that I won't go into. All I will say is, it's very hard to find a bathroom when you need it in Florence. It very negatively affected our time in Florence. I blamed it on the city at the time, but it was probably the fault of a restaurant, not the city of Florence.

* * *

Amsterdam was a beautiful and interesting city, but the greatest discovery I made in Amsterdam was that French fries dunked in mayonnaise or warm peanut butter are amazing. I also had the most amazing breakfast I ever had in my life at a guesthouse owned by a wonderful older woman. The way to man's heart is…

Oslo, Norway was not what I thought it would be. When we got off the train, we were shocked that we had to step over the bodies of many drunk and filthy men to get out of the station. The scent of urine permeated the air. I hear it's better now but it's still an issue. People in Norway don't drink for the taste: they drink to get drunk.

We were so unimpressed that we decided not to spend the night there. It was cold, dreary, and depressing with all the drunks passed out everywhere. We got a feel for Oslo and jumped back on a train heading back south.

As we were wrapping up the European trip, I started getting excited about getting back to the Good Ole USA. I started missing the ease of living in America and some of the things I took for granted, like driving a car and riding my motorcycle. I had written notebooks full of new comedy material on the trip and I was anxious to get back on stage and see how well my new material would be received in Los Angeles.

Chapter 20—Back From Europe/On To L.A.

Once we were back in Illinois, we needed to return a few remaining wedding gifts and buy a car powerful enough to pull a U-Haul trailer over the mountains on our trip to Los Angeles. We also wanted to spend time with our families since we didn't know how long it would be before we would be back.

Where does any person from the Midwest go when they first hit Los Angeles? Malibu, of course. We secured a room in a dumpy little motel that was across the road from the beach; that was all that mattered to us. For the next 24 hours we lived on the ocean.

It took a few days to find a short-term lease on a furnished apartment, so we ended up staying in another dumpy motel in Santa Monica because it was only $16, instead of the $25 in Malibu. We hadn't been spoiled yet, so as long as it was cheap, had a mattress, and was in a reasonably safe neighborhood, we were happy.

We found a three-month rental on a furnished apartment through an ad in the Los Angeles Times. We knew nothing about Los Angeles and had no idea where we would be working, so we picked a nice apartment that was not far from downtown or Hollywood. It was a newish apartment complex with a nice pool and fairly nice furniture. Unfortunately, it was not close to the beach or the West Los Angeles area.

We both wanted to secure employment right away so we wouldn't have to use our savings to live. Liz was immediately hired by Hertz Car Rental near Hollywood and Vine, right in the middle of the craziness of Hollywood Boulevard.

I needed the same flexibility I had found in San Francisco by waiting tables. I didn't really like being a waiter for many reasons, but most of those reasons had something to do with ego. It wasn't easy for me to set my ego aside to work in a restaurant again, but I had to put my entertainment career ahead of my ego. That meant making the most money in the shortest amount of time. There was also the beauty of being able to trade shifts, or just call in sick if something really important came up.

My research told me the restaurants in the Westwood area were very busy and the average guest was reasonably sophisticated, so there was good money to be made in those restaurants. Also, those restaurants were within two blocks of the theatres where most major movies were premiered.

I walked into the Hungry Tiger, a fresh fish restaurant literally one hundred yards from the entrance to the UCLA campus, and I walked out with a job and a work schedule. The manager loved that I had great experience in San Francisco and knew a lot about wine. He also appreciated the fact that I had a college degree and lots of sales experience.

It was a union house, so I got full health insurance after sixty days. Unlike the world of servers today, we were paid full minimum wage, received excellent free employee meals, and 50% off at any of the other many restaurants the company owned. Most important of all, we only had to report 10% of our tips. I came home with lots of cash.

I waited on many celebrities: Sean Connery (my favorite James Bond); Alan Alda multiple times; Tom Selleck twice, Jerry Lewis (was not nice) three times; movie star George Segal (*The Owl and The Pussycat*), who left me an empty pack of *Gitane* cigarettes with half a joint in it; Michelle Lee from *Knots Landing*, who would request me; Valerie Harper from Rhoda and *The Mary Tyler Moore Show*, who would always want me to escort her to the door. The list could go on and on.

In fact, I think I will. Indulge me for a bit.

Chapter 21—Celebrity Disappointments and a Few Nice Guys

Jerry Lewis was one of my two biggest celebrity disappointments. He wasn't nice to me or anyone else in our restaurant. He was not the man I had admired for his work on the Muscular Dystrophy Association Telethons. He treated me like I was a total annoyance to him. He was just too cool for school. Maybe he put on that act so people wouldn't try to engage him in a conversation, but it was wrong. This happened to me more than once with Jerry. Lucky for him there was no social media back then; I would have trashed him.

But Art Linkletter takes first prize as the number one jerk. He was nice enough, but it was all a show. He showed his true colors at my table.

Harry, the manager of our restaurant, came to me and said he wanted me to wait on a large party hosted by Art Linkletter. I was excited because I grew up watching him on television. Art was a Canadian-born American radio and television personality and pioneer of TV talk shows. He was the host of *House Party*, which ran on CBS radio and television for twenty-five years, and *People Are Funny*, which aired on NBC radio and television for nineteen years. One popular feature of his *House Party* program was the *Kids Say the Darndest Things* segments. People in America would have trusted him with their money and their children, but they didn't know him like I came to know him.

Harry seated Art and his guests, one of whom was an actress that had been very famous in the '40s & '50s, in a room separated from the other guests. I started out by asking if anyone would like a cocktail or wine. Art immediately stated, "I know I don't want a cocktail. Personally, I don't know why anyone would need to drink alcohol before a meal. But if anyone would like a drink, please go ahead."

No one dared to be the person who "needed alcohol," so that cut drinks and wine out of Art's check.

Then I asked, "Would anyone like an appetizer? Oysters on the half shell, oysters Rockefeller, shrimp cocktail..." Art cut me off saying, "The portions here are so large that you can't even eat the whole meal with all the rice pilaf, baked potato, salad, and the entree." That pretty much put the whammy on the addition of any appetizers added to the check.

I mentioned the different fresh fish of the day, the cheapest of which was red snapper. We always had red snapper and Art seemed to know it because he announced to the party, "The red snapper here is amazing. It's the best I've ever had." I now had Art pegged as "One of Those Guys." First of all, I hate red snapper, and even if I liked it, I'm sure it wasn't the best in the world.

After everyone was finished, or not finished, with their red snapper, I asked if anyone would like an after-dinner drink. Of course, the answer was no. I started to list the choices for dessert, but Art piped up saying, "Oh my, I could hardly finish my meal. I can't even think of dessert after that meal. Would anyone like dessert? No, I think we're good. Just the check."

This was my only party for the night, and my whole tip income was going to be based on a check for eight people eating the cheapest thing on the menu with no drinks, appetizers, after-dinner drinks or dessert. Surely, Art Linkletter noticed that I was devoted to his party and would leave me a very generous tip.

Art paid the bill with large bills. I brought back his change and he immediately put a large tip in the middle of the table—for his guests to see. He and his party started leaving with Art ushering everyone out of the room ahead of him. After his guests were out of sight, he reached back and grabbed much of the tip he had left on the table and put it in his pocket. He didn't see me watching him, but I don't think he really cared about what I thought.

When I counted what was left of the tip, he had barely left 10%.

I was just stiffed by Art Linkletter? I was so disappointed I called my parents the next day and told them to never, ever watch Art Linkletter if he ever got another TV show. He didn't.

He did the exact same thing with a different group of people a few months later. Harry wanted me to wait on his party again because Art told him he really liked the service I gave his party the last time. I told Harry I wouldn't do it again. Harry promised he would make it up to me somehow.

He never did. And needless to say, Art did not get the special treatment the second time. I didn't spit in his food—but I wanted to.

* * *

James L. Brooks has been writing, directing and producing hit TV series and movies since the '70s. Shows like: *Mary Tyler Moore, Rhoda, Lou Grant, Phyllis, Room 222, The Associates, TAXI,* and *The Simpsons.* Later he wrote and directed such films as: *Terms of Endearment* (three Academy Awards); *Broadcast News*; and *As Good As It Gets.* The list goes on and on. I had waited on James and another writer/friend before. They were super nice to me and gave me a very generous tip, partly because they knew I was staying late just to take care of them. He was a fun, funny, regular guy with no attitude who obviously loved what he did for a living. They usually came in later in the evening as business was winding down in the restaurant. This meant I would need to stay until they were ready to go, but I was happy to do it for them.

On one of his visits, I told him I really enjoyed his television shows. I could tell he appreciated my compliment. I was sincere with my praise, but it was also a conversation starter that I hoped would lead to more talk and maybe some career advice. He asked me if I was involved in the entertainment business, probably because a great percentage of waiters in those days were trying to break into the business on some level. Knowing he was a comedy writer, I decided not to mention the actor/standup stuff. Instead, I told him I had a comedy play I had written called *Thousand Island,* that was being considered by The Hudson Guild Theatre in New York and another theatre in Los Angeles. He graciously said he would be happy to take a look at it. He gave me his assistant's name and told me I could drop it off or mail it to his offices at Paramount Television, where his company was based.

I was flying high on my way home, which usually meant I was riding my motorcycle well above the speed limit. After all, this was my first real contact with someone that was wildly successful in "The Business." In fact, I had not really made any contacts that had a medium amount of success in the business other than the actors I had served at the restaurant. I thought to myself, "This is my man, and my big break."

I made sure that I didn't waste any time. I showed up with my play in hand at his offices at Paramount on Monday morning. I knew I wouldn't see him but I wanted to make sure that I physically delivered it to his assistant.

Now, I just needed to wait for James L. Brooks to read my play and recognize my comic genius. I say that jokingly, but I'm sure I thought I had a lot to offer as a comedy writer back then. Nothing wrong with confidence.

Two weeks later I called James's office to see if he had had the opportunity to read my play. I was told they would leave a message.

Two weeks after that I still hadn't heard from James, so I called again and left another message, reminding him how we met and what he said.

Two weeks later, my bruised ego was starting to get in the way. I decided I would try one last time to shame him into reading my play that he suggested I send to him. Still no response. At that point, I gave up and stopped calling. My ego couldn't take it anymore. I felt like I was begging and I worried he would think I was a pest.

Now, I realize that was one of my biggest mistakes in my entertainment career. I should have persisted. I believe he would have eventually read it. After being in the business for years, I understand what it's like to be so busy that you can't do everything you want to do, when you want to do it.

I let my ego get in the way. I tell my students not to do what I did. Be persistent and don't give up. If someone like James L. Brooks says he will read it, he will read it someday. But you have to be patient, along with being persistent.

CHAPTER 22—I NEVER REALLY WANTED TO BE A COMEDIAN IN THE FIRST PLACE

The standup comedy world can be a real ego buster. One evening I was scheduled to go on at The Comedy Store at 9:00, which was a coveted time slot. Just before I was supposed to go on, Jimmie "JJ" Walker, the star of the hit CBS television series Good Times, came in the club and wanted to try out some new material. There's a rule at most comedy clubs: if a big comedy star comes in and wants to perform, they get to go on next. The audience loves it and they can tell the world how they got a big surprise performance by a TV star at the club. It's the best kind of free publicity for the club.

The club manager told me I would go on as soon as Jimmie was done. Jimmie ended up experimenting for two hours. By the time he finished it was 11:00 and all but five people left the club. One of the five was Liz. I can't be funny for four people plus my wife; it just doesn't work for me. Plus, Liz never laughs when she's watching comedy. Even if she thinks it hilarious, she doesn't laugh. It's weird. She says she's too busy listening to laugh. It was no fun at all.

The last time I ever appeared as a standup comedian was in 1978 at Ye Little Club in Beverly Hills. When I got to the club early that evening, I found out I was going to be following Garry Shandling. I immediately went into panic mode because I was a Garry Shandling fan. I had seen him several times on *The Tonight Show* as well as other national television shows, and always thought he was hilarious. I'd never followed a star before. I don't count the night following Jimmie Walker. I couldn't riff after a pro with a very tight act. I started editing my material knowing I needed to pull out my very best material and performance; but making changes right before you go on is a sure way to crash and burn. You have to stick with the plan. As I thought about each of my bits, I couldn't help comparing them to Garry's material. I knew my material wasn't at the same level. I was an amateur and he was a professional. I really let it get in my head. Watching him kill was so painful.

Then I heard the emcee say, "Our next comedian is here for the first time. Let's give Alan Dysert a big hand."

My legs felt wobbly and my brain wasn't working right. I was going through my edited bits but they weren't hitting. I was in my head too much to be funny. The audience can't have fun if the comedian isn't having fun, and I was definitely not having fun.

Unfortunately, Liz had invited a couple of people from her work to come that night. I have never liked performing for people I know, but it was especially unfortunate that they came that night. To make matters worse, we had to go out to eat with them after the sinking of my ship.

I never get depressed, but I'm sure the next few days were the exception. Liz said, "If you're going to go through this every time your performance doesn't go well, you shouldn't do it." A friend chimed in with, "You don't look like a comedian anyway, Alan. You look like an actor."

I said, "Ok. Where do I do that?"

CHAPTER 23—ALAN THE ACTOR

A friend told me his girlfriend had taken acting classes at a little ninety-nine seat theatre called Theatrecraft Playhouse behind The Sunset Grill. Yes, the same Sunset Grill made famous by the Don Henley song, *Sunset Grill*. I ate a double cheeseburger there every week from little old Joe, the owner.

I called Theatrecraft Playhouse and scheduled an interview with Rick Walters, the owner/acting coach. He had me do a reading to see if I had any acting chops. I'm sure I showed very little acting ability, but I was accepted into the program. I'm not sure anyone was ever rejected.

I was a nervous wreck when I first started taking classes. Rick's rule was that if you showed up more than ten minutes late, you wouldn't be allowed to perform that day; you would only be able to watch the other class members perform. I tended to be late a lot in the beginning. Sometimes, I was actually sitting in the parking lot waiting so I could walk in late. I needed a few weeks to get comfortable. Sometimes I would drink a sixteen-ounce beer through a paper straw (makes it go to your head faster) to get the courage to go in. I'm not proud of that, but that was my reality and an example of how much I was affected by my performance anxiety.

My performance anxiety became a problem after I choked badly at a piano recital when I was thirteen. The issue was never mentioned or addressed at the time. Everyone acted like it had never happened. I just buried it deep and vowed to myself that I would never let myself feel that humiliation again. It was the last time I ever played piano in public and the beginning of a decades-long problem.

Most of the members of my class were pretty good. Some of them had been in class for a year or two, and some had studied acting in college. Others were just pretty people who had been told they should be actors. Then there was me, who had been told I should get out of stand-up comedy because I looked like an actor.

I wasn't a total novice: I had been in four plays in high school and had taken some acting classes at the University of Illinois and San Francisco State University, but I didn't feel like I really knew much about the craft of acting. I'm not a big fan of the way most colleges teach acting. Most programs have nothing to do with acting for film and television. There is often a lot of wasted time learning techniques that don't work in the modern acting world, and usually the teachers have never worked professionally.

I knew absolutely nothing about the business side of the acting world when I started taking class, but I was picking up a lot listening to the people in my class. I was so green, I didn't even know what a headshot was. One of the guys brought in his new headshots and was showing them to another student/actor sitting in the row in front of me. Eavesdropping, I realized this was something I was going to need, so I asked him who did his headshots. He gave me the name and number of his photographer, Buddy.

My photo shoot with Buddy went very well. He took some very flattering professional photos and even helped me piece together my performance resume. Buddy knew I didn't have an agent, so he introduced me to a bottom-of-the-food-chain agent he knew. He told me upfront the agent didn't have any power in Hollywood, but said maybe he could get me started: any agent was better than no agent.

The agent was possibly the worst agent in town and had no known actors on his roster, but somehow he managed to have an attitude anyway. The first thing he did was pick me apart. He said my forehead stuck out too far and told me I had a "sibilant s." I had never heard of a "sibilant s" before that. He made me feel like I had a terrible speech impediment and no one would ever hire me. But he still took me on as a client.

He only got me one audition, but the casting director on that show thought I had some talent. He asked, "Why the hell are you with that agent?"

I told him the story of how I ended up with the guy but expressed how desperately I wanted a better and more pleasant agent. The casting director gave me the name of a much better agent and said, "Tell them I said they should sign you." I did exactly as he suggested and the agency signed me. The new agency was on a whole different level than the first loser.

* * *

The same casting director told me my resume would look a lot stronger if I were training with one of the very best acting coaches in Hollywood, like Jeff Corey. He said Jeff was picky about who he let in his class. Once again, he said I could use his name when I contacted Jeff.

I was a little nervous about calling Jeff Corey because I had seen him in many old movies and television shows. Jeff had coached major movie stars including: James Dean, Jack Nicholson, Kirk Douglas, Rob Reiner, Jane Fonda, Leonard Nimoy, and Tony Perkins, to name a few.

Jeff started teaching acting in 1951, the year I was born, after his career had come to an end when he was blacklisted because he refused to name names before the House Un-American Activities Committee. Jeff did manage to re-boot his acting career in 1962 and was cast in such movies as *Butch Cassidy and the Sundance Kid* with Robert Redford and Paul Newman, *True Grit* with John Wayne, and *Little Big Man*, in which he played the legendary Wild Bill Hickok.

When I called Jeff and told him casting director Al Onorato had suggested I audition for his class, Jeff asked me to come to his home in Malibu to meet with him. We sat and talked about my background and my goals for about fifteen minutes before he had me read a scene with him. The reading went well and he was complimentary, but I had no idea what he really thought. He told me he would let me know within the week if he had a spot for me in his class. I was very excited when I got the call a few days later saying I had been accepted into Jeff Corey's class.

Jeff didn't mess around. If someone was overacting, being too cute, or not listening to their scene partner, Jeff was very rough on them. Sometimes he would cause women to cry and leave the studio with Jeff yelling to them, "And don't come back until you're ready to take acting seriously."

I didn't always agree with Jeff's approach because it put too much fear in everyone. We worried about how Jeff would want us to do the scene rather than go with our feelings. It made it harder to be creative. I learned a lot from Jeff's class but most of the time we were watching other students do scenes, since he would only schedule two scenes per session.

This meant each student only performed about once every six weeks. We would rehearse with our scene partner outside of class for weeks before our scheduled performance. This was not ideal for me because I really need-ed to perform on a more regular basis to help with my performance anxiety issues. I also found it boring to watch Jeff beat up on a scene for an hour or more before moving on to the second scene.

It was good discipline for me, and Jeff definitely knew the craft of acting. His class also prepared us for working with directors and producers who would be expecting a lot from us and wouldn't put up with any BS: some directors can be even more brutal than Jeff, so get ready for the real world of a working actor.

When I started teaching, I took a totally different approach. I taught based on what I thought would have helped me most as an actor. I felt it was best to have each student perform on camera in every single class. The actors need to be comfortable in front of the camera and lights before working on more complex aspects of the craft.

I've always taken a very gentle and positive approach to working with my students. Actors are easily bruised, so a coach has to be very careful not to damage the student and cause them to fear performing. I tell my students I want them to have fun learning the craft, not worry about what will happen to them in class.

* * *

My first real acting job came from a contact Liz made while working at Hertz Rental Car. Her office was on Hollywood Boulevard and, due to their location, they rented lots of cars to production companies. Sometimes a project would need as many as ten cars. One of the guys who often rented cars asked Liz what her husband did. She told him I was doing comedy but had decided to focus on acting. He told her I should drop off a headshot and resume at their office. He said they did lots of commercials and maybe they could call me in for a casting session sometime.

Liz came home and told me about the guy, and even though I assumed he was just trying to get to know my wife, I dropped off my headshot and resume at the commercial production company, Paisley Productions, the next day.

You can imagine my surprise when I got a call from the commercial agent at my new agency saying he had a request for me to audition for a Chrysler commercial to be shot by Paisley Productions. I hadn't even met the commercial agent at my new agency yet, only the theatrical agent who had signed me.

I went in for the audition the next day. There was a little small talk and a few questions about my acting training. Then they asked, "Can you drive behind a camera truck?"

They explained this was crucial for car commercials. Not realizing it was an actual skill, I replied, "I'm a farm boy and I can drive anything with wheels." Everyone got a good laugh out of that. I felt like everything went well but knew they were auditioning lots of actors for the commercial. It was going to be a two-day shoot and a very important commercial for Chrysler.

I was shocked when the commercial agent called me and said, "I haven't even met you yet, and not only did you get a big audition, they want to hire you for the shoot." Then he said, "All I need is your Screen Actors Guild card number."

I said, "Oh, I'm not in SAG yet."

"What? They think you're in the union."

"I never told them that," I protested.

The agent was not happy. He ended by saying, "Let me call them and see if they will Taft-Hartley you."

A Taft-Hartley letter basically says the producers of a project can't find the actor they need for their project from actors in the Screen Actors Guild and want to hire a specific non-union actor for their project. If the producers are willing to sign a Taft-Hartley letter, the non-union actor is then allowed to do the job. That actor is also able to join the union at that point. I got lucky; the producer said, "No problem."

Not only was I going to be acting in a big Chrysler commercial, I was going to be legitimate. It made me eligible to join The Screen Actors Guild, which is very tricky to get into because you're required to have worked on a SAG project before you can join. But you can't get the SAG job unless you're in SAG. It's a "chicken or the egg" situation. What needs to happen is exactly what had just happened with me: someone has to want an actor bad enough that they're willing to sign a Taft-Hartley letter. Every actor in the union has a story something like mine.

My new agent was very happy with me since I was cast in the first audition they sent me on. They were also aware the audition hadn't really come from their efforts; it had come from Liz's contact at Hertz Rental Car. Once I arrived on location for the commercial, I realized I was the only actor in the commercial. I would be doing a lot of driving around the very picturesque Griffith Park for the commercial. The ad was for the popular Chrysler Volare. It was a two-day shoot, which meant the initial session fee would be double, and the residual payments would be higher as well. My agent told me some Volare commercials in the past had run for months and the actors made over $100,000 in residuals. My agent should never have told me that, because I started looking at expensive cars and considering the purchase of a bigger house.

The shoot was nerve-racking. Once we got started, I realized following a camera truck was an actual skill. It meant I would have a walkie-talkie sitting next to me so I could take direction from the director, who was riding on the back of a camera truck telling me when to accelerate from one speed to another speed over a certain number of seconds. During this acceleration, I was to stay the exact same distance from a camera that was mounted on the back of the camera truck. One false move and I could easily crash into the camera truck and seriously damage a very expensive camera lens.

During this process, I was supposed to keep a very happy smile on my face since I was portraying a man who loved his Volare. It was traumatizing. This all had to happen in the late afternoon when they could catch the "beauty light." This short period of time is when the sun is low, but not down, and the natural sunlight is most flattering for filming cars. It can make even an ugly car look pretty good. Almost all national car commercials are shot this way.

We rehearsed for hours and every preparation possible was made to ensure, once we had the beauty light, we could start filming the commercial. When they said, "Let's go," there wasn't even time to pee, since the only place to pee was the Winnebago back at the production base camp. I had no choice but to hold it, which isn't easy when you're nervous.

Anyone seeing that commercial was going to see a very nervous young man who was about to pee his pants. The filming went on for what seemed like hours, but mostly because I was about to burst. In the end, I didn't break any equipment and they never said, "You don't really know how to follow a camera truck, do you?" I must have pulled it off because they told me I did a great job.

All I had to do was wait for the Brink's truck full of money to roll up in front of my house once the commercial started airing. Unfortunately, it didn't happen that way.

We were told the exact date the commercial was supposed to start airing. Chrysler's plan was for the commercial to debut during the USC-UCLA football game. I was thrilled about seeing my spot on national television. I was performing in a play at a small theatre that day, so I brought my television to the theatre and put it in a dressing room backstage.

There was no way to record programming in 1979, so if I didn't catch it in real time, I wouldn't see the debut. When I was on stage, I had another actor watching for the commercial; and when I wasn't on stage, I would watch. We never saw the commercial. Maybe we missed it?

Trying to be positive, I decided it was probably going to air during one of the NFL games the next day. I watched every game on Sunday and still no Volare commercial starring Alan Dysert.

On Monday, I decided to call the producer of the commercial at the offices of the advertising agency, Young & Rubicam. He and I had hit it off during the shoot, so I knew he could give me the scoop on when the commercial would be airing. There was no small talk: he came right out with, "I have some very bad news, Alan. The commercial is never going to air. Lee Iacocca just took over Chrysler and he canned all the commercials we've shot recently. He wants to be in all the commercials for the Volare himself. They're going to shoot all new commercials with Lee as the spokesman for Volare."

There went the new sports car and new house.

I was sick to my stomach. Sure, I was going to make a nice chunk for the shoot, but the residuals would have been twenty-five to fifty times that amount over time. This was the very first major disappointment in my acting career.

* * *

Once I was in the Screen Actors Guild, I became even more aggressive about marketing myself. I used what I had learned as a real estate guy to promote myself as an actor. I had a headshot, a resume, and I was taking acting class. In those days, that made me an actor.

I regularly bought all the trade magazines, looking for any address where I could send my marketing materials along with a cover letter introducing myself and requesting to be considered for any projects they might be casting. I had my "marketing department" set up in my garage and any time I could find an address I would go out to the garage, put a packet together, and send it off. All my friends said my marketing campaign would never work, but I kept it up.

Eventually, what my actor friends said wouldn't work, did. The first job I got was on the number one soap opera, *The Young and The Restless* on CBS. It was two days as a glorified extra, playing an EMT. I was actually glad I didn't have lines because I was totally intimidated by their enormous studio with its hundreds of lights, six cameras, twelve sets, and at least one hundred people working on the production. It was exciting but a little overwhelming. Soaps use more cameras, lighting, and sets than any other type of production. David Hasselhoff was on *The Young and the Restless* at that time and was the biggest soap star in the world. David was in "my" scene, which made it even more intimidating since I had watched him on the show many times.

Next, I was cast in a movie starring one of my all-time favorite Irish actors, Richard Harris. This was also a gig that came from a packet I had submitted myself. I was cast as a SWAT squad guy who had very little to do, but, for some reason, I was asked to eat with the main cast. The leading lady of the movie (who I won't name out of respect for the lady) sat across from me at dinner. We had a fun and lively conversation. I felt like she was hitting on me, but I assumed she was just kidding around. Now, I realize she was hitting on me; I was just too naive to realize it at the time. Maybe that's why I was invited to eat with the main cast?

It was all very exciting, even if I was an unimportant part of the film. I learned a lot about how a big film is put together—and a lot about the star of the movie, who was a biggie at the time.

* * *

Shortly after the Richard Harris film came one of my biggest breaks. I got a message through my answering service that the hit ABC-TV comedy series, *Soap*, had called and wanted me to call back. I was super excited because *Soap* was my favorite show at the time. It was wacky and way over-the-top.

I had sent another of my self-marketing packets to them; my agent hadn't submitted me for a role on the show. I immediately called back and was asked if I could work as an extra on the show. I jumped at the opportunity. I didn't care that it was just an extra role. I wanted to be on that set even if it meant mopping the floors.

It was so exciting to walk through that soundstage door and see my favorite actors running lines and walking around the sets that represented the world I knew from watching *Soap*.

Alan's Headshot From The 80s

I was taken to a holding room where all the extras were hanging out.

I was there for about fifteen minutes before a frantic producer came in and said they had forgotten to cast Father Tim's best man. That's how wacky the show was; the young priest was getting married in that episode. He looked around the room to see if there was a candidate for the role in the room. There were only two possibilities that made sense.

He looked at me and said, "Alan, come with me to the business office." I didn't know what that meant, but I knew it was good news.

The producer gave me the details of my role in the scene as we walked to the business office. He explained the situation to the woman there and said he would be back for me in a few minutes. She clarified the contract I needed to sign and told me what I would be paid. I was very excited to see I would be making almost ten times what I had expected to be paid as an extra. Then she said, "And of course you'll also be getting residuals if the show goes into reruns." I had very little knowledge of how residuals worked at that point because it had never applied to my career until that point, but I knew it was a good thing.

The producer showed up just as we were finishing up and asked me

91

to follow him. He said, "Sal Viscuso, who plays Father Tim on the show, is a method actor and wants to feel like you really are his best friend. He wants to hang out with you today to get that relationship going before the scene in the church."

I said, "Cool!" Then he took me to meet Sal in his dressing room.

Sal was a great guy! He took me under his wing and introduced me as his best man to Billy Crystal, the fabulous Doris Roberts, Katherine Helmond, Diana Canova, Richard Mulligan, and other members of the show. We even had a bite to eat in the commissary with some of the cast. He treated me as an equal, not just a guy that was coming in for a bit in one episode. He also introduced me to the director, Jay Sandrich, one of the all- time great comedy directors.

I was one of the gang at that point. Everything Sal did made me feel very comfortable. I would've been a basket case if they had just brought me on cold to rehearse the scene. Sal even had me improvise some conversations that he thought the characters would have before the wedding. He was the first actor I had met that put that kind of effort into his character and a scene. He taught me a lot in a short amount of time and set a very high standard for what I would look for in my next scene partners.

The fact that the priest on the show was getting married gives you an idea of how outrageous the storylines were on *Soap*. That's what made it so much fun.

In "my" scene, I was standing at the altar with Father Tim (Sal) and Corinne (Diana Canova), who in real life ended up marrying my future record producer.

The ceremony was about to begin when Father Tim's mother (Doris Roberts--best known for her role on *Everybody Loves Raymond*) frantically runs into the church to stop the wedding. My job was to intercept her, struggle with her with lots of improvised grunts and groans, and then drag her out of the church kicking and screaming. It was magical working with those professionals. They were all so believable and invested in their characters.

When the episode aired, I was so excited that nothing was cut. Not only that, the director thought the look on my face was so stupid, he rolled the credits over a freeze frame of my face. I don't know if any other show's credits ever rolled over someone's face that was originally brought in as an extra. I got lucky.

I've been getting residual checks for that episode of Soap for forty-two years: every time it airs on Comedy Central, airplanes, free TV, or when someone buys a DVD collection. That's the beauty of residuals.

CHAPTER 24—CHEECH AND CHONG
GO HOLLYWEED

Not long after the *Soap* gig, I was cast in a movie with Cheech and Chong.

I'd just performed a scene from a comedy play I had written at a comedy showcase. As I was getting dressed backstage, someone came to the door and said two casting directors from Universal wanted to talk with me. I knew their names immediately because I had tried, unsuccessfully, to meet them many times.

The casting directors told me they loved my performance and were casting me in the new Cheech and Chong movie.

What? Did I hear that right?

I felt like I was dreaming. The Cheech and Chong movies were the kind of outrageous, over-the-top comedy projects that made me want to come to Hollywood in the first place. They said they had already called my agent and the deal had been made. They just wanted me to come to their office the next day to talk about my role in the movie.

When I got in my car, my hands were shaking and my mind was racing. I couldn't believe what had just happened. My world had just changed. I was legit. I didn't know what to do first. I wasn't sure I was in any condition to drive. I just sat there in my car until I felt like I could make it home safely.

The meeting was really a formality, but it was a good chance to establish a relationship with the casting directors. They told me there was a script, but said Cheech and Chong rarely stick to it. "Expect a considerable amount of improv," they said.

They also explained that my ability to play guitar was important since my character would end up being the guitar player in Cheech's Vegas band. I was totally cool with all that and excited to see how it was all going to come together.

I was still working in the restaurant at the time, so I had Liz call me in sick. I knew Harry would try to tell me he couldn't let me off work to do the movie. Of course, I would've quit if I had to, but calling in sick was easier. Little did I know that I would be "sick" for weeks.

When I showed up at the Universal Studios lot, I felt like I was really in "The Biz". An associate producer met me at the gate and took me to my trailer. I couldn't believe I had my own trailer. It wasn't a special place, but it was mine. He told me they were running behind and might not get to my scenes that day. In the meantime, he said to just hang out and come into the soundstage anytime I wanted to watch what was going on.

There was lots of time to explore since they weren't going to get to my scenes. I had asked the associate producer if I could get a copy of the script. "Don't worry about it," he said. "Things are changing rapidly. You'll probably get a copy tomorrow." This didn't seem normal to me, but I surely wasn't going to complain, since I was being paid by the day.

I loved walking around the studio lot. It was so exciting to be on a real studio lot with actors from different movies walking around in costume. When the other films would take a break, some of the actors would come outside and have a smoke on their soundstage steps. They were shooting the original *The Blues Brothers* movie on the sound stage right across the little alley from our sound stage. I couldn't believe it when I saw John Belushi and Danny Aykroyd out on the steps in their *Blues Brothers* wardrobe that I had seen many times on *Saturday Night Live*. I felt like I had finally made it. I was in a Cheech and Chong movie and hanging out on the steps of a sound stage a mere fifty feet from The Blues Brothers.

The producer came to me later in the afternoon and said they wouldn't be getting to my scenes that day. He told me to report back at 7:30 in the morning.

The next day was the same as the first day with no script and no filming of my scenes. But as I was killing time walking around the lot, I ran across a woman in her twenties sitting outside another trailer. I stopped to ask her what she was working on.

She said, "I'm working on a movie with Cheech and Chong."

Turned out, she was a comedic actress who just happened to play piano. She said she had come across a young black actor hanging outside another trailer who told her he was a comedic actor who played bass. As we walked further, sure enough, we found a guy who was a comic actor who played the drums.

Then it hit us, "We're a band." Nobody had mentioned to any of us that we would be part of a band.

All three said they'd been told they would be doing improvisational comedy scenes with Cheech and Chong. There was concern amongst the group in that some had slightly exaggerated their musical abilities. It wasn't so much that we had exaggerated; we hadn't been asked to elaborate on the information that was on our resumes. We could all play pretty well, but we were by no means studio musicians. I can play most any song if given a little time, but I was used to playing only my original songs.

We still didn't have scripts and we didn't know what our characters were doing in the movie. We were all feeling a little less important as time went on, knowing we were sharing the limelight with three other comedic actor/musicians hired to do "improvisational comedy scenes with Cheech and Chong."

This went on for days before they were ready do our scenes. Our scenes weren't scripted and none of us had even seen a script. The film was Tommy Chong's directorial debut. Tommy gathered "the band" and explained the story behind the scenes: Cheech, Chong, and Cheech's girlfriend walk into a music store where they find me trying out a guitar, as well as the other musicians testing out instruments. Cheech improvises with us and then we all start jamming. Cheech goes into a fantasy where he becomes Elvis and we are his band in Las Vegas. Tommy told us we would be going to Vegas to film that part of the movie. He said to follow Cheech's lead and have fun winging it.

At this point, everyone involved with the movie was aware the film was way behind schedule, which meant they would be going over budget. The budget was already higher than any comedy movie had ever seen. They were able to get the big budget because all their previous movies had been very successful.

It was easy to see why they were behind schedule once we started working on our scenes. It was extremely loose and Tommy didn't seem to be fazed by the fact they were burning through lots of money as we continued to wing our scene over and over again. We would try stuff and then have a little meeting. Then we would rehearse another idea and throw in some music. This went on and on.

On the second day of getting almost nothing done, Tommy decided he wanted us to do some serious jamming as a band. Oops! That's when Tommy realized the casting directors had cast actors that could play instruments, not great musicians with a little comedy ability. We weren't the kind of band that could play anything he wanted on the spot. He needed very good studio-type jazz players to achieve what he was asking us to do.

Once he realized what he had to work with, he decided to call the musicians union and bring in a real jazz/blues band to help us out a little. It took four hours to find qualified musicians that were available and get them to our set. We were at a standstill until they arrived.

Once the "real musicians" arrived, Tommy had some fun jamming with the guys; he was a good amateur guitar player himself. After they got warmed up, it was time to knock off for the day. Nothing was achieved that day.

Those days were excruciating. Nothing was working and what was getting done wasn't very funny. I would come home every night more and more frustrated that my part in the movie wasn't turning out to be what I had expected. Sure, I was getting paid very well, but I had wanted to make a mark with the film. I decided I needed to be proactive.

I started writing funny scenes for the movie each night at home that prominently included my character. Early in the mornings, I would slide the scenes under the door of Cheech's Winnebago. I decided Cheech was the way to go because he was fun and friendly; Tommy was always very serious and less approachable.

I realized I might get reprimanded or fired, but I felt like I didn't have a lot to lose at that point. I also thought Cheech might like the scenes or at least appreciate the fact that I was trying to help. It was no secret that they were struggling and there was a lot of concern amongst the crew about how far behind schedule we were.

Not one word was ever said to me about the scenes I was slipping under Cheech's door. When I would see him, he would just smile and say hello.

Two days later, the producer came to me and said, "You won't need to come back tomorrow, Alan." My first thought was that I was being fired for shoving the scenes under Cheech's Winnebago door.

Before I could ask why, he said, "Universal has taken over the film. The budget has been spent. Behind the scenes, the studio has been planning a takeover if Tommy continued to blow through the budget. They've given Tommy six scenes that he's allowed to finish. After that, they're shutting the production down and they'll have to make the movie from what they have. This means the Vegas shoot won't be happening, and the music store scenes may not make the cut. Those scenes probably won't make sense without the Vegas scenes."

I was devastated. This was supposed to be my big break.

My scenes did end up on the cutting room floor. This was probably the biggest heartbreak of the many I've had in the entertainment business. But the good news is that I've been getting checks for working on that movie for forty years.

Side note #1: Three years later, I saw Cheech across the lobby at a small concert. I waved and he smiled back. I had been on *All My Children* for two years at that point. He either knew me from *All My Children*, or he remembered me as the goofy, aggressive actor who was shoving scenes under his Winnebago door. I will never know. I actually like the second scenario best.

Side note #2: Cheech and Chong were *not* druggies. They were big into working out and eating healthy organic foods. Pretty much health nuts.

CHAPTER 25—ALL MY CHILDREN CALLING

Early November of 1979, I got a call from my agent asking what I thought about doing a soap opera. I told her I really hadn't thought about it because my focus had been on comedy. My next question was, "How much does it pay?"

I was shocked to find out it paid two hundred dollars more per day than I was paid on the Cheech and Chong movie, and I thought that was a lot.

Now I was very interested in what she had to say. "They would like to read you for a part on ABC's *All My Children*," she said. I knew it was a very popular show but I had never watched *All My Children* because the ABC station came in fuzzy at our house when I was growing up. The only clear channel was CBS, so that was the channel we watched.

I said, "Sure. Throw my hat in the ring." She told me a freelance casting director, Barbara Remsen, would be doing the first reading. In the '70s and '80s, all auditioning was done in person, unlike now where all auditions are taped, and often actors are required to self-tape and submit their auditions through an online service.

I made it through the first cut with Barbara. By the next week, Barbara whittled the group of candidates down to a reasonable number for Mari Lyn Henry, the head of all daytime casting for ABC-TV, to meet and read. I was told there were about 200 actors still in the running at that point.

My reading with Mari Lyn went very well, as did my conversation with her before and after. We really hit it off and I was starting to feel like I actually had a chance. Mari Lyn told me there were very big plans for the character. I really wanted the part after hearing what she had to say.

After the reading with Mari Lyn, I was picked as one of thirty actors to screen test for the part. This was my first screen test ever, so I was very excited… and nervous.

For some reason, they did the screen test at the *General Hospital* studio in Hollywood. I was never told why GH wasn't filming that day, but their whole studio was devoted to auditions to find the right actor for the character, Sean Cudahy, on *All My Children*. The right casting meant better ratings and more advertising dollars.

It was very stressful sitting around the *General Hospital* actor's lounge waiting for my turn to screen test. I wasn't so sure it was a good idea, but they had the television in the actor's lounge tuned into the internal video feed; we were able to watch the other actors during their tests. I tried not to watch, but it was impossible to resist the temptation to see how the other guys were doing.

Mari Lyn was doing a short interview with each actor through the camera lens after they finished their scene. From the control room, she would ask the actor to look directly into the camera lens and answer a few questions about themselves. The actor would hear her ask the questions over the studio's PA system. The purpose was to get a sense of the actor's personality outside of what they could see from the audition scene.

I was surprised at how uninteresting and weak most of the actors came off due to their boring answers to her questions. There was nothing fun or exciting about their answers. I thought it was humorous that several of the guys were acting very serious and dramatic, like they were in a soap opera scene. I wanted to find a way to stand out and have some fun with it.

Her very first question to me was, "Where are you from and what does your father do for a living?"

I immediately saw my chance to liven things up a little. "My father is a salmon fisherman in Illinois."

There was a long pause before she responded with, "I didn't know there was salmon fishing in Illinois?"

"Oh, God, yes!" I shot back. "It's huge. My family's been fishin' for salmon there for over a hundred years."

I smiled and then she said very loudly, "You asshole. You lied to me." Then I heard Mari Lyn and all the people in the control room laughing.

At that point, I knew I had made a very good choice not to play it safe. In the end, I think this played a huge part in me being cast in the role: I was cocky enough to play the overconfident Sean Cudahy.

I was picked as one of two actors from the Los Angeles screen tests to go to New York City to do another taped audition for *All My Children's* executive producer and others at ABC. It was very exciting to have ABC paying for me to fly and stay in NYC. Even if I didn't get the part, it was definitely something to write home about and let the folks know I hadn't squandered my education.

When I got on the plane, I was very surprised to see I was sitting next to an actor I knew. In fact, he and his wife had been at our house for dinner a month before the *All My Children* auditions started. We thought it was just a strange coincidence, until we realized we were both headed to New York to audition for the same part. We were the last two actors standing from LA.

After we got over the shock, we talked about the character and helped each other with lines. We both wanted the part, but neither of us had come to Hollywood with the intention of being on a soap opera. Not that we didn't respect the soaps, we had assumed we would be doing movies and episodic television. But the money was great and we knew getting the part would put us "on the map." At the time, neither of us was even close to being on the map. I think we both had the right attitude: If we didn't get it, it was great practice and a big confidence boost.

We had been told that there were actors in New York that were also in the running. We assumed this meant two actors, but when we got to the audition, there were ten New York-based actors. That sure changed the odds. I liked the one-in-four odds much better. One-in-twelve was a whole different ball of wax.

I looked around the room and saw at least four guys that I thought were way cooler than farm boy Alan Dysert.

They didn't have available studio space for us to do the audition at *All My Children* that day, so our auditions were held on the *ABC World News Tonight* set two blocks away, where Peter Jennings co-anchored the evening news every weeknight. That was weird in itself. We all read two scenes with Richard Shoberg, the actor who had been playing Sean's brother, Tom, for three years. We weren't allowed to watch the other actors this time, which was a relief; I didn't want to see any of those studs nail the scene before I got a chance to do my thing.

My audition went very well, and Richard and I seemed to have a natural connection. Maybe it had something to do with us both being close in age, from very small Midwestern towns, and former athletes. It actually felt like we could be brothers.

After the auditions, they told us it would probably be a week or so before they made their decision. The other actor from LA and I were staying in the same hotel and going to the airport together the next morning, so we decided it only made sense to check out the Big Apple together and have a little fun.

It was early November, so there were no leaves on the trees, very little grass, and people were not picking up their dog's poop, even though they had passed a law. We both found the town to be ugly, smelly, dirty, and not inviting compared to the beauty of Southern California. We were spoiled. We both ended up thinking maybe we didn't want to give up what we had in LA for a soap opera part in New York City. That was probably just a defense mechanism and a great excuse if we didn't get it.

After coming back from New York, I realized I really did want the part. I went back to work at the restaurant because most of my income in Los Angeles was still coming from waiting tables. There was no doubt in my mind; I would much rather be making a lot of money on a soap opera in New York City than selling fresh fish to a bunch of random people in Los Angeles.

All My Children told my agent they would make their casting decision right after Thanksgiving. I was starting to overthink it at this point; It was hard for me to think about anything else.

Then I got a call from CBS's #1 rated *The Young and the Restless*. They wanted me to audition for a big contract role on their show. When I was with their casting director, he told me he knew I was up for the part on *All My Children*. I asked him how he knew about me since they had called me directly instead of contacting my agent. He said, "Your acting coach, Jeff Corey, called us and told us we better take a look at you before you sign a contract with our biggest competitor." The reading with the casting director went very well, so I was brought in later that week to meet the producers.

At that point, it looked like I might have to make a choice between the two shows. It was a good spot to be in, but it just messed with my head even more. What if I said no to *The Young and the Restless* and then the part at *All My Children* didn't come through, or vice versa? I was definitely overthinking everything. Maybe neither show will want me. Maybe I was destined to sell fresh fish.

Christmas was getting close and still no decision from *All My Children* or *The Young and the Restless*. All My Children said they would definitely make a decision before Christmas, but that didn't happen. Then they said right after

Christmas. That didn't happen either. Sean, the character I was up for, was already written into the show starting January 9th. That date wasn't flexible, so they were pushing it to the limit.

I couldn't believe it when New Year's Eve came and we still didn't have an answer. There I was selling fish again on December 31, 1979. It was driving me crazy. I just wanted to know one way or the other. Everyone would say, "No news is good news, Alan."

I would respond back, "No news is bulls—t!" I felt like I was being jerked around.

New Year's Day, I got a call from my agent saying, "They want you! You got it!" I was floored. The torture was over.

"They need you in New York on January 7th for wardrobe," she continued. "They'll be sending your flight and hotel information later today. They're putting you up at the Mayflower Hotel on Central Park West for two weeks until you find a place to live. There are six scripts on the next American Airlines flight to Los Angeles. You need to meet the plane to pick up the scripts. Congratulations, Alan! You're going to be a soap opera star." I honestly don't remember what happened right after that other than my mind immediately started racing, in a good way. It was the kind of excitement that most people never get to experience. With one phone call, my life had just changed in a very big and wonderful way.

The first thing I did after telling Liz was call my parents. They were so excited for me, and for them. Now they could tell people their son was an actor on *All My Children*. I was no longer a waiter and never would be again. That was one thing I knew for sure.

Next, was my favorite call: I called Harry, the manager of the Hungry Tiger, to tell him I got the part and I would no longer be working there. For you to understand the kind of man I was dealing with, Harry responded, "I think you're making a big mistake leaving the restaurant."

And he was serious. Never again did I have to listen to the stupid orders that Harry would bark around the restaurant.

I did go back into the restaurant the next night to say goodbye to all the nice people I worked with there. They were all very excited for me, except for the other actors. I could tell from their fake smiles that there was some jealousy. They all thought they were better actors than I was, even though they'd never seen me act. That's actors for you.

When I picked up the six scripts *All My Children* had sent via American Airlines, I immediately ripped open the package to see what I would be doing in my first episodes as a soap opera actor. All I knew was what I'd been told at the readings and what I could glean from the screen test scenes. I couldn't believe how many lines I had. I was in so many scenes. I counted 110 pages of dialogue I would be doing the first week I was on the show.

I started to worry since I had never done anything close to that much dialogue: almost twenty pages per day. I thought I might be in over my head, but I couldn't turn back now. The train had already left the station. *What had I gotten myself into?*

I found out a year later during a lunch with Mari Lyn Henry that my agent had nothing to do with ABC finding me. They learned about me from a marketing package I had sent myself a few months before they started looking for the right actor to play Sean Cudahy. This meant I had been paying my agent 10% of my income for a part she hadn't even thought to submit me for. Of course, she never mentioned that to me. I had to pay her for the entire time I was at *All My Children* because she negotiated the contract. I dumped her as soon as my contract ended.

So, what all my friends had said would never work, sending out my own packets, brought me the biggest acting opportunity I ever had. That made a total of four acting jobs I got from my own efforts.

I tell my students that story as an example of how they must be aggressive. "You are the captain of your own ship; and you need to take the helm. No one else will have the time to focus on your journey like you will. Waiting for the phone to ring won't work."

CHAPTER 26—WELCOME TO NEW YORK AND *ALL MY CHILDREN*-1980

I flew to New York by myself for six days of shooting and wardrobe buying trips. After that, they gave me four days off to fly back to Los Angeles to gather up Liz, clothing, and what we thought we couldn't live without for the next few months. Everything else was stored in the garage and a storage facility.

Once I hit New York City, it was a whirlwind. ABC picked me up in a limo and took me to the Mayflower Hotel, a New York classic. I loved staying at The Mayflower because it was so old school New York, right on Central Park West, and a short walk to the *All My Children* studio at 67th and Columbus.

I got up early the next morning. The excitement and anticipation of the upcoming day got in the way of a good night's sleep. It was a day devoted to creating the physical image of Sean Cudahy. First, I had a meeting with the executive producer, Jorn Winther, followed by a wardrobe buying trip with costume designer, Carol Luiken.

My meeting with Jorn, who some called "The Viking," was very strange. In his heavy Danish accent, he smiled and told me, "I just want you to know that you were not my pick to play Sean. Mari Lyn Henry pulled rank on me, as head of casting for all ABC soaps. She told us we had to hire you. She thinks you have something special that I quite frankly didn't see in your audition. So, I want you to think of this first week as a probationary period. We will see how you do this week, then I will decide if I am going to keep you. And don't tell anyone I told you this."

I was shocked by his words but acted like it made total sense to me. I refused to let him see me sweat. I walked out of his office thinking, "What the f—! As if I don't have enough pressure on me with 110 pages to perform this week on a hit television show."

But the human spirit is surprisingly strong and I was determined not to go home with my tail between my legs. And why was I not allowed to tell anyone I was on probation?

There was no time to dwell on the nuclear bomb The Viking had just dropped on me because I was immediately whisked away by Carol to spend a fortune on designer clothing for Sean. We had a mission: we were on our way to create the image of Sean Cudahy.

The buying trip was a fashion-conscious man's dream. We went to Saks, Barneys, and Bergdorf Goodman, where they had "studio services" departments. At each store, they rolled out everything to make us comfortable and ready to spend lots of ABC money, including wines, cheeses, and other goodies.

Carol told them what she had in mind for the character, and they commenced an eye-popping parade of designer suits, sport coats, shirts, sweaters, shoes, outerwear and accessories.

Carol decided the Armani suits and sport coats fit me like a charm, so that was the foundation on which she built the image of the character, Sean. When I saw the price tags on the clothing, I was shocked. She laughed when I told her I knew of stores where we could buy designer suits for a lot less.

Carol taught me a very important truth: nailing the wardrobe for a character is crucial. Sean's wardrobe would be a major part of who he was as a person. Sean would spend whatever it took to achieve the image he wanted, whether he could afford it or not.

Carol had won three Emmy Awards for "Outstanding Costume Design for a Drama Series," so she knew exactly what she wanted. I kicked back and chimed in on what I liked and didn't like. I decided it was okay to spend ABC's money like it was going out of style.

Carol was definitely having fun creating my character, but sometimes the spending did seem a little reckless and unnecessary to the farm boy in me. I asked why we were spending so much on shoes when they would never show on camera. Carol explained, "The clothes make the man, Alan. Even though no one else will see the shoes, you will feel special when you put on a pair of $400 shoes. You will no longer be Alan Dysert: you will be Sean Cudahy."

She was right. I felt like a different person every time I suited up in Sean's wardrobe.

* * *

I was very nervous on my first day of filming. Sean was in twenty pages of the show that day. Luckily, Richard Shoberg, who played my brother

Tom, was great about guiding me through the process and making me feel more comfortable. He was also my dressing roommate, so I was able to watch his routine and see how he prepared. Most of my scenes the first few days were with Richard, so that really helped. I had no idea what I was doing, but I think I did a decent job of faking it.

I had a ridiculous amount of dialogue the first few days, but somehow I got through it without passing out. The first day wasn't too bad. They needed to ease Sean into town, set the tone for the character, and tell the audience who he was and why he was in Pine Valley, the fictitious hometown of *All My Children*. But the second day was a day of bad decisions.

The second day of shooting had Sean crashing at brother Tom's apartment, drinking all his beer, eating pizza, and turning his living room into a pigsty. There were multiple scenes where I was to be slamming beers. Before the dress rehearsal, the props guys said they could give me real beer or fake beer. I said, "You know what, a beer would taste good right now." I thought the beer would help calm my nerves a little.

But there were three scenes with me drinking beer and they wanted me to guzzle them in each scene. By the time we finished those scenes in dress rehearsal, I was definitely feeling the alcohol. I wasn't over the edge, but I knew I shouldn't have any more.

When it was time to actually tape the first scene, I told the props guy I needed to switch to the fake beer for taping. He said, "We don't have any. You didn't tell us you wanted to switch. It's too late to go out and buy any now. We're already taping the show."

Oops! I ended up drinking six beers in total, and I'm not a big beer drinker. Two, maybe. But six?

Somehow I got through the scenes, and I didn't even throw up the many slices of pizza that I had to eat with the beer. But no one seemed to notice. Maybe they thought I was acting. I knew how much I was affected when I started walking back to the hotel after filming. I was really lit, but I got away with it. I vowed never to do that again.

The rest of the week went well but I found myself in survival mode. I came to New York City as a vegetarian who worked out most days and did yoga on a regular basis. But after my NYC arrival, I found myself never doing yoga, never working out, and eating meatball heroes. I told myself I would get back to my old routine after my week of probation.

All My Children *Bank Robbery Scene— Julie Barr, Alan, and Taylor Miller*

On that Friday morning, I asked Jorn's executive assistant if I could talk with him. I wanted to find out if I had passed his test. She said, "Jorn's in Connecticut on a location shoot all weekend."

I told her, "It's urgent that I see him. He told me we had to talk before I leave for Los Angeles on Sunday. I have to get things settled there so I can move here next week." She said, "Can't it wait until you get back from LA?"

I wanted to tell her about my probationary period, but I was sworn to secrecy. I told her it couldn't wait. She said, "I guess you could go to the location and talk to him there." She gave me the address of the mansion in Connecticut where they were shooting.

I got up early the next morning, rented a car, and drove to the location in Connecticut. Once there, I found Jorn, but he was very busy directing the shoot. I waited around until they took a break for lunch. He asked me why I was there. I told him I was headed back to Los Angeles the next day and needed to know if I was supposed to come back. He asked what I meant.

"You told me I was on probation and you would tell me if I passed your test by the end of this week."

Jorn laughed and said, "I just did that to make you work harder. You did very well. See you next week when you get back."

I walked away relieved but also thinking, *What an asshole!*

A month later, I mentioned the whole probation thing to my agent and she told me that wasn't even allowed by my contract. Jorn could have been in big trouble for playing that power game with me. If Mari Lyn Henry had known, she would have really been pissed. I guess that's why he told me not to tell anyone.

* * *

Being the new guy on any job is tough, but being the new actor on a hit national television show is really rough. Some of the actors were big stars and had been cast members since the show's beginning, ten years before I arrived.

At *All My Children*, they had what they called "Red Chairs" after the dress rehearsal, right before the actual taping of the show. The props department would bring out red director's chairs for all the actors to sit in while the director gave each actor notes on the scenes they had just performed in dress rehearsal. Sitting there with fifteen known soap stars, waiting to have my scenes critiqued by the director, was very intimidating.

The other actors seemed to enjoy the time together since there was no other time during the day when the whole cast was assembled like that. One director, Henry Kaplan, was particularly rough on actors, but in a humorous way. There was a lot of laughter when he would pick on actors. No one was spared, not even Susan Lucci, the biggest soap star in the world. I didn't know Henry like they did, so I just thought he was mean.

When it came time to critique my scenes, Henry turned to me and said, "Now for Mr. Hollywood." The cast found that very funny, knowing ABC had shipped me in from Los Angeles to join the cast. He proceeded with, "I didn't see it in the first scene. In fact, I didn't see anything on your face to tell me how you felt."

I jumped in with, "I was taught to be subtle with my on-camera performance."

Time stopped after I said that. Henry looked around at the cast and pointed at me as he said, "Take a good look, cast. We have a real trained Hollywood movie actor in our midst."

They all thought that was hilarious. Then Henry explained to me that the television screen was no more than 24 inches (this was long before big screens) and my head would be very small on the screen; and the viewers were often doing something else while they watched. He concluded with,

"So sometimes we have to make sure they see what we're feeling. That is what your face is for."

I wanted to say, "So you want me to overact?" but I knew it was best for me to shut up and take it. I was humiliated. Richard Shoberg told me, after my beatdown, that Henry does that stuff all the time to lighten the mood. He told me I would get used to it. But I was too new and too vulnerable.

After that, I always dreaded the shows that would be directed by Henry. The other directors were all very kind and realized they were working with sensitive and often insecure humans. The directors that came from an acting background were particularly great to work with because they knew how to explain what they needed in a scene without being cruel.

In all fairness to Henry, when I came back to *All My Children* six years later and found myself working with Henry again, I realized he was a very sweet man. We actually ended up having a great relationship. I think he felt he had to put up the hard and semi-cruel front so the actors wouldn't take advantage of his true kindness. His shows always looked great because he forced the best performance out of all of us. We all wanted to please Henry because we knew he would be tough on us if we didn't put 100% into our scenes. In the end, Henry made me a much better actor.

* * *

I had never seen myself on television before I started on *All My Children*. It's hard for my young students to believe there was no way for the average person to record a television show in the 1980s. If you didn't catch it when it was happening, you would never see it. Our show was on at noon when we were on lunch break, so we would try to catch ourselves in the actor's lounge or in the makeup room. Some of the veteran actors didn't care if they saw their performances, unless it was a big event in the life of their character. They were past watching themselves and realized they weren't going to love what they saw. I looked at it as a way to improve my on-camera acting skills. I usually wasn't crazy about what I saw. Watching yourself on national television is very painful, especially knowing that millions of people are watching and scrutinizing the new actor on "their" soap.

During my first week of shows, I noticed I wasn't getting many close-ups. I went to Reggie, my favorite camera operator, and asked him why the directors weren't giving me more close-ups.

"You're dancing around too much, so they told us to back off on you," Reggie answered.

"Why didn't anyone say anything to me?" I shot back. "I think they just thought it was your style."

"Style?" I said. "I have no style. I don't even know what I'm doing most of the time."

That was a great lesson for me. From then on, I planted my feet and didn't move my base unless they told me to move to another mark. I got my close-ups after that. I still can't believe no one told me.

I learned another lesson from a crew member in the props department. I think we were talking about a football game or something backstage at the time. He said, "I really like your acting because it's not like all the other guys on the soaps."

I thanked him but had to ask him what he meant. He said, "You know how you let your voice go up real high when you get excited or get mad? Nobody else does that. They keep their voices down in that low, manly, soap opera voice. You're different."

I had no idea what he was talking about until I watched a few shows after that. He was absolutely right. I was appalled. Yes, it was real, but I found it almost comical. It would have worked great on a sitcom or in a comedy movie, but I was on a soap. I made that adjustment immediately. My character was written to be sexy, and that floating pitch thing I had been doing was not sexy at all.

The writers brought my character's storyline in strong and fast. I was taping five shows a week, which is usually not the case. A soap contract guarantees the actor a certain number of shows per week; and it also sets the amount the actor will be paid per show. This allows the actor to budget for the worst case scenario. In my case, my contract also set forth how many first class tickets ABC would give me per year to travel back to California, since that had been my home base when they hired me.

For a new soap opera actor like me, the guarantee was usually one and a half shows per week. But the guarantee didn't give an accurate picture of how many shows I would do, or how much I would earn. If I filmed five shows on a particular week, I was paid for five shows. Also, if a show ran past 5:00 P.M., the whole cast and crew went into "Golden Time." The overtime was very expensive for the show. As you can imagine, the show and the network hated it when an episode went into Golden Time. Overtime pay for the actors was excellent, so I was always happy when we went into Golden Time.

I was making more money than I had ever seen in my life, but I would have given up some of the money for a little breathing room the first few months. I was doing five shows a week for a long time, which is brutal. My storyline became very popular, so they ran with it. The show was all- consuming. It was exciting but I was running on adrenaline half the time.

ABC and *All My Children* were very happy that Sean became popular from the moment the character debuted on the show. They started setting up talk shows, interviews, and magazine shoots very quickly to boost the character's profile even more. It was a whirlwind, and my head was spinning.

Imagine, on December 31st, a person could sit at one of my tables in Westwood, California and order fresh fish from me. Fourteen days later I'm walking out of the *All My Children* studio at 67th and Columbus in New York City and fans are screaming my name because they had just watched me on television the day before.

It was a total mindf—k. I felt like this was some kind of drug in-duced dream/nightmare. How could a man's life change so drastically in two weeks? But it did.

* * *

My first big storyline came very quickly. It was a love story with my character, Sean Cudahy, and Devon McFadden, played by Tricia Pursley. Jorn, the executive producer, called both of us in for a meeting to tell us how important the storyline was going to be for us and the show. Our storyline was planned to stretch over several months, making it the summer storyline the network would use to attract teens and college students.

If the storyline was popular and increased our viewership, not only would it help the ratings of *All My Children*, the larger audience could carry over to the next two ABC soaps, *One Life To Live* and *General Hospital*. The hope would be to dominate three full hours of network television with the three very popular ABC soaps. Big ratings meant big dollars. That's exactly what ended up happening. The three ABC soaps were cash cows for ABC. The profits were enormous and made up for the losses in their news, sports and primetime divisions.

Jorn said he needed to be sure we were prepared to handle the intensity of the highly emotional scenes, of which there would be many. He told us that we would be working five shows a week for a long time. To make sure we were prepared, the show hired an outside acting coach, Hal, to work with us individually each Sunday afternoon to analyze every scene from each of the scripts for that week. I wasn't sure I liked the idea at first, but in the end, Hal taught me a lot about preparation, script analysis, and on- camera acting skills.

Our story was about a 20-year-old woman who had married her husband, nice guy Wally, only because she was pregnant. She cared for Wally and their new baby, but there was something missing in her life. Devon decided to try out for a play at the community college, where she met the charming cad, Sean Cudahy, who had just moved to town. Sean and Devon were cast as lovers in the play.

Sean was a heartless wrecking ball. He took advantage of Devon's vulnerability, charmed her, and developed what became a very destructive affair that ruined her marriage and damaged her relationship with her family. There would be many love scenes for the two characters as well as some very disturbing, physical breakup scenes.

The intensity of our work brought Tricia and I together in a way like two people stranded on an island, or sharing a war experience would be. Neither of us had faced material as challenging as what we were about to experience. We worked with Hal separately on Sundays and rehearsed our scenes over and over when we were at the studio.

Neither one of us wanted to look like we didn't know what we were doing in the love scenes. We wanted to make it real, knowing how cruel the audience can be. Tricia and I were both married, which made it a little awkward at first, but we were actors and it was our job to make our love scenes believable.

ABC promoted the Sean/Devon story heavily with television ads and magazines articles, once our storyline was on the "front burner." The front burner is when a storyline is being pushed heavily for weeks or sometimes months. If the story hits big with the audience, they push it hard; if the audience doesn't like the story, the show will cool the story down or abandon it completely. Ours turned out to be a hot storyline, so they pushed us and the storyline heavily.

Our characters spent a lot of time in bed. The scenes may have looked sexy, but under the sheets, we were wearing sweatpants and Tricia also sported a camisole. The way they carefully arranged the sheets gave the impression that we were naked.

Also, it doesn't look good if your head is smashed into a pillow, so it's necessary to hold your head slightly off the pillow during the bed scenes; this isn't comfortable or sexy. To add to the difficulty, the director would choreograph the scenes so we didn't get in each other's key light.

The direction might be, "Say your first line, then kiss her lightly. Then pull back and give me three beats, followed by Devon's line. Kiss her again for two beats and pull back." All in all, it was pretty uncomfortable and it didn't feel sexy at all. We often found ourselves laughing about our scenes. We did have some fun, but it seemed so odd knowing an audience of millions would watch us doing something that appeared so intimate.

Many actors' wives and husbands find it difficult to accept their mate doing love scenes for a living. Liz, however, said to me, "I don't want people thinking my husband is a bad kisser, so get in there and kiss her like you mean it." I guess I was lucky she didn't freak out about it, but I do believe there were times when she questioned the relationship I had with Tricia. But we never crossed the line; we were friends that kissed a lot because it was our jobs.

The irony of it all was that I had always been uncomfortable with public display of affection in my real life; but here I was making out on national television to entertain millions of people.

"Irony is a disciplinarian feared only by those who do not know it, but cherished by those who do."—Soren Kierkegaard.

Tricia and I were both uncomfortable when we got to the ugly and disturbing breakup scenes. They wrote scenes with Devon begging Sean not to leave her, and him saying very cruel things and treating her horribly. We knew they were only scenes, but she hated what they were doing to her character, and I didn't like being the bad guy. The thought of a few million fans thinking that I might be like Sean really started to bother me.

Alan With Castmate Tricia Pursley (Devon)

CHAPTER 27—SWINGOS CELEBRITY HOTEL

When our storyline was going full throttle, ABC sent Tricia and me to make appearances on popular ABC affiliate morning and afternoon shows. One trip of note was to Cleveland, Ohio.

We were scheduled to appear on the Cleveland affiliate's afternoon show. Our flight got in around 11 o'clock, so they set us up with a room at the famous Swingos Celebrity Hotel, where we could freshen up and relax until our appearance later in the afternoon (yes, I think it is an odd name for a hotel).

Tricia and I were excited that our check-in would allow us enough time to go to our room to watch ourselves in the *All My Children* episode that was airing that day. The episode included our first big love scene, and if we didn't see it air that day, we would never see it, since there were no VCRs in 1980. In that episode, Sean and Devon were checking in at the somewhat sleazy Pine Cone Motel.

When we tried to open our room at Swingos, we couldn't get the key to work. We were getting nervous because it was 12 o'clock and our show had already started. I was trying to get the key to work when suddenly a woman opened the door from the inside. She looked at us like she had just seen a ghost or we were going to kill her. We apologized profusely but she couldn't get words out of her mouth. We walked away saying the desk clerk must have told us the wrong room number.

Once we found ourselves in the correct room, we immediately turned on the TV. As we started watching, we realized we had missed the first scene where Sean and Devon check into the Pine Cone Motel. At that point it hit us: the woman in the other hotel room had been watching *All My Children*. She had seen Sean and Devon check into the Pine Cone Motel on her TV, and then Sean and Devon showed up at her hotel room door. No wonder the woman was speechless. She probably thought she had lost her mind. I hope someone explained it all to the poor woman.

* * *

I had just flown into Detroit for a personal appearance and was reading the Detroit newspaper in the limo on the way to the hotel. I saw a full-page ad for a Diana Ross concert that was happening that evening at Pine Knob, a large outdoor concert venue about 35 miles from Detroit. Being a huge fan, my mind went into hyper drive to figure out a way to see Diana perform live.

When we arrived at the hotel, we realized Diana and her entourage were staying at my hotel because there was a Rolls-Royce convertible in front of the hotel and my driver said it was the car Diana was driving while she was in town. He knew that because she had rented it from a friend of his who owned the only one like it in Detroit.

As fate would have it, I ran into Diana's backup singers in the lobby as I was checking in. They were *All My Children* fans, so when I told them I was a huge Diana Ross fan, they said they would set me up with a great seat and bring me backstage afterwards, if I could find my way to Pine Knob. They told me to go to the "Will Call" window and have them call Deedee as soon as I arrived. That was all I needed to hear. I was going to Pine Knob to see Diana Ross even if it killed me.

I wanted to see the concert even if things didn't work out like the backup singers had suggested, so I decided to buy a ticket before I went. The only ticket service was several miles away at a Sears store. The hotel shuttle driver was kind enough to drive me to the Sears store, where I found a very long line for tickets.

As I started to get in line, one of the men in the line yelled out, "It's Sean Cudahy from *All My Children*." Others recognized me and started clapping. The man yelled again, "We aren't gonna let Sean Cudahy stand in line in our city." The others agreed and insisted that I move to the front of the line. Another man yelled, "I'm not gonna let Sean Cudahy buy his own ticket in our town." I tried to resist as he came up and paid for my ticket, but he was determined.

It was embarrassing but very sweet. I could tell it meant something to the man and I didn't want to take that away from him. I thanked all of them over and over again as I walked out.

I called the hotel to see if they could pick me up, but they said their driver wouldn't be available for an hour or so. I tried to get a cab, but they told me it was rush hour and it would be a very long time before they could pick me up.

There was supposed to be a rental car for me when I got to the hotel, but that was no help. I had to get back to the hotel or I was going to be too late to catch Deedee before the concert started.

I decided to do something I had never done in my life: hitchhike. I knew the hotel was a few miles straight down the very busy road in front of me. I thought a fan will see me and gladly pick me up. I put out my thumb and hundreds of cars passed me by. No one would even give me a look. I was invisible.

Finally, a young couple picked me up and had me sit in the front seat with them because the backseat was filled with all kinds of crap. They were very nice and asked me where I was headed. I told them right up the road a few miles to the Hilton Hotel.

Then the girl turned to me and said, "You know who you look like? That guy Sean on *All My Children?*" Her boyfriend looked over at me and said, "He does kinda." Deciding it would be fun for them to know it was me, I said, "I am him."

"Right," she laughed. "Like Sean's gonna to be hitchhiking in Detroit."

I was never able to get them to believe me. To this day, I'm sure they tell the story about the Sean Cudahy look-alike hitchhiker that tried to make them believe he was really Sean from *All My Children*.

* * *

Due to the popularity of the Sean/Devon storyline, I was often hired to make appearances at malls, theme parks, and even casinos. It was crazy. I was making as much from appearances as I was on the show at times. I really enjoyed being paid to see the country while traveling first class all the way.

I was usually booked to travel with a female star of another ABC show, but occasionally from a CBS soap. We always had fun entertaining the crowds and hanging out together for the weekend while being treated like royalty. We often had crowds of a few thousand crazed fans.

One weekend, my travel partner/co-star for the weekend was Kim Zimmer from *The Guiding Light*. The limo driver picked me up first and then Kim. Next, we were to pick up our MC/handler for the weekend, who was also a columnist for multiple entertainment magazines.

Kim and I were having fun getting to know each other in the back of the limo, but after fifteen or twenty minutes we noticed the driver seemed to be driving around in circles. I asked him if there was a problem and he admitted he was lost and unable to find the apartment building of the MC/ handler. There were no cell phones at the time, so we had to find a pay phone to call and get directions. By the time we arrived to pick him up, it was obvious we were going to miss our flight. The MC/handler went back into his apartment and called the promoter, who called the mall developer that had hired us for the opening of his new mall.

The mall developer had invited the top executives from the mall's anchor stores as well as several politicians to the grand opening and dinner. The festivities were to start in just a few hours and Kim and I were the big attraction for the events. If we didn't show up, the grand opening would be a big bust.

The developer instructed the MC/handler to tell the limo driver to head to Teterboro Airport, the most popular executive airport in the New York City area. He was sending his private jet to pick us up. Wow! That was pretty wild. Neither one of us had flown on a private jet before, so we were very excited. I was shocked at how small the Learjet was inside. It was very low to the ground and felt more like we were taking off in a sports car than an airplane. Unlike what I was used to with commercial flights, the Learjet felt like we went from takeoff to going straight up into the clouds. I was glad I hadn't had a lot to drink because there was no toilet, at least not one I was going to use. Neither of us peed our pants.

CHAPTER 28—BULLETPROOF VESTS, BODYGUARDS, AND DEATH THREATS

They say there is a 3% nut factor out there in the world, meaning 3% of the population could snap at any time. I was told this when I first started working for ABC. They felt the need to warn me because they knew I was making personal appearances all over the country with audiences sometimes numbering in the thousands.

They weren't trying to scare me. They wanted me to be aware that the soaps had millions of wonderful fans, but there were some that become obsessed with the shows and individual characters. The line between what is real and what is fantasy is blurred and they think the actors are really the characters, and everything they do on the show is real. Since my character was one of the characters people "love to hate," I was more of a target than the good guys.

Alan With Castmates Susan Lucci (Erica) and Richard Shoberg (Tom Cudahy)

The events were free to the public so anyone could show up. The events were also heavily advertised. We were often in towns that rarely or never had a celebrity show up. People could easily figure out what hotel we were registered at and where we would be taken for dinner. The concern was that someone might see it as an opportunity to make a name for themselves by killing or just punching someone famous.

Alan and Leslie Charleson (Monica Quartermaine) of
General Hospital *at Opryland Soap Opera Festival*

I was approached on more than one trip by a drunken man in a bar saying something like, "My girlfriend says she watches you on TV. I told her you're just a sissy actor and I could knock you out with one punch. Why don't we just go outside so I can show her you ain't sh-t."

Sometimes there were very sketchy people in the audience, and it seemed like they were always in the front row. One weekend, I was making a mall appearance with Jackie Zeman, from *General Hospital*, somewhere in the heartland of America. The crowd was excited, loud, and unusually row-dy. This created an energy in the mall that felt like something was going to boil over, more so than at any other appearance I had made. The mall had stationed an armed security guard on each corner of the stage to discourage anyone from jumping up on the stage.

Jackie and I had just started getting our show rolling when "pop-pop-pop" echoed like gunshots through the crowded mall. We ducked as people started screaming, and then ten or more people jumped onstage past the distracted armed guards. They were screaming and aggressively pulling at us and our clothing. Instinctively, I pulled Jackie to me and sheltered her head next to my chest as I forcefully pushed people away from us. Realizing we needed to escape, I carried Jackie off the stage and fought my way to the nearby escalator. The mall manager and another security guard met us at the top of the escalator and took us to the safety of the mall office. It was crazy!

That was the way our show ended. It was chaos. We found out later someone had popped several balloons, not realizing the sound would echo in the cavernous center court. I'm sure the audience was disappointed that what was expected to be a fun show and an autograph session turned into almost no show and a lot of crowd mania.

* * *

Sometimes you look at a human being and they seem normal and harmless, but if you dig a little deeper, you realize that's not the case at all. You find they don't have the slightest grip on reality. I've been told this is true of 6% of the population.

Such was the case with a woman in the audience when I co-hosted the Detroit ABC affiliate's *Morning Show*. Their show had a live audience of about seventy-five or so that sat about fifteen feet from me and the show's regular host. At one point, the audience was asked if they had any questions. One lady asked me, "Where in Detroit do you film *All My Children?*"

I looked at her and then turned to the host who was as confused as I was. I turned back to the woman and said, "We film our show in New York City."

The lady said, "That's not true. I know it's filmed in Detroit because it's on my television and I live in Detroit."

The host, the audience, and I were all in shock, realizing this woman thought all the shows on her TV were filmed in Detroit. I very carefully explained, "We really do film the show in New York City. Then it's broadcast to all the ABC affiliates around America. This station is one of those affiliates. I don't live here. I flew here from New York yesterday

At this point she looked like she might hurt someone as she said, "Don't tell me it's not filmed here. It's on my television." At that point the host decided to go to a commercial break.

CHAPTER 29—ME AND THE BEATLES

Soon after my character became a major part of the show, I started getting fan letters from a young woman in her late teens from Texas. The letters started increasing in frequency after I responded to a couple of the early ones. At one point, I was getting a letter almost every day. Then she started calling the studio every day asking if she could talk to me. She told the receptionist at *All My Children* that she had something urgent she needed to tell me. The front office gave me the messages and asked if I could do something about getting her to stop. They did suggest that I be very careful. They had seen this pattern before, but they gave me no guidance on how to handle the situation.

Bodyguards Escorting Alan At Mall Appearance

I decided I would call her and have one nice conversation with her and then tell her I would not be able to call again due to the fact that I was married. I made the call and she seemed very nice and not nutty at all. She did end up telling me that she loved me and she also said The Beatles and I were her whole world. At that point, I knew there was a serious problem. She told me she was going to send me photos of her bedroom so I would know just how devoted she was to me.

I was shocked and freaked out when I saw the photos she sent. She had made at least one hundred copies of my acting headshot and wallpapered two walls of her bedroom with them. She had papered the other two walls with photos of The Beatles—mostly John and Paul. Not knowing how to react, I sent her a short letter telling her thanks for her support, but said nothing to encourage her to pursue anything further. I started trying to wean her off of the letter writing by taking a very long time to answer her letters and making my responses very short.

On December 8th, 1980, everything changed. At 10:50 P.M. that evening, John Lennon was murdered outside The Dakota at 1 West 72nd Street, where John and Yoko lived. New York City went silent the next day as the news hit that the beloved Beatle had been murdered by a fan, Mark Chapman.

Not only did New York City go silent, so did the fan that was obsessed with me and The Beatles. I never heard from her again. Once I put the two together, I wanted to call her and see if she was okay, but I was urged not to reach out to her. For one, she might have killed herself or possibly been hospitalized. If she was still alive, reaching out to her might make her obsession worse, especially since John Lennon was dead. I'll always wonder what happened to her.

After John Lennon was murdered, it seemed like the world became more dangerous for all celebrities, and possibly more so for those of us who were on TV three to five days a week. Mark Chapman was a perfect example of how a random, disturbed person could become famous by killing a celebrity. Not that we were at the celebrity level of John Lennon, but we were easy to find and most cities in America didn't have famous people at the level of John Lennon appearing at their local mall. The possibility was now a reality.

Fans knew where our studio was, what time we started coming into the studio entrance, and the approximate time we would be leaving the studio. It would have been very easy to secretly follow us to our homes because many of us lived in Manhattan within a couple of miles of the studio. In my case, I was making heavily publicized appearances in cities all around the country. Many of us started changing up our routines. I started leaving the studio from the back loading dock. I looked for the strange ones and made sure I always had an exit plan.

I was starting to get death threats in my fan mail. The studio would often open and read our fan mail (not sure if that was legal) so they were aware of the letters. The executive producer called me in to discuss the threats. They were concerned about the multiple letters that threatened my life, especially since I was doing more personal appearances than any of the other actors on the show. They explained what can happen and had happened in the past with obsessed and sometimes mentally disturbed fans. They told me there had been many close calls and several actresses had been stalked. One very dangerous stalker was convicted and sent to prison.

I asked what ABC could do to help protect me. They told me there was nothing in the budget for security like that: I was on my own as far as security went. I was shocked they were telling me my life might be in danger but they weren't willing to help protect me. They could only suggest I be careful and curtail some of my public appearances.

Thanks a lot, ABC!

The most concerning letters I received came from a gang in New Haven, Connecticut. The letters warned me, "Stay away from Nina or you will bleed." Another letter said, "Come to New Haven and you are a Dead Man." They knew I was going to be at their local mall, so I would be an easy target.

It seemed like something you would see in a comedy movie: this gang is sitting around watching *All My Children*, thinking what was happening on their TV was real and they could affect it by killing me, an actor simply doing his job. If they didn't want me to touch their beloved Nina, they needed to talk to the producers and writers, not me.

I didn't want to limit my appearances since it was a great source of income. I also knew the popularity of the storyline that was driving the invitations wouldn't last forever. I decided the best way to protect myself was a bulletproof vest.

Shopping for a bulletproof vest brought up a lot of different emotions, fear being the dominant one. I was doing more than just taking precautions. I would be going on stage with a very serious bulletproof vest under my clothing. I must have thought getting shot was a possibility because they weren't cheap—and it was going to make me look fat.

I started wearing the bulletproof vest onstage at personal appearances. Winter worked better for the vest than summer, because I could wear a sweater over the vest, and top it off with a sport coat. It looked a little bulky, but at least it didn't look so out of place that people would think I was wearing a bulletproof vest.

Summer was a whole different story. I still had to wear the heavy sweater and sport coat or the outline of the vest and the straps would show. I would excuse myself right before going onstage saying, "I need to use the restroom one last time before going on stage." I had the vest and sweater in my leather bag that was the size of a mail carrier's bag. When I came out of the restroom, I would be wearing all the heavy clothing over the vest.

At one weekend appearance in Nashville, the temperature was almost 100 degrees. When I came out of the restroom, the MC/promoter, Joyce Sugarman, said, "Why the hell are you wearing a winter sweater and a suede sport coat when it is almost 100 degrees?"

"I think I'm coming down with something. I have a chill."

She bought it at first, but later in the show she gave me a big hug. I could tell she felt the vest. She stopped in her tracks and whispered in my ear, "What is that under your clothes?"

I whispered back, "Don't say anything. I'll explain later."

I continued to protect myself at personal appearances until I left the show at the end of my contract. When I came back to the show six years later, I wasn't doing as many appearances and it seemed like the country was not as crazy. I was no longer getting death threats. I have kept the bulletproof vest to remind me of how strange that time was in my life.

CHAPTER 30—ON THE COVER OF
PEOPLE MAGAZINE

One crisp morning in early 1981, I got a call from Maxine Levinson, the head of public relations for all the ABC soap operas. She asked, "Would you be interested in being on the cover of *People* Magazine?"

I thought she was kidding. Once I realized she wasn't joking, I said, "Why would I not be?" Maxine told me that it wasn't a done deal, but *People* was considering doing a cover on "The Soap Opera Cads" for a March issue. They needed to know if I was interested.

"Absolutely!"

Maxine called me later that day to tell me we were on for a shoot later in the week. She explained that *People* had three possible cover story ideas they were considering for that particular issue. They planned to shoot all three and then decide which to run with after all three shoots were completed.

The shoot was at an amazing loft photo studio in Lower Manhattan. They catered food and wine since the shoot was planned for several hours. I'm sure the wine was supplied to loosen us up for a more relaxed vibe during the shoot. The cover was to be myself, Michael Corbett from ABC's *Ryan's Hope*, and Christopher Bernau from CBS's *Guiding Light*. The wardrobe department heads from all three shows showed up with the very best designer suits and dress-casual clothing from each of our character's wardrobes. The public relations people from both networks were there as well.

Before we started shooting, there was a big discussion with the PR people about the three of us not wanting to be portrayed as "hunks." I don't remember why, but at that time in the entertainment business, it was a big negative to be called a hunk. I guess we thought it would be a career damaging image for some goofy reason; we wanted to come off as serious actors, not just pretty boys from the soaps. Our concerns were passed on to the photographer. He assured us that wasn't what *People* had asked for anyway.

We should have realized we were in trouble when we were told our photographer was a world-famous German wildlife photographer. We spent hours doing serious and smiling poses with many different wardrobe changes. We were all having a good time with the photographer and felt he was getting some great stuff that featured all three of us equally. Even though we weren't sure we would make the cover, it was quite a thrill thinking we might be on the cover of *People* Magazine. We had all been featured in the soap opera magazines, but this was The Big Time.

After hours of shooting, the photographer said, "That's a wrap. Great stuff, guys." At that point we were very loose and happy with the way everything had gone. Then, just as we were starting to get undressed, the photographer came to us and said, "I just realized I have a few frames left on this roll of film. Let's just have a little fun and take some wacky shots for ourselves, not for the magazine."

We thought that would be fun, so we came back on the set.

He said, "Alan, let's have your shirt and tie askew as if you're getting dressed after having very boring sex with some man's wife. Michael, let's have your shirt unbuttoned looking like you just had the most amazing sex of your life. And Chris, you are shocked when your best friend walks in on you getting dressed after having sex with his wife."

Proud Dad Marion Dysert Reading People Magazine With Alan On Cover

We yucked it up and did exactly what he asked us to do. It took all of ten minutes. The photographer loved the fun shots and said he would make sure we got copies.

Later that week, I got the call from Maxine saying *People* Magazine had decided to go with our cover. She said they needed to do an interview to go with the cover. I was so excited. I couldn't believe I was actually going to be on the cover of *People*.

I told Maxine I wanted her to be there for the interview and I also wanted to record the interview to keep the writer honest and make sure I was not misquoted. I had been seriously misquoted in a newspaper once before and I didn't want it to happen again. Maxine agreed that it was a good idea for her to be there.

The interview took place at our apartment on 88th Street between West End and Riverside Drive. The writer brought a photographer to take a few shots during the interview. I felt like the interview went great. I was very happy with the questions the writer had posed. We talked about life on the farm, my parents, how I ended up being an actor, life as a soap star, being married, and some topics I had suggested for the interview. She was very complimentary after the interview and said she felt it was going to be a great piece.

I didn't tell many people at the studio about the cover; I knew some of the actors that had been on the show for years would not be excited for me. There was definitely an underlying, but little talked about, competition between the actors on our show. I'm sure that's true on any soap opera or television show where there is a big cast.

The weekend the cover was to come out, I was in the Chicago area for a personal appearance with Brynn Thayer from *One Life to Live*. Since our farm was less than three hours from the event, my parents came up to see us and experience one of the soap opera festivals they had heard so much about. My parents were excited to be there and meet Brynn, who they had seen many times on her show. Waiting to see that magazine cover was excruciating. I kept trying to imagine what the image would be.

The morning the magazine was expected to hit the stands, Mom, Dad, Brynn and I went into a supermarket to see if they had a copy. I was very nervous when I walked up to one of the checkout stands and saw the cover for the first time. There I was on the cover of *People* Magazine. That was the good news.

The bad news was that the cover was one of those wacky shots taken after the shoot was supposedly finished. I realized the damn "wildlife" photographer had totally duped us. He knew all along he was not going to present a bunch of boring shots of three guys just standing together smiling. He had a vision of what would get him that cover and he made sure he got it.

I was devastated at first because I thought we all looked goofy—and a little "hunky." The article was not accurate, and the writer had totally misquoted me and exaggerated one story saying, "My dad watches all my shows on his tractor." I never said that.

In the end, none of that mattered. Everyone thought the cover was fun and light-hearted. After getting over the initial shock, I totally understood why the photographer did what he did, and it's probably the reason they ran with our cover instead of one of the others. No matter what, I was on the cover of *People* Magazine, and no one can ever take that away from me.

CHAPTER 31—IN THE UNEMPLOYMENT LINE: "IS YOUR LIMO WAITING OUTSIDE, SEAN?"

1981 couldn't have been better. There was the *People* Magazine cover in March, a nice boost in money for my second year of the contract, and I was making a lot of money for personal appearances. I had done *The Merv Griffin Show*, co-hosted *The Mike Douglas Show* and many others. It was all limos, first class, and hotel suites.

We had all heard that there was an exciting storyline involving my character coming up, but the show and the network were being very secretive about it. I did know this big storyline meant I would be working extra shows, which would translate to lots of extra money. It would also guarantee my character and story would be promoted heavily on ABC Daytime as well as Primetime. This would translate to even more appearances since my story would be expected to drive the ratings higher.

We started hearing rumors that someone was going to be killed on the show, but at first, there were no rumors about which character that would be. I knew I was safe because my character was very popular at the time and ABC was promoting me very heavily.

Then we got the news that Sybil, a beautiful and fun nurse that my character, Sean, had dated/slept with occasionally, was going to be killed by Daisy Cortlandt, played by Gillian Spencer. Daisy was jealous of Sean's occasional dalliance with Sybil. Daisy was quite a bit older than Sean and also suspected that he was secretly pursuing her daughter, Nina.

It's a soap opera—what did you expect?

I was hanging out in the makeup room with a few actors talking about how much we were going to miss Linda Gibboney, who played Sybil, when a production assistant came up and told me Jorn Winter, the executive producer, wanted to talk with me in his office.

This wasn't the way things were usually done, but I thought he probably wanted to pat me on the back and tell me how much he and the network appreciated all the traveling and promotional appearances I was doing. Or maybe talk about how great the ratings were, partially due to my storyline.

When I walked into his office, it reeked of "doom and gloom." It felt like someone had died, and the look on Jorn's face confirmed it. I asked him what was up and then I saw a tear in his eye. This was not a good sign since he was a very macho Norwegian.

Jorn responded, "You killed Sybil."

After a very long pause, I said, "No, Daisy killed Sybil." "The story has been rewritten."

In total shock, I asked, "Why? What happens to Sean."

"He goes to prison for a long time," replied the choked up Jorn.

Jorn had told me shortly after my arrival on the show that he thought of himself as a Sean type of guy. So, I guess it was hard for him to see the character leave the show. He had no control of the situation. The network and Agnes Nixon had all the power.

Jorn explained that it was nothing that I had done wrong. Basically, there was a pissing contest between Agnes Nixon, the creator of the show, and the head of ABC Daytime.

Agnes wanted to create a storyline that put Sean, the show bad boy, together with the show's angel/virgin ingénue, Nina Courtlandt, played by Taylor Miller. The network was afraid the audience would hate the pure Nina being tainted by a relationship with Sean, the cad. Nothing a network and its executives fear more than a story that their audience hates and causes ratings to tumble.

But Agnes, who created *All My Children, One Life to Live, and Loving,* knew more about soap operas and what audiences liked than anyone in the history of soap operas. She knew that the audience would hate Sean being in a relationship with Nina, but that would make them want to watch even more.

Agnes had actually owned *All My Children* for many years and then sold it and *One Life to Live* for an absolute fortune. But she retained the right to control the stories that would be written.

She told them if they wouldn't let her have the storyline with Sean and Nina, she would write Sean off the show because she didn't have any other great story ideas for Sean. They said if she didn't write a new story for Sean, they would not pick up the option for the last six months of my contract.

Thinking Agnes would never let Sean be written off the show, they called her bluff. They didn't pick up my option and I was to be written off after a long and drawn-out murder investigation and trial. In the end, Sean was sent to prison for accidentally murdering Sybil Thorne.

Here's how they could do that: At that point, we were into the third year of my three-year contract with ABC. Since my contract was the standard contract ABC offered all new actors on one of their soaps, there were many options built in to protect the network. There were no protections for the actor. The network could get rid of an actor at the end of any thirteen week period during the first year. During the second year and third year, they had options every six months.

After the trial and a week or so of prison scenes, I found myself an out- of-work actor.

* * *

Since I didn't quit the job at *All My Children* and I hadn't incorporated, I was eligible for unemployment. At that time, unemployed persons were required to physically show up at the unemployment office to fill out paperwork, etc. Each time I thought about going in to apply, I would come up with a great reason not to do it that day. I had a vision of standing in line with people that knew me from the show. I knew it would be a giant ego buster. But there was money waiting for me and I had paid into unemployment, so I wanted the money. I think it was about $600 to $800 at the time and I would have been an idiot to just ignore it.

I finally sucked in my pride, pulled my shoulders back, and marched in to get the money I was entitled to receive. But it was much worse than I had imagined. First of all, the office was incredibly dull, drab and depressing. Then a woman yelled out, "Sean, what are you doing in the unemployment line?" Another woman seriously asked, "Is your limo waiting outside?"

Then, to top it off, some of the people started asking for autographs, even if they didn't watch *All My Children*. It was straight out of a comedy. It was so bizarre that I had to laugh. I couldn't have written a more humiliating experience for a prideful actor like myself. It was a serious life lesson for me. I think I needed to experience it to understand what millions of Americans go through every day.

* * *

When my first contract ended at *All My Children*, I was totally focused on "the record deal," songwriting, and the recording project I was getting ready to start with my producer, Elliot Scheiner. That record deal was orchestrated by legendary artist manager, Irving Azoff (The Eagles, Stevie Nicks, Jimmy Buffett, John Mayer, Harry Styles, Dan Fogelberg, Gwen Stefani, Van Halen, REO Speedwagon, and countless others). Irving was all in for my project, the funds were in place, and then an unspoken battle over publishing and song choices caused the project to seriously stall.

What turned out to be a long and uncomfortable "stall" created plenty of down time, so I decided I should keep working the acting side of things, knowing there were no guarantees to what was in the works musically.

I was shopping for new representation at the time, since I had dumped the agent that defrauded me into thinking she got the *All My Children* gig for me. I knew I was in a good position to move to a better and more powerful agency now that I was a known commodity from the soap. I had a great PR package to send out to the agents that would, of course, include my *People* Magazine cover to attract their attention.

I made some calls myself, but some friends that were well connected also made calls to a few of the bigger agencies for me. All the mid-level agencies were willing to take meetings with me. The process was the same at every agency. I would meet with one of the agents whose mission was to get a feel for who I was and determine if I was a good fit for the agency. I always passed the first test with flying colors.

The next step was always a group meeting with all the agents in that agency. After a little small talk, the agent in charge would ask what I wanted to happen with my career. I was 100% honest with them. I told each agency that I didn't want to do anything with a long-term contract: I wanted to do movies, movies of the week, and guest starring roles in television series.

At one agency I was asked, "But what if it was a great, new, intelligent series like *M*A*S*H*? Wouldn't you want to do something like that?"

"Don't get me wrong," I answered. "I love many of the series, but I believe this is the right time for me to try to take a big step up. A series would be a half step."

I noticed the disappointment in the room, but they still acted like they were excited. The meeting ended with, "Thanks for coming in, Alan. Let us talk together and get back to you."

After the third agency rejection call in a row, the agent who had first interviewed me at The Gage Group was kind enough to call me and give me some great advice.

The Alan Dysert Band

"Alan, you have to stop telling agencies you don't want to do a television series. That's where the big money is for an agency. They see you as an actor who could be a lead on a series making $100,000 plus per week. The agency would get 10% of that each week. But you're telling them you want them to help you build a movie career. That can take years. And guest starring roles pay less than $5,000 per week. You are tying their hands. You can always say no to a series you don't like. Look, you need a good agent now, and no good agent is going to take you if you tell them you won't consider doing a series."

It was very nice of him to tell me that before I ran out of good agents to contact. He opened my eyes to the fact that agents are there to make money, not have fun building a movie career for me.

Chapter 32—Escape From L.A.: Nashville Here We Come With Baby Cody-1986

When we found out we were going to become parents, we decided Los Angeles didn't make sense as the place to pursue my music career. Both of our families were 2,000 miles away in Illinois, but only 325 miles from Nashville.

Everyone in Los Angeles had been telling me I needed to take my music to Nashville anyway, so we decided to sell our house and move ourselves and our new son to Nashville, only a six-hour drive from our families.

Nashville was at the end of our 2,005-mile cross-country road trip with our six-month-old son, Cody. He was a great traveler, having slept in his car seat almost every minute we were on the road. We decided to rent an apartment in Nashville for six months to give us time to find the right home, since we knew nothing about the Nashville real estate market.

We looked at many different styles of homes in many different areas of Nashville with our realtor, Susanne O'Connor, wife of the legendary fiddle player, Mark O'Connor. We had fun with Susanne, but I'm sure she thought we were crazy. We had originally told her we absolutely had to have four bedrooms but ended up buying a two bedroom home simply because it was made of stone, really cute, and not too expensive.

I had some connections in Nashville, but I was also not shy about playing the *All My Children* card to get appointments with publishers, producers, and record companies. It was my handle and I was not shy about using it.

Within two months I was writing with some of the top writers in town and cutting demos. I was learning a lot fast and also starting to realize my strengths and weaknesses as both a writer and a singer. It was a special time for me artistically, but I wasn't making any money; I was only spending it and it was flowing out quickly.

* * *

On two different occasions it seemed like something very big was going to happen. Garth Brooks's producer, Allen Reynolds, invited me into his studio to listen to some of my music. My friend and Garth's manager at the time, Pam Lewis, set up that meeting.

When we finished listening, Allen asked me if I would be interested in spending a couple of days with him in his studio to see what we could come up with. I knew it was a great offer that so many artists would have dreamed to have, but Allen's studio was filled with more smoke than Tootsie's Bar. I even sneezed a couple of times when I was there. I told him I would love to come work with him, but I knew the smoke would be a major problem for Mr. Allergy Dysert.

I walked out of the studio having serious reservations; it wasn't like I could tell him not to smoke in his own studio. I tortured myself trying to convince myself it could work; but in the end, I backed out of the offer to work with Allen. I knew I would have terrible nose and throat issues in that environment. I can't remember what fib I told him to get out of it. I do know I didn't mention the smoke.

There was another big producer that was talking about doing a project with me at the same time, but as we got close to starting the project, his wife filed for divorce and his life fell apart. All conversations were put on hold.

* * *

Then, in 1988, destiny took a hand, to paraphrase Rick from *Casablanca*. Taylor Miller, who played Nina on *All My Children*, surprised me with a call early one morning.

She said the show was planning to bring Sean, my old character, back and they were in the process of auditioning actors. She explained that she had accidentally seen an audition script in the rehearsal room that someone had left behind. She said, "Everyone at ABC thinks you never want to do a soap opera again, so they didn't bother to ask you. If you want me to tell them that you may be interested in coming back, I will."

Considering the fact that I was making no money at all in Nashville at the time, I saw no reason not to talk to them. I asked Taylor to tell the powers that be I was interested in talking.

Taylor had a conversation with the executive producer, who exclaimed, "Why didn't someone tell me the original Sean was out there somewhere! Let's get him in here and talk about a possible deal."

Taylor called and asked if I could fly in that Monday to talk.

Steve, the executive producer, and I decided it would be a great idea for me to come back. He called the ABC attorney and I called a great New York entertainment attorney to handle the contract negotiations on my side. I managed to do the deal with no agent involved, which saved me the ten percent commission I had paid to the undeserving agent from my first contract.

My weight was up twenty pounds, so I hired a trainer from the Vanderbilt University football program to get me back to looking more like I had six years before. It was painful and I thought I was going to starve, but I didn't want the fans of the show to say, "Sean's back but he's fat now." My hair was long, curly, and showing a little grey, so I brought in a top Nashville stylist to get me back to a more conservative style and the classic, almost black hair Sean was known for in the early '80s.

Within thirty days I was back in NYC working on the same show, in the same studio, playing the same character, wearing Armani again, with the same TV brother, but six years later. It was very surreal. It was like time had stopped for six years and then started back up again.

Sally Jessy Raphael Show with Tim Reid, Harry Smith, David Brenner, Chuck Woolery, Alan and Cody

Taylor was actually getting ready to leave the show, get married, and move to Chicago, so she asked if I wanted to rent her apartment. Taylor wasn't leaving for about a month so she said I could live with her until she left. Once Taylor was gone, I flew Liz and Cody to Manhattan. It sounds complicated, but it went very smoothly and it was great to have a big check coming in again.

* * *

While I was away from *All My Children* for the six years, ABC had been acquired by Capital Cities Communications. The new owners were very bottom line focused and didn't spend money wildly like ABC did when it was simply "ABC." I knew things had changed drastically when they picked me up at the airport on my first trip back to New York City with a brown Buick limo.

At first, I thought it was a one-time mistake, but the next time ABC sent me for an appearance at an affiliate station, the same brown Buick limo showed up. I realize it sounds like I was spoiled, and I guess I was, but it was an indication of how things had changed since I left ABC. Before the Capital Cities takeover, ABC made every effort to make its soap stars feel appreciated.

Those days were gone.

In the old days, the limos were black and in spectacular condition; the parties were extravagant; the contracts were generous; and no cost was spared for wardrobe. One year we took over the top floor of the World Trade Center for a party. But that was when ABC was ABC and we had three of the top four soaps on television. We were such a cash cow that the profits from *All My Children, General Hospital* and *One Life to Live* paid for all the losses in news, sports and primetime. Still, the primetime executives looked down on our shows—the ones that paid their salaries.

CHAPTER 33—HALCION BLUES

My 1988 return to *All My Children* was good for many reasons, mostly financial, but bad for me psychologically. I had been gone from television for six years, and coming back to the same show with many of the same cast members, directors, producers, sets, dressing room, dressing roommate, crew and production staff was freaky and surreal.

I had developed a lot of anxiety about performing on national television and started obsessing on the memorizing of so many pages of dialogue for each and every show. I don't know if it was because of the new responsibilities of having a family or a desire to make the show work well for me and not have a surprise ending like I had with the first three-year contract at *All My Children*.

The anxiety was causing me to have serious sleep problems. One of my castmates, Gillian Spencer, said she had a great primary care doctor that could probably help me, or at least suggest someone that could. On her referral, I made an appointment with her doctor.

Based on what I told him about my inability to sleep more than four hours, he prescribed a sleeping medication, Halcion. In all fairness to the doctor, he did make me swear that I wouldn't take it more than twice per week.

The Halcion definitely knocked me out for the night. At first, I was good about taking the medication only twice per week as the doctor had insisted. But it didn't take long for me to come up with excuses for taking the medication three, four, and sometimes six times per week, based on my workload and personal appearances. I found a way to justify each day I took the medication, even though the reason may have been weak: the personal appearances are a major source of added income, and I don't want to screw that up by being tired onstage; I have lots of heavy dialogue in tomorrow's show and I don't want to screw it up; I don't want to ruin the day with the family. I found so many reasons to take the Halcion.

I told Liz I was having very dark thoughts; I'm talking seriously dark. She tried to convince me that everyone has dark thoughts. I explained to her that this was a whole different animal. I knew I should be happy, but I definitely was not.

I did some research and found a psychiatrist. He was terrible. He kept saying, "I'm not sure. What do you think, Alan?"

I asked him if he thought the dark thoughts could be from the Halcion. He told me he thought it would take twelve sessions to figure that out. That's when I decided he knew Halcion was the problem, but he wasn't about to pass up an opportunity to milk my problem for as much cash as possible. Plus, I had seen him on the street one day, when he didn't know I was watching him, and I could tell he was definitely crazy himself.

I did some research on my own and discovered Halcion was a notoriously dangerous medication. Halcion can cause paranoid or suicidal thoughts and impair memory, judgment, and coordination. Combined with alcohol, it can slow breathing and possibly lead to death. I was pissed! That psychiatrist should have been put in jail for not telling me that.

I decided I was going to try to go cold turkey on the Halcion. I knew it would be rough and I wouldn't be sleeping much, so I decided I should let Jimmy Mitchell, my dressing roommate, know since we spent hours together each day we both worked on an episode. At the time, Jimmy was having big health issues and had been told he had Epstein-Barr Syndrome. When I told him about the Halcion situation, he said, "I've been taking that sleeping pill for 10 years."

After doing some research on Jimmy's symptoms and the side effects of Halcion, we decided his issues were probably caused by the Halcion. We decided to do the cold turkey thing together. Although neither of us got much sleep, we didn't feel worse during the day than when we took Halcion. With Halcion, we were knocked out for hours, but never felt rested in the morning. I read a few years later that Halcion keeps the user from going into REM sleep, which really takes a toll over time.

After two weeks, the darkness lifted. I felt much better even though my sleep left a lot to be desired. The very dark thoughts that sent me to the bad psychiatrist in the first place went away.

I still never slept that well while I was on *All My Children*. I worried way too much about my lines and my performance. I wanted it to be perfect and please everyone, but that isn't possible on a soap opera. There are just too many lines and the material isn't exactly great literature. I was always trying to figure out how to turn the soap into a movie, when it was exactly what it was supposed to be: a soap opera.

Chapter 34—I'm Going To Make Love To Nancy Karr? 1988

After three months back on the show, I was asked to come to the executive producer's office to discuss my upcoming storyline. My character, Sean, was in a serious romantic relationship with a young woman from a very rich family, Cecily. Rosa, who played Cecily, was actually in her late twenties, but was playing eighteen or nineteen. I was thirty-eight playing late twenties. The executive producer wanted to tell me that in addition to that relationship, I would also be having an affair with Cecily's mother, Bitsy.

My first thought was, "Here we go again with the mother and daughter affair thing." They had done this to me during my first contract at *All My Children*. I had to wonder if there was something about me personally that caused them to write this kind of story for my character twice.

My mom even asked me, "Why do they have you doing these things, Alan? You're such a nice young man."

The executive producer said they were bringing in an amazing veteran soap opera actress, Ann Flood, to play Cecily's mother. He told me she was a beautiful and sophisticated lady in her fifties. In the story, her character, Bitsy, would come onto Sean without him knowing she was Cecily's jet-setting mother, who had rarely been in Cecily's life.

Bitsy's jet-setter lifestyle had always been more important to her than her daughter. She spent most of her time in Europe and rarely had time for Cecily. Cecily lived with her filthy rich great-aunt, Phoebe, and dealt with abandonment issues. But when Bitsy heard that her daughter was engaged to Sean, an older cad/ex-convict/murderer, she decided to finally be the mother she should have been along.

Her plan was to orchestrate an affair with Sean, who wouldn't know she was Cecily's mother. She knew her plan would work because Sean was known to be obsessed with rich people and getting rich himself. After she had slept with Sean, she planned to blackmail him into breaking up with Cecily. If he didn't break off the engagement, she would tell Cecily what he had done, proving to Cecily what kind of terrible man she was about to marry.

Even though she knew her scheme might damage her relationship with her daughter forever, Bitsy had known too many men like Sean in her own life and wanted to save her daughter from a life of pain and heartbreak, even if it meant Cecily hated her for it.

Yes, I know that was a long and convoluted story, but give me a break, it's a soap opera and I felt it needed a little build up to the punchline.

The executive producer told me the actress, Ann Flood, would be coming by that afternoon and wanted to meet me. I said I would love to meet her and told the executive producer to have her knock on my dressing room door when she got to the studio.

An hour later there was a knock on my door. I opened the door and there she stood with the biggest, most wonderful smile. As she introduced herself, I immediately knew who she was. I don't know if I had a shocked look on my face, but my first thought was, "You've got to be sh*&#ing me! It's Nancy F&*%ing KARR from *The Edge of Night*!"

When I was a young boy, I was sick a lot; I mean a lot. I was always in the hospital for something: hepatitis, appendectomy, pneumonia three times, extreme hives twice, kidney issues, prostate issues, and several other hospital stays. I spent months in the hospital and months out of school. My teachers brought my homework to the house and the hospital, but there were many hours during the day to kill. Television became my best friend, and in those days, if you were watching television during the daytime, you were watching soap operas. I was hooked on the CBS soaps because it was the only clear signal in our area.

My favorite show was *The Edge of Night*, and my favorite character was Nancy Karr. I was in love with Nancy Karr. Even as a young boy, I dreamed of marrying a woman just like Nancy Karr.

So there I was, at my dressing room door staring at my childhood TV dream woman, knowing I was about to have an affair with her and make out with her on national television. I was sure it was a sign that I was actually dead. This couldn't be happening in real life; it was too bizarre. Who would believe a story like that?

It was a little awkward for me at first, but she made me feel very comfortable. To add to my reasons to be nervous, Ann's husband, Herb Granath, was the President of ABC Sports at the time. I hoped he wouldn't be upset about me being under the covers and kissing his wife.

In 2001 Herb received the *Sports Emmy for Sports Lifetime Achievement Award*. He also served as Chairman of the Board for ESPN, *The History Channel, Lifetime Television* and Disney/ABC International.

We had worked together for three months before I told Ann my childhood crush story, what she had meant to me, and how she got me through some very rough times when I was a sick boy.

Ann and I became great friends and had tons of fun working together. She was a true professional. Herb didn't think a thing about our lust-filled scenes on television. I guess he was used to it, since they had both been involved with television for most of their lives.

Chapter 35—Surprise! Miracle Pregnancy #2 And No Job!

After three surgeries, multiple in vitro failures, and $100,000 of medical expenses, our fertility doctor told us there was little hope that we would have children. The doctor talked with me about the possibility of using a surrogate. Liz said he never mentioned that to her, but I remember the conversation very well. Liz's very fertile sister, Sally, even volunteered at one point, but Liz wasn't interested in that idea.

So Liz's surprise pregnancy with Cody was considered a miracle by all. Even the fertility doctor couldn't explain how it happened. He said, "Don't question it. It's a miracle. Enjoy your baby."

Those early years of Cody's life were special. I was there most of the time since I didn't have a "real job" at that time. We filmed every little thing he did and took hundreds of photos. We had fought hard to get him and we wanted to enjoy the gift we'd been given. He was adorable, fun, funny, and happy. To me, he was the perfect child.

You can imagine everyone's surprise when Liz became pregnant with Cooper. It was a total shocker. We were very excited but baffled as to how we could be so lucky two times.

When we found out our second miracle child was going to be a boy, we knew the rare tradition of only boys being born into the Dysert side of the family was continuing. Since then, my brother had a son, Ethan, and my oldest son, Cody, and his wife Brianna had a son, Jack, in 2019. That's four generations of Dysert boys over a 100-year span—and not a single girl. At that point we hoped someday to see a Dysert girl or two so people wouldn't think there was some kind of witchcraft involved. .

We had already moved to a house in the very preppy Darien, Connecticut, before we found out Liz was pregnant again, so we had more than enough room in the home we had rented. We had planned to rent first to see if we liked Connecticut and if I could handle commuting to New York City to work on *All My Children*.

* * *

To add more stress, ninety days before Cooper was born, the executive producer called me to her office to tell me they couldn't renew my contract yet because they had just fired Lauren Holly (later married to Jim Carrey), whose character was planned to be Sean's next love interest. She went on to explain they didn't have time to bring in a new character and write a whole new story, since soap operas plan their storylines six months to a year in advance. She said they would be working on possible new story ideas for Sean, but ABC wouldn't allow her to renew my contract without a storyline. It was terrible news at a very inconvenient time. The network kept emotions out of their decisions: it was just business.

Happy Grandma (Faye) With Grandsons Cody and Cooper

In the old days, they would have renewed my contract and waited for the story to be developed, but the "new ABC-TV" was owned by the very bottom line-focused Capital Cities, who would never approve that. This meant I would have to wait around unpaid and trust they would come up with a new storyline for me.

I decided two times was enough. I didn't like the way they handled the end of my first contract, and I definitely didn't like it this time. There I was, second son on the way and about to buy an expensive house in Darien, Connecticut. Thank God we hadn't signed a contract on the expensive house we had been seriously considering.

The fact I had no control over the situation infuriated me, but that's the life of an actor, unless you're the star of a successful primetime series or a bona fide movie star. I was neither, and farm boys are not raised to let other people control their lives. I realized I needed to somehow take control of my life, not only for me, but for my family. I needed a plan and prayed for a sign.

Alan and Sons, Cody and Cooper

* * *

The first three months after being blindsided by the bad news about my contract were focused on preparing for Cooper's arrival and finishing my commitment at *All My Children*. The show worked me heavily on the way out the door, which helped build up the bank accounts, but I knew the savings would dwindle quickly once the checks stopped coming in.

The cost of living in Darien and working out of New York City was an expensive proposition. Sometimes, I would find myself hitting the ATM twice in one day, each time thinking I had plenty of money in my pocket for the day.

I was very lucky in that we had enough money saved to get us through a couple of years, but I had worked very hard to save that money and hated to see it disappear with nothing to show for it.

Alan and Sons, Cody and Cooper

It made no sense to leave Connecticut with a baby on the way. We had already readied one of the bedrooms for Cooper's arrival and didn't want to take away from the joy of his arrival. I decided I could gain control of my career from the New York area as well as anywhere else. I could always travel for meetings or recording, and ship in the grandparents if Liz needed help. Uprooting everyone with no particular plan in place would have been a huge mistake.

I kept myself busy helping with Cody and Cooper, writing songs late at night, playing the stock market, going on occasional auditions, and working on treatments for comedy projects I hoped would give me the control I wanted in my life.

CHAPTER 36— *COCONUT GROOVE* – MY COMEDY SERIES

I was excited about a comedy project I was developing. A primetime comedy series. At a neighborhood party, I ran the concept past one of my new Connecticut acquaintances, who was a fast-rising executive at Paramount Television's New York office. He loved the concept and offered to set up a meeting with the Senior Vice-President of Development for Paramount's Los Angeles television division.

Music was a big part of my show, and I envisioned the music being heavy on Latin and Caribbean rhythms. I thought, in a perfect world, the ideal people to bring in on the music side would be Gloria and Emilio Estefan.

At that time, Gloria was a three-time Grammy Award winner and hugely popular internationally. Her husband, Emilio, produced all their music and headed up their very successful entertainment company. Emilio was the original founder of the Miami Sound Machine and later added Gloria as the vocalist.

I managed to get a meeting at Estefan Music in Miami after getting past my own negative self-talk. I knew Estefan Music was the perfect company for the project, but I really had to fight my negative thoughts to make the initial phone call.

I was amazed at how easy it was to get the appointment, after I got out of my own way. Having the *All My Children* / ABC-TV handle was a big help in getting that door to open.

The meeting went very well, and Emilio told me they would like to be involved with the music if I could get network interest in the show. Knowing this connection with Estefan Music made my project much more attractive, I made plans to head to Los Angeles for the meeting at Paramount.

January 14, 1991, I headed to Los Angeles to pitch *"Coconut Groove"* in a meeting with Steve Nalevansky, Senior Vice-President of Development for Paramount. He hadn't been told anything about my project; he only knew a top executive from their New York office thought the project was viable.

I got on the plane with a splashy presentation I had worked on for two months. In addition to the written presentation, I included colorful graphics I thought would represent the fun and wacky personality of the project. If a picture is worth a thousand words, I squeezed in another 10,000 words. Since I had never pitched a show and didn't know anyone who had, I didn't know what to expect or what would be expected from me. I wanted to be prepared for anything.

During the flight, I started thinking it would be a good idea to have a backup project just in case he wasn't grabbed by *Coconut Groove*. They say creative people often do their most imaginative work when under pressure or experiencing insecurity. That was exactly what was going on with me when I came up with the concept for *Alvis* on the flight to LA. Alvis is an Elvis impersonator/auto repair shop owner who lives in the desert just outside Las Vegas, so close he can see the lights of the Vegas strip from his shop. Alvis's band consists of four weird guys that work at his auto repair shop, along with his 10-year-old son, who is the brains of the family.

My brain was in hyperdrive cranking out page after page of character descriptions and episode ideas for a full season. It was four hours of the most intense focus l had ever experienced. I had to finish by the time I got off the plane to allow enough time to have the project professionally typed and printed for my meeting the next morning. I was writing it by hand since I had no computer or word processing skills at the time.

* * *

I walked into Paramount the next morning nervous but feeling very good about both of my projects. After a short wait, I was escorted into the office of Steve Nalevansky, a very nice, high-energy guy I liked immediately. After I reminded him who had suggested we meet, Steve said, "Tell me about your show."

My explanation was far too detailed, which made my pitch about three minutes in length. I didn't realize at the time, but was enlightened later, a good pitch should grab the listener in the first two or three sentences. If you don't have their interest in 30 seconds, you've probably lost them.

Looking a little confused, Steve said, "It sounds fun, but I wasn't quite able to wrap my head around all that. I'll have to read that one." That made sense to me, so I handed him a copy of the project.

At the time, I didn't know, "I'll have to read that one," is the kiss of death. They probably won't ever get around to reading it. An idea has to hit very hard and fast. Pitching series and movie projects is an art—and I was not a pitch artist.

Then he asked, "You got anything else?"

I proudly said, "As a matter fact I do. It's called *Alvis*. It's about a wacky Elvis impersonator/auto repair shop owner who lives in the desert just outside Las Vegas: so close he can see the lights of the Vegas strip from his shop. Alvis's band consists of a bunch of weird guys that work at his shop along with his 10-year-old son, who is the brains of the family."

I saw Steve's eyes light up more with each word that came out of my mouth. After a three beat pause, Steve said, "That is the funniest f—king idea I've heard in the last three years."

Then he rattled off all the name actors he could see playing the part. He was totally into my project. The room filled with creative energy as we started bouncing ideas back and forth. The meeting ended with him saying, "I'm taking this straight to Frank" (the Head of Paramount Television at the time).

He walked me to the elevator going on and on about how funny the show would be. As the elevator doors were closing, Steve yelled, "Funny f—king show, Alan. Funny f—king show! I'm goin' straight to Frank. I'll call you tomorrow."

I have never been more excited about anything in my creative life than I was in the Paramount elevator that day: more than when I was cast on *All My Children* or the Cheech and Chong movie. It was a validation of my ability to recognize and put on paper a good comedy project. I was amazed the project that had blown him away was not the one I had worked on for months; it was the one I had created and developed on a five-hour flight from New York to Los Angeles. I felt like I was about to get some control of my professional life.

The next day I didn't get that call from Nalevansky. I stayed positive knowing it probably took some time to meet with Frank and discuss *Alvis*.

On the second day I started getting nervous, so late in the day I called Paramount and asked to speak with Steve.

When Steve came on the line I said, "Steve, it's Alan Dysert." There was silence. I said, "Alan...with the comedy show *Alvis*."

Then Steve responded, "Oh, Alan. Funny show. Very funny show.

Frank says we're not doing any new comedy shows this year. Sorry."

I was in shock as I hung up the phone. Everything looked peachy at Paramount a mere 48 hour earlier. Now what?

Steve had just dropped a giant s#%! bomb on the model of my new world, but I wasn't going to let my vision be destroyed by one rejection. I decided to stay in Los Angeles for a few days and see what other meetings I could put together using my many contacts.

But two days later, the United States and its many allies started dropping thousands of bombs on Iraq, and our entire country, including the entertainment business, was focused on nothing else for weeks. The upstart network CNN was covering Operation Desert Storm 24 hours, every day of the week.

I couldn't buy another meeting with anyone after that first bomb went down that smokestack in Iraq. I left town very disappointed that the amazing reception I first received at Paramount didn't turn into a series commitment.

* * *

Once back in Connecticut, I was disillusioned and even more aware of how little control I had. I hated asking people for help and then facing what seemed like endless rejection.

I decided to push harder with my music project because I felt I would have more control. I believed that if I started my own record label, I could stop kissing ass and depending on others to give me work. Now, I realize how naive I was about the music business, but it made sense to me at the time.

While I was on the East Coast, I was still writing songs and had continued flying to Nashville to record on a very regular basis. I finished recording a pop-rock album of all original songs that I planned to be the beginning of my company, Notown Music. This was all part of a bigger plan to have my own company with music and television divisions.

It had made sense financially to go back to *All My Children*, but it was very disruptive to our lives and what I was trying to achieve musically. In the end, it probably killed it. Historically, it has always been very tough to sell the "TV star wants to be a recording artist" thing.

Chapter 37—NBC-TV's
Working It Out With Jane Curtin

I was still going on a few auditions in New York. I scored a guest starring role on *Working It Out*, an NBC sitcom starring Jane Curtin (*SNL*) and Stephen Collins (*7th Heaven*). I played an old friend of Stephen Collins's character who was still performing and emceeing at the same Greenwich Village club where they had both performed in the '70s. My character, who was stuck in the '70s, sang a song and then invited Stephen Collins's character to come up and sing a song for old times' sake.

The taping ended up being a very traumatic event. At first, I was excited because they had told me I could sing one of my original songs on the show. I sent the producer a recording of the song I wanted to do three weeks in advance, and he said it would work fine.

The director decided it would work best if they recorded the singing part of my performance after the full rehearsal the evening before the taping of the full show. Since they did the show in front of a live audience, he felt it would save time and be cleaner if they did it that way. I actually liked the idea of singing for just the crew and staff and then lip-synching to my recorded track during the live filming.

The rest of the cast left after the rehearsal while they set up to record my vocal and guitar accompaniment. Once everything was set, the stage manager gave me the action cue and I started to sing. After about thirty seconds, the stage manager yelled, "Cut."

He asked me to hold on; there was a discussion going on in the control room. He was listening very intently through his headset to what was being said. Then he looked at me and said, "They want to know who has the publishing on that song?"

"I do," I answered. "I was told three weeks ago that it would be fine for me to sing it."

He asked me to hang on for a minute while he went into the control room. A few minutes later he came out and said the producers and the director needed to talk with me in the control room.

In the control room, I was first told that the mistake was theirs, not mine. They acknowledged they should have asked me about the publishing information weeks ago. They explained that the NBC legal representative was watching the taping and realized NBC didn't have a license to use my song without paying me a sizeable amount for its use.

Then I was asked, "Would you be willing to give the publishing rights to your song to NBC?"

"No. I can't do that."

I wanted to scream at them for letting it get this far without realizing they would have to pay me. I had realized all along that they would have to pay me for the use of my song and I was looking forward to the chunk I would make from it. I couldn't believe the experienced producer hadn't thought of it when I had asked if I could play one of my songs.

They apologized and totally understood my not wanting to give up publishing rights to my song. They had a powwow and then someone brought out a multi-page list of songs that NBC had rights to use. They asked me to look at the list and see if there was a song on the list I could play.

I immediately knew it wasn't going to work because I'm not one of those guys that sits around playing a thousand cover songs. The song list was a very odd collection and I saw not one song on the list that I could just walk out on the set and record; and none of the songs would have made any sense for the scene. This was national television and I didn't want my performance to be slapped together at the last minute.

Then they brought out another list that included several Jim Croce songs. I knew I would sound good singing any Jim Croce song, so I told them I could do "I Got a Name" if they could find the sheet music or chart for it.

At that point, we all realized the recording was not going to happen that night. They asked if I could come in at 8:00 A.M. to record it. I said yes, but I needed them to understand that I lived in Connecticut, would need to drive home, learn the song, get up very early, and then drive into Manhattan to record the song; and it was already 8:00 P.M. I made it very clear that they needed to furnish the music because I had no idea where to find it at 8:00 P.M.

One of the associate producers tracked down the sheet music at the historic Colony Music Store in Times Square and got confirmation they would hold it as long as someone picked it up before they closed at 9:00 P.M. The producer said they would send someone for it who would then bring it to my house in Darien.

Realizing this might turn into waiting up all night for a lost delivery person, I decided it would be much less stressful if I headed over to Colony Music myself, since it was only about ten blocks away from the NBC studio.

After I picked up the music, I drove to Darien, ate a quick, very late dinner while I worked on the lyrics, and figured out the most interesting way to play the song on my guitar. This got me in bed late. After a very restless night, I got up at 4:30 A.M. to get ready, practice a little quietly as not to wake the family, and drive into Manhattan to tape my performance.

The producers were happy with the way the performance came off and I was relieved that part of the saga was over. The acting part and lip-synching were the easy part. The hard part was faking the guitar playing. We had recorded my guitar performance in the morning along with the vocal, but now they needed it to look like I was playing the guitar live. I couldn't actually touch the strings or the noise would leak into the audio. I can't remember exactly why it had to be that way, but I do know it felt very odd. The good news: it looked and sounded good in the edit and that's all they cared about.

Chapter 38—A School Goes Up For Auction

In the summer of 1991, Dad called me in Connecticut and said, "They're going to auction Fithian Grade School in about ninety days." I asked him if it was in good shape. He said it was just like it was the last day the kids attended school there. I told Dad I needed to talk with Liz and would call him back. He knew that I was disappointed when I had missed out on the sale of my old school that sold for $5000.00 the year before.

Liz and I had talked about the possibility of moving back to Nashville many times but had never talked about moving back to Illinois. Moving back to Los Angeles for my acting career was never a consideration. We had a serious discussion about my vision of buying the school, making it a fun living environment, and running my music operation from the school as well.

There would be room for music equipment, a sound system, and touring vehicles in the gymnasium, and a full stage for rehearsals and filming live music videos. The boys would have the gym to play in and they could go wild riding bikes up and down the hallways.

Liz was up for the change and loved the idea of being around family with the boys. She also knew the cost of living would be much less there, so our savings and investments would last a lot longer there while I made my career transition.

I called Dad back and told him we were going to move back home and would like to buy that school. He asked, "What in the world are you going to do with that school?"

"Live in it and set up my music company there. Use the stage for rehearsals and the gym for a garage and equipment storage. Turn two of the classrooms into bedrooms and cook in the giant industrial kitchen."

Dad and Mom were very excited about the idea of having us and their grandkids near them, but I'm sure they thought I was a little crazy with my idea of "living in a school." Where I come from, people don't usually think outside the box: a school is school; a house is a house; and a barn is a barn.

Having lived in San Francisco, New York City, and Los Angeles, I had learned the art of thinking outside the box, where space is space and land is land. My vision was to take a very large, well-designed, solid brick structure

156

that was tossed aside and transform it into something exciting, creative, and wonderful.

I told Dad not to let anyone know about our plan. If the school board heard their "local boy makes good" was coming home to buy the school, they would set a higher minimum bid. We told our parents to tell people we were coming back for a visit to spend time with both families, and to let them get to know their grandchildren.

* * *

I hadn't realized just how much stress I was under until I left Darien in the rental truck full of furniture and household stuff, with five-year-old Cody riding shotgun as we headed to the farm in Illinois. There was a peace that came over me the minute we left the driveway in Darien.

Cody and I took two days to make the trip to Illinois. It was so much fun having my son road tripping with me, and it was quite the adventure for a five-year old boy. He was so excited about riding in the big truck and staying in a hotel with his dad, as we traveled hundreds of miles.

After two days on the road, we reunited with Liz and Cooper, who had flown into Indianapolis from New York two days earlier. We received a huge welcome from both families and then unloaded the rental truck at a storage facility.

We settled in at my parents' house ready to work on our master plan while enjoying the calm country life; we even put in a garden. The plan was to stay with Mom and Dad until we achieved our secret goal of buying the school and making a few alterations to make it livable.

The decision to move to Illinois was good in so many ways. It was a much needed and refreshing break from the hustle and bustle of NYC, Connecticut, and Los Angeles. It was also a relief to be away from the stress of doing a soap opera and the politics at ABC. I needed some breathing room and time to focus on the next phase of my professional life. For Liz, being in the same town with both sets of grandparents, her two brothers and their children, aunts, uncles, and cousins was comforting.

We managed to make it to Illinois without anyone finding out about our secret plan to buy the school. The school district ended up deciding not to set a minimum bid. Everything was going as we had hoped.

First, we needed to find a way to get inside the school without anyone knowing we were doing an inspection. Luckily, Dad, as a politician/local farmer, knew everyone in the area. He confidentially reached out to the former custodian who said he would be happy to sneak us in to look around. I loved looking around the empty schoolhouse thinking it could all be ours for a song. It was exactly as I had remembered from my childhood.

The more I looked around, the more excited I got. I could just see the boys riding their big wheels in the gym and all of us performing on the stage.

Liz was not as excited as I was. She could see the vision and was not against living in the school, but she had very different ideas than I did. She decided two "regular" bathrooms needed to be added, as well as a "modern" kitchen in one of the classrooms. Liz didn't want her boys using the large, multi-urinal bathroom that was there. She thought it would be too weird. I thought it was cool. She refused to cook in the large industrial school kitch- en. Then she told me she wanted a two-car garage built onto the existing structure. She didn't want to unlock the large, metal doors to the gym every time she wanted to pull in the car.

I got rough bids on all the changes she wanted, which inflated the cost of moving into the school drastically. Then we were told the school had some asbestos in the furnace room and on some of the pipes. This would need to be removed by professionals, so we got a bid. The guy started at $35,000. I told him, if that was the case, forget it. He came back the next day offering to do it for $20,000. Again, I said forget it. His last offer was $3,500 to do what he had originally asked $35,000. At that point, I refused to work with him because he obviously tried to screw me at first.

By the time the estimates came in for the changes Liz wanted to make, my $5,000 school was turning into a possible $150,000-$200,000 white ele- phant that we would be stuck with if we decided we didn't want to stay. The way I had wanted to do it, we could have packed up at any time and unloaded the property. If we put in the improvements, we would have been sitting on the property 'til the end of time.

That was the death of my beautiful and very creative idea. Compro- mise is hard to swallow sometimes.

Just in case you're wondering: The school brought $1,000 at the auc- tion. That's not a misprint. The school on five acres sold for one thousand dollars to a man who turned it into a model train museum.

* * *

Once the original idea to buy the old elementary school was scuttled, we decided to stay in Illinois for Liz and the boys to have the added support of both families while I was traveling back and forth to Nashville to write and put a band together.

All four grandparents were retired and more than willing to take care of the boys anytime we asked. My parents were in heaven. It was a great situation for everyone. Liz and I needed that reconnection with our families that we hadn't experienced in the seventeen years of being in Los Angeles, New York and Nashville.

There were no nice houses to rent in Danville, so we ended up buying a house.

I have to admit it was a better setup for Liz and the boys than living in a giant school when I was out of town. This also meant we didn't have to be distracted by all the construction it would have taken to retrofit the school.

But I still love the idea of having a property like that school.

Chapter 39—Scrambling And Scattered, But Music Got Me Out of NYC

I was scrambling and scattered, but I was following my heart, and my heart was telling me to continue on the path and have faith.

Music is what got me out of the New York area and away from the temptation of doing another soap. Taking another soap opera gig would have made me feel like a prostitute: just doing it for the money. I believe it would've been a huge mistake to stay there. I never felt like I belonged in New York. It was fun as a twenty-nine-year-old actor without children in the early 1980s, but I was faking it the second time around. Thank God, I got out of there before I stayed until there was no other choice.

I made decisions for my family I will never get credit for, and the biggest ones were the decisions to get the hell out of the NYC area and never do another soap again.

I was offered another soap opera gig on a CBS soap right before we left the East Coast. I told them I wasn't interested. I never mentioned it to Liz because I was worried we might talk about it and decide to stay for a couple more years just for the money. I was on the way out of town and I didn't want to look back, so I pretended it never happened.

* * *

I had never planned to travel back and forth to Nashville for five years and drive over 250,000 miles, but that's exactly what I ended up doing. I completely wore out two new cars going back and forth in all kinds of weather. I would usually leave around 4:00 A.M. to drive the six hours to Nashville.

I never questioned why I was making that drive every week; I just got in my car and drove. It was like I was being guided by God and The Universe. I knew it was my mission.

It was the most creative period of my entire life. I was writing song after song as I drove through the peaceful highways in Indiana, Kentucky, and Tennessee. I never took I-65: too many tractor-trailers and lots of people driving like they were Nascar drivers. I always took the less traveled

Route 41 in Indiana, to the Pennyrile Parkway in Kentucky, and connecting to I-24 that rolled me into Nashville.

Dysert Family Mother's Day 1991

I was recording every song idea, lyric, or melody with two different handheld cassette recorders. It was like I was purging myself of every idea, thought, and emotion, of the creative side of my soul. I have over 200 cassettes of material that I recorded, mostly while I was driving back and forth from Illinois to Nashville, and Nashville back to Illinois.

Every two weeks I would log the tapes in spiral notebooks. Now, those tapes and notebooks are very neatly organized at a storage facility. When I die, I assume my sons will throw it all away, but it would be nice if they at least leafed through them to know more about who their father really was and how his mind worked. I don't think they know the tapes and notebooks exist.

Sometimes, I would find a song half or two-thirds finished that I had no recollection of writing. It was so exciting when I would find one of those songs that I didn't remember, knowing I had written them when I was in the middle of one of my creative trances.

It seemed like an obsession, but I was desperate to express myself. I found it much easier to do through a song than writing a script or a book. I was cranking them out. Some of the songs were very good, and some were not.

A couple of times, in the middle of one of my "right brain hurricanes," I completely lost track of my location. I came out of my trance thinking, "Where am I?"

I had made that trip at least 400 times. I knew every building, house, road sign, and exit along the way, so if I didn't recognize where I was, something was wrong. One time, I had gone fifteen miles past my exit before I realized nothing looked familiar. I guess my left brain took care of the driving while my right brain was working on song ideas. I realize it sounds dangerous, but my eyes were focused on the road the entire time. If it had been dangerous, I assume I would have crashed many times.

CHAPTER 40—THE THINGS WE DO FOR MONEY

As I was going through a stack of bills I had just found in the mailbox, I got a phone call from a Nashville video producer who offered me a way to pay all those bills and more. I didn't know the producer but I had heard of him and knew he wasn't a big player in the Nashville production scene. He told me his production company had been hired to handle the television production and broadcast of the Miss South Carolina Pageant, that would be seen by an audience of several million in the Southeast. He said he had pitched me as the emcee for the four-day event.

Normally, I would have said no, but they were offering me $5,000, all expenses, and some extra perks. I desperately needed a cash infusion at the time, so I went for it.

I had no idea how popular this event was until I got involved. Apparently, people in South Carolina have been obsessed with beauty pageants for decades. Men sit around barber shops, coffee shops, hardware stores, and fire stations discussing the possibilities and odds on who might win. They follow pageant girls from their youth until they're ready for the big show: the Miss South Carolina Pageant. I was told there is more money wagered on the Miss South Carolina Pageant than the Clemson vs. South Carolina football game each year—and that's a lot of money. I found it all very weird and a little creepy.

The producer told me there would be three days of live competition and the last day would be a live broadcast via a state-of-the-art broadcast truck.

The producer of the show was a former preacher who had just been forced to leave his church due to a scandal involving his wife: she left him for a woman in their church. A couple of friends suggested I insist on being paid in cash as soon as I get off the plane, since everything sounded a little sketchy. The producer/ex-preacher agreed to pay me in cash, half when I arrived and the other half before I went onstage for the broadcast.

When I got off the plane, the producer, who seemed like a very nice man, handed me a check. I told him a check was not going to work for me.

He told me he didn't have time to go to the bank before he picked me up and they would be closing soon. I said we needed to go to the bank because I would not accept the check and would not start rehearsals until I had cash. I watched the producer and the banker go back and forth for over thirty minutes. The banker didn't want to cash my check because the $100,000 check from the pageant owners to cover production expenses hadn't cleared yet. Finally, the banker coughed up $2,500 in cash for me.

After the uncomfortable bank episode, I felt it necessary to remind the producer that I would insist on cash for the other half before the broadcast started. He said he totally understood and promised me he would make sure the cash was there.

The rehearsals went pretty well even though they were trying out a ridiculous concept they hoped would increase viewership. If it worked, they would use the same concept in other state Miss America pageants. The concept was to weave the participant's talent and interviews into a very stupid story with a group of children from the future on laptops looking back and telling the story of the current pageant. Not only was I emceeing the pageant, it was necessary for me to give acting lessons to the kids and make changes to the ridiculous dialogue.

I was promised a Teleprompter but it hadn't arrived. Each day I was told the Teleprompter was coming, but every evening I ended up being forced to go from memory and cues I had written on my hands or the podium.

I was also promised a stage manager, but each day there was a different excuse for why the stage manager had not arrived yet. This meant I had the added responsibility of timing all the segments and making sure we were getting in and out of commercials on time. At that point I realized I was very underpaid. It was not the walk-in-the-park I had anticipated. It was the work of three people and very stressful, to say the least. I would have quit if I hadn't needed the money.

It was turning into a nightmare and there were rumblings of problems between the family that owned the Miss South Carolina Pageant, the producer, and the owner of the production company who was directing and broadcasting the pageant. They promised me everything was being worked out and all would be smooth as silk on the final night. Once again, I was promised a Teleprompter and stage manager.

On the night of the final performance, the producer and my money were nowhere to be found. They begged me to go on without the cash, promising me he was on his way. I said no. If I didn't get my money, they needed to figure out a way to do the show without me, which I knew was impossible.

Then they told me that they never got the Teleprompter and the stage manager wasn't coming. I was on my own for the broadcast.

Finally, the producer showed up. The bastard handed me a check saying he didn't have time to get the cash. He begged and begged and promised I could cash the check on Monday. Everyone was begging me to go on with the show.

I caved and went on with the show knowing how much it meant to all the young women and the cast of kids. I did threaten the producer that I would hunt him down and kill him if the check didn't go through. I reminded him that he also owed me my per diem.

The show was a disaster: the audio kept going in an out on the broadcast and we had feedback so loud on stage that the contestants couldn't hear themselves sing. At one point, there were two minutes of broadcast with no audio. I was told the director was in the broadcast truck drunk and had no idea what he was doing.

I did manage to bring the show in exactly on time, without a stage manager, a clock, or a Teleprompter. I considered that a huge success on my part, but the pageant owners were so upset with the botched broadcast, they put a stop payment on the $100,000 payment to the producer.

This was no surprise to any of us because the owners of the pageant were as crude and slimy as a family could possibly be. I have no idea how they ended up with that pageant franchise. Everyone hated them. The sons were sloppy, disgusting pigs who constantly made crude and suggestive comments to the contestants.

To top it off, their mother was a kleptomaniac whom I witnessed steal a server's tip right in front of us and then scream horrible, racist insults at the African-American server when she very nicely said, "I'm sorry, but I believe that tip was left for me."

I needed to fly out on Sunday, so I had to deposit my check in Tennessee. I wasn't shocked when it bounced. I immediately got a massive adrenaline rush. I also wasn't surprised when the producer/preacher didn't answer the phone for two days. When I did finally get him on the phone, he apologized profusely and told me the story about the pageant owners putting a stop payment on the $100,000 that was to pay everyone. He said no one had been paid yet. He told me to deposit the check again and he would cover it.

Three days later, the check bounced again. This time I told him I wanted a cashier's check FedEx'd to me immediately or I would call every church in his hometown, everyone I had met there, and put an ad in his hometown newspaper to let everyone know what a dirtbag he was for not paying me and everyone else that worked on the horribly flawed pageant.

Two days later, I received the cashier's check. No per diem, but I considered myself lucky to get the rest of the $5,000 at that point. I heard the production company, the professional dancers, and the young actors were never paid.

I guess I made bigger threats than they did.

Chapter 41—Me, An Acting Teacher?

Teaching the craft of acting was not something I ever planned or wished to do.

I made my living as an actor, but I had no idea how to teach someone else to do it. I was by no means an expert, and sometimes I even felt like a gatecrasher.

It all started with a meeting with the executive director of the Nashville branch of SAG/AFTRA, Randy Himes. The meeting was to introduce myself and ask for some music business advice. He was aware that I was an actor from *All My Children* and was excited that I had moved back to Nashville.

In the meeting, Randy said, "You must surely know 'Joe Blow' (not his real name). He was an actor on *All My Children* as well. In fact, he's been teaching acting here for three years."

"I don't recognize his name," I answered. "What character did he play?" "Bob," Randy answered.

"Characters on soap operas have last names. Let me do some checking.

I don't remember a Bob."

I called the casting director at *All My Children* and she said 'Joe Blow' had never been a regular on the show. 'Joe Blow' had only worked on *All My Children* as an extra. He had exaggerated the importance of his participation on the show and then lost control of his lie. He had bumped himself up from an extra to a show regular, and it would have been too humiliating to 'fess up.

So he ran with that lie for three years. They even put him on the union board of directors because of his false vast experience at *All My Children*. That couldn't happen now, but it was pre-internet, pre-Google, and pre-IMDB, so it wasn't easy to check an actor's credits. People just assumed it was the truth. I found out even my music attorney had taken acting classes with 'Joe Blow.'

Once the executive director learned the truth, he wanted to put 'Joe Blow' in his place by having a "real" *All My Children* actor teach a workshop at the union.

I really didn't want to do it, but Randy said they would do all the marketing and give me the meeting room space for free to hold the workshop: it wouldn't cost me a penny. To be honest, I only agreed to do it because the money was going to be good.

I immediately started getting nervous about standing in front of a group of people pretending to be an expert. I had made my living as an actor for years but I didn't feel like I was a very crafted actor. The idea of teaching the craft felt like asking me to teach astrophysics. Time for Alan to start reading acting books.

My first class included three women who were country music legends. Anyone who ever watched the Grand Ole Opry knew Jan Howard, Jeannie Seeley, and Carol Lee Cooper (The Carol Lee Singers). It was two weeks before I found out who they were because they never mentioned it and I hadn't watched the Grand Ole Opry in twenty years. They didn't want special treatment; they simply wanted to learn how to act. The rest of the class was mostly women, and several of them had watched me on *All My Children*.

I was very nervous because I didn't know what they expected from the class, and I wanted them to feel like they were getting their money's worth out of the class.

* * *

From the first class I taught, I used cameras to film the work of the students. I wanted them to get comfortable working in front a camera and learn from watching their performances. It's the best way to learn the technical side of acting for the camera. I had always wished I had been able to take classes that were filmed when I was an acting student, but they didn't exist; cameras were far too expensive.

Unfortunately, I had to learn my craft in front of a national television audience. I always tell my students they will know more about working in front of a camera after their first class with me than I knew when I worked on my first television show.

In the early years, I was able to use cameras that taped directly to VHS tapes. This allowed me to hand each student their work at the end of class. They could take their tapes home and watch what they did in class. Ninety- nine percent of the time, everyone over the age of nine hates watching themselves. But I believe it's necessary for them to watch their tapes until they desensitize themselves to what they look like, and anything else that has nothing to do with the actual craft of acting.

The ego and vanity have to go first. Then the student is able to move on to the little things they would change if they did the scene again. Eventually, it all starts to work and the acting starts to become more believable. They also start to pay a lot more attention to the performances of professional film and television actors; then they incorporate what they learn from the pros into their own performances. It works. If it didn't, I wouldn't have taught acting this way for thirty years.

Of course, the technical side is only part of what an actor does. Learning to build a character, understanding the scene, the relationships, digging into all elements psychological and emotional, all take lots of time. The serious students will continue their studies because they love everything about acting, whether it's for camera or stage. It's totally fine with me if someone wants to take class just for fun, to meet people, it's on their bucket list, or they want to prove something to someone. But if they want to compete professionally, I always tell them it's like training for the NFL, NBA, NHL, MLB, ballet, or piano: other people are training all the time, so they need to hustle and put out 110% to get noticed. If they don't, someone else will.

I'm not going to get into acting technique or methods because there are teachers and directors who are better at that than me. There are also those teachers who write books about acting who are totally full of s#^t.

But, I really don't think any acting teacher cares more about helping their students feel better about themselves or getting them over stage fright than I do. I believe it's my mission, and it feels good.

In the modern world, there are multiple websites with hundreds of full movie scripts and every episode of popular TV shows. In 1991, I had little access to scripts of any kind. I had lots of *All My Children* scripts at my disposal, but to get other material, I had to watch movies on a VCR and transcribe the dialogue. This meant lots of stopping, starting, rewinding, and then typing of scenes. It was very tedious, but I learned a lot about the scenes, the way they were shot, the directing, the editing, and pacing by doing it that way. I did this every week for a long time, because I didn't want them to hear the same material over and over.

After we finished the first six-week workshop, some of the students wanted to keep working with me. The union said they would love to have me continue doing classes in their conference room and offered me a ridiculously low rental rate for the room.

After a few years, I had taught a lot of students and had a long list of actors who wanted more training. I started bringing in local and national casting directors to teach specialty workshops. At first, I called on casting directors, directors, and producers I knew, but as the school grew, I started getting calls from industry people from Los Angeles and New York that wanted to teach workshops at my school.

I got to the point where there were multiple workshops going on each weekend, plus we had a voice-over program that we were doing at Nashville-based audio producer, voice-over artist and teacher Joe Loesch's recording studio. We have been doing that program successfully for over twenty years. Then I added songwriting, guitar, and studio singing at another recording studio.

I ended up building out a 4,000 square foot facility with two large rooms for classes and videotaping. Another room was 2,000 square feet of unobstructed performance space with a full stage and great sound equipment for live music performances. We could easily seat an audience of 80 to 100.

Chapter 42—I Own A School?

I always loved school, so I guess it only made sense that I would end up creating one. I was a learning sponge in high school and college, and I loved the social aspect, the exchange of ideas, and meeting students from other countries and backgrounds. As a young man, I would think about teaching sometimes, but I didn't feel I knew enough about any subject to teach others.

I was by no means an acting expert, but I had years of on-camera experience and others wanted to learn from me. Thirty years later, I feel like I am an expert of sorts. Not "*the* expert" but "*an* expert." You can't talk about acting and work with actors for thirty years and not know a lot about the process. I think I know what works and what doesn't after working with 4,000 people.

I also know a lot about people in general from observing and serving them for so many years. I understand their fears, their body language, and their insecurities. I know a lot about how women think that I didn't know before. They've told me their innermost secrets, desires, fears, and often very sad stories. I know that a smile can hide much tragedy and pain: things I never knew before.

I may be addicted to the analysis of people now. I may also be addicted to helping people conquer their fears. I have witnessed amazing transformations and have helped many heal very deep wounds. I wish I had found someone to do that for me.

I have had several hundred teenage girl students and many of them have come to me with problems. I was flattered that they would trust me to listen to their troubles. Often, we were able to work on their problems using acting as a way to help them get through tough times. I may have learned more from them than they learned from me. Coming from a family of nothing but boys for the last one hundred years, I had no idea what it's like being a teenage girl, especially in the 21st Century.

I've had girls who started acting classes with me when they were eight years old and studied off and on until they went to college. I'm still in touch with some of them after twenty years and others I will see at Whole Foods with their children. It freaks me out, but I love the fact that I've been a part of their lives for years and maybe I had a positive impact on their lives. High school, elementary school, and college teachers usually work with a student for a year or two, but I get to watch them grow up into women in my acting studio.

Alan Teaching One Of His 6000 Classes

I've been blessed with the opportunity to be part of so many lives helping people pursue their acting dreams, or find another dream if it's not acting. Many of the biggest successes I've witnessed with my students have had nothing to do with acting. Through acting class, they were able to remove blocks and barriers that had kept them from moving forward in their lives. Once those blocks and barriers were removed, they were able to get past the negative expectations that had been built from early life experiences. Often, those past negative experiences kept them going in circles and repeating the same failed approach to their lives. Clearing out those fears often cleared the path and let them continue in a new, more positive direction.

I have been so impressed with the efforts that many of my students have made to study with me. Efforts I never made in my own career. It fills my heart when I see some of my students travel for hours to get to class. I have a student now who has driven six-and-a-half hours round trip most Thursday evenings for the past three years to come to my two-hour acting class.

I had a woman who would drive in from Virginia to Nashville to take my classes. I had another woman who flew in from the state of Washington to attend class. I've even told some of these determined students I don't think it's worth it for them to travel that far to take my class, but that hasn't deterred them. They tell me they want to train with someone who has actually been there, and they can't find that training anywhere close to their hometown. They also like the positive and supportive environment at the school. These people are warriors.

I figured out early on that I was teaching people to be brave as I taught them about acting. I want my students to not care so much about what other people think, and not dwell on succeeding. I want my students to have fun learning in a very supportive environment with other like-minded people. There is no judgement allowed in my studio.

It isn't really about acting; acting was the vehicle, not the end result. I'm not trying to make them stars; I want them to be fearless. I want to give my students the opportunity to try something they have always been afraid to try before.

I want my students to feel they are working with someone who cares about them as a fellow fragile human being. I know what many of them are going through because I fought performance anxiety most of my life. I knew my fears were imagined but I would still dwell on possible negative outcomes. Sometimes the fear of "what if" would stop me in my tracks or cause me to procrastinate doing something I really wanted to do. I don't want my students to avoid trying anything due to their fears.

I've been touched by the hundreds of parents that have sacrificed to allow their children to explore their dreams of becoming a professional actor. One woman paid me weekly with change from her tips at Waffle House. I would have given her the money back, but I knew it was a matter of pride; she didn't want charity. It meant a lot to her that her daughter knew she was doing everything she could to give her a shot at a better life. Even though my classes are very reasonably priced, and I haven't raised the prices in ten years, I have become very aware that a great percentage of Americans are living paycheck to paycheck and simply don't have an extra $195 for five acting classes, let alone continue studying after the initial session. Yet many of my students have been with me for years and they are by no means rich.

I witnessed my students become much braver in the classroom and in front of the camera. But more importantly, it was spilling over into their lives outside of my studio.

One young woman, with a slight stutter, had never had the confidence to take an acting class or do any kind of performance. She had been in the same job with a catering company for a few years and had never been given a promotion. After eighteen weeks of classes, she had been promoted three times. She told me, for the first time in her life, she was proud of herself. She started to speak up at work and tell her superiors her ideas. Then, I noticed her stutter was gone.

After a few months of training, she told me she had been cast in a play and would not be in class for a while. I'm always excited when my students have to leave classes due to an acting gig. I miss them, but I understand it means they're succeeding. I know it's a big deal for them and I celebrate that.

It is my belief that a person's core personality can be changed in a very positive way using acting as a vehicle. I've had so many students who walked into the studio as extreme introverts learn to enjoy expressing themselves in ways they never had. I've seen it happen in my studio hundreds of times. I've also seen many students find a reason to get in their best mental and physical health in their lives.

* * *

I've had more than 4,000 students at my school over a thirty-year period.

I've gone through some very tough times with my students: one student died in a car accident trying to get to class in icy weather; many students have gone through battles with cancer; one died of cancer; another died from a sudden onset of a lung disease; one student's home was completely destroyed by a tornado; another student's daughter-in-law and granddaughter were killed in a tornado; many divorces; three suicide attempts, one successful. There were drug overdoses; hundreds of heartbreaks; rehabs; and one former client died of COVID-19. I was part of the lives of my students, and they knew it.

I have also experienced thousands of special moments with my students. I've had students meet in my class, fall in love, and marry. I've taught three generations of one family over a period of twenty-five years, and the children of several former students have studied with me. I've had students start studying with me at age seven or eight and continue taking classes until they went to college, and then come back when they were out of college.

Before class one evening, a fairly new student, Sandra Molina, came up to me with a photo and said, "I wasn't going to show you this, but I decided you might appreciate it." It was a snapshot of a much younger me and a much younger her hugging. I smiled and asked her where the photo was taken. She said, "Outside the *All My Children* studio. I was one of those fans waiting outside the entrance to get your autograph."

I was so happy she told me. Sandra ended up studying with me for the better part of nine years. She is a very good actress and a sweet, hardworking woman who would take a bullet for me.

I was working in my office one day when a man in his early 50s walked in with a six-year-old boy. He introduced himself and his grandson, Perris. I asked how I could help them, and he said, "Perris has been dreaming about taking acting lessons with the same man who taught his mother."

I asked, "Who was his mother?"

The man said, "His mother was Peezo. It was about six years ago." Before I could respond he said, "Remember…she was killed in a car crash trying to get to your class from our home in Alabama. The roads were icy but she tried to come anyway."

I was speechless. He said, "Don't you remember?" as he showed me her photo. I definitely remembered her. She was a beautiful, young woman around twenty.

"I'm sorry," I said. "Can you excuse me for a minute?" I stepped out of my office and into the teaching room to pull myself together. Looking at that little boy and knowing he had lost his mother when he was just a baby, and seeing him look at me like I was some legendary character, was too much for me to handle.

Once I got it together, I went back in my office and told him I had no idea Peezo had died in an auto accident. He said he thought I'd been told. I told him I would have never forgotten a tragic event like that. I must have told them how sorry I was five times or more.

We made plans for Perris to follow his dream of studying acting with the same man who taught his mother. They would drive up from Alabama whenever they could for Perris to take class with me. It was obvious that it meant a lot to him, and I wanted to help him pursue his dream in any way I could.

I have a photo of Peezo in my studio with a plaque that says, "My Most

Devoted Student." That young woman lost her life following her dream of being an actor.

CHAPTER 43—ACTING TEACHER TURNED MUSIC PRODUCER

In 1996, a brand new student, Jamie Brantley, came up to me after class and told me he was country music superstar Ronnie Milsap's guitar player. He said the reason he had signed up for classes was because Ronnie was developing a splashy show for a Ronnie Milsap Theatre that was being built by investors in Myrtle Beach, South Carolina. Jamie told he was an introvert and very concerned that he might be involved in the show in ways other than singing and playing guitar. He thought acting classes would help him with his anxiety.

When he found out I was a singer/songwriter and had experience in production, he suggested I meet with Ronnie. Ronnie had been procrastinating and had not found a producer for his show. He had been performing for years and really didn't see the need to have a lot of production even though the developers and investors expected it.

Ronnie was blind from birth and didn't have a visual sense of his show, so he was at a huge disadvantage. For Ronnie, it was all about how the show sounded. Nobody knew that part of a show better than Ronnie. His world was all about sound. But he needed someone he felt comfortable with to put together a visual show that matched the level of his amazing talent. It was also important for that person to be able to communicate the visuals to a man who had never had the ability to see.

The first meeting was at Ronnie's recording studio, which was sonically the best in Nashville. I was escorted into Ronnie's office, where Ronnie sat behind a large desk in semi-darkness. He had been told quite a bit about me before we met; but he wanted to find out what kind of guy I was and if I had a personality he could work with. We really hit it off, so Ronnie handed me several videotapes of past shows and asked me to watch them and come back in two days to tell him what I would do differently if I were to produce a new show for him.

I was surprised at the lack of production with his shows. There was nothing going on visually other than a band standing and playing with Ronnie at his piano. The music was great, but there was no "show." One show in Branson, Missouri had everyone lined up in a straight line across the stage, which I had never seen in my life.

I went into the next meeting with Ronnie planning to tell him exactly what I thought, but being careful not to offend him. I told him his show needed visuals and pizzazz added because the audience expects it. I suggested opening up with a splashy three-minute video on a huge, drop-down screen with a great voice-over artist introducing the audience to Ronnie's vast achievements and Grammy Awards. This would be followed by stage smoke and then, at the top of a long ramp, a large spot would hit Ronnie as the video screen vanishes. The crowd goes crazy as Ronnie walks down the ramp to his concert grand piano.

Country Music Superstar Ronnie Milsap And His Show Producer, Alan

Ronnie got it. He said he loved everything about it except the ramp. "I can't walk down the ramp by myself," he said. Ronnie's bodyguard, Phil, had always escorted him to his piano.

"I can get you to your piano by using clear fishing line," I explained. "The line will go from the top of the ramp to your piano. It will be at a height where you can hook your left index finger around the line as you walk to the piano. About four feet from your piano, there will be a large knot in the line that you will feel with your finger to let you know you have two steps to your piano."

This totally sold Ronnie. He said, "I've always dreamed of walking to my piano by myself. Let's do it." I was hired. Somehow, I had just become a show producer.

There was lots of writing and planning to be done before heading to Myrtle Beach. There was video to be shot and edited, photos to be picked from archives, giant backdrops to be designed and painted for different show segments, wardrobe to be designed or purchased, props to be designed or purchased, a ramp for Ronnie, risers for the band, song order to be decided, comedy skits to be written, and a comedian to be hired.

It was a big and expensive show, and I couldn't believe I had been hired to put it all together as the writer, producer, director, and designer. I was very surprised that it seemed to come naturally to me. I think one reason I'm good at producing is because I get bored very easily. If I'm bored, something needs to be changed, whether it's a pacing issue, song order, or too much talk.

The theatre was not even close to being finished when we arrived in Myrtle Beach: The sound system and stage lighting were still being installed; the 1,800 plus seats hadn't been installed; the parking lot, landscaping and concession areas were not even close to completion. Everyone knew there was no wiggle room. There was a Grand Opening date set and we had to make it work because the governor of South Carolina and other special guests were coming.

We were there for two weeks before we could even get a full rehearsal in. When we did start rehearsals, we had to rehearse without Ronnie. When he came to the first full rehearsal, he could hear a noise in one of the moving lights in the back of the theatre that only he could hear. He said he couldn't rehearse until they fixed the light noise.

Ronnie's hearing was so acute due to his blindness he would often amaze us with what he could hear that we couldn't. It took three days to get a technician in from the company that made the lights. Once the light noise was fixed, we found ourselves very behind with our rehearsals. That was worrisome because the show was complex with comedy bits, wardrobe changes, video segments, different lighting looks, and music and lighting cues that had to be practiced over and over until the timing was perfect. It was looking dreadful for a week or more.

Even though we had lost two weeks of rehearsal, the show started to come together and the theatre was getting closer to being completed. It was going to be tight, but all the contractors were promising it would be ready for the Grand Opening.

It was a nail-biter because the last seats were installed thirty minutes before the fire marshal came to make the final inspection. The fire marshal signed off fifteen minutes before the doors opened to the governor and the other guests that included my sons, Cody and Cooper, and Liz.

It was amazing: The show went off *perfectly*. It was everything we had all dreamed it would be. Ronnie, the band, the comedian and the technicians were such pros that night. These amazing musicians weren't actors and comedians, but you would've never known that night because they rallied to the occasion. I was so proud of the show and everyone involved. We had pulled off a miracle.

At one point in the show, where Ronnie was to do a short talk to the audience, he asked me to stand from where I was seated with my family. He told the audience I was his amazing producer and I had written, directed and produced the show they were watching. It was one of the proudest moments in my life. I was so glad that my family could be there for that moment and my sons could see what their father had been doing while he was away from home for weeks at a time.

I continued to work with the show for the first three weeks the theatre was open. Ronnie wanted me to stay because they were doing eight shows a week and he wanted to make sure the show stayed fresh and see how the regular audiences were receiving the show. We made a few adjustments but basically the show stayed intact for almost two years.

After a few months, they called me and asked me to produce a Christmas show. I accepted the challenge, so when the holidays came around, I found myself back in Myrtle Beach for three weeks to pull that together. It called for lots of new video, the addition of Christmas songs, and Christmas comedy bits.

This also meant the challenge of completely decorating a huge stage, seating area, and lobby with Christmas decorations. I had planned on focusing on the actual Christmas show myself but outsourcing the decorating to a professional decorating company. Unfortunately, the bid from the only professional company within a hundred miles came in at $75,000. We didn't have that kind of budget for Christmas decorations.

Decorating was going to be a very big project, because we needed twelve fully decorated trees to fill the stage, not to mention the decorating of the lobby and auditorium. There were also going to be added production costs for the Christmas show that we needed to consider, but we had spent almost all of our production budget on the original show, not realizing the investors were counting on a Christmas show later in the year.

Then I made a huge mistake and told Ronnie and his wife, Joyce, I could handle the decorating myself. I suggested a theme of red bows and large candy canes; we would use no hanging ornaments to save a bundle. After they signed off on the idea, I had a new problem: no one in the area sold bows big enough to look right on our huge trees. Some of the trees were twelve and fourteen feet tall. It was going to take at least two hundred large bows.

There was only one solution: *make the bows myself.*

After I found the right ribbon material, my next task was to learn how to make a bow that would look good from the seating area. The bows didn't have to be perfect because distance covers a lot of mistakes. I experimented until I figured out how to make a bow that would work and then set out making lots of them.

It took a few days and nights to accomplish the task. Some nights I was in the theatre by myself until 4:00 A.M. working on the bows, setting up the trees, and then decorating them. In the end, no one but me had any idea how much time, effort, and near panic went into getting the job done. But I had opened my big mouth and said I could do it—so I did.

Everything looked great once we put the fake snow down and added the effects of the stage lighting. In the daytime it was not impressive; but it was all about how it looked during the show. I will never get that cocky again. I'm sure it took days off my life.

I worked with Ronnie on and off for almost three years and have great memories of working with him and his entire organization.

* * *

About two months after our show opened at The Ronnie Milsap Theatre, I got a call from another country legend, Lee Greenwood. Lee introduced himself on the phone and said his manager had seen the show I produced for Ronnie. His manager told him if I could do that for Ronnie Milsap's show, Lee needed to hire me to help with his show at the new Lee Greenwood Theatre under construction in Sevierville, Tennessee, a popular vacation area in the Smoky Mountains near Dollywood.

I helped Lee with his show until it opened and then I moved on to another project that had been offered to me by an investor group that had just purchased The Music Mansion in Pigeon Forge from Dolly Parton.

* * *

This wonderful theatre had been purchased to feature a show by the notorious Anita Bryant. Anita had been a very popular singer, TV personality, and spokesperson for the Florida Citrus Commission when I was growing up. However, her anti-gay rights activism and extreme religious beliefs had ruined her career, driven her into bankruptcy, and destroyed her first marriage.

I had major reservations about working with her because of her ugly past and extreme political leanings, but Anita addressed my concerns immediately and assured me she was a totally different person. I thought I should give her the benefit of the doubt: everyone deserves a second chance. But in the end, it was a mistake to do so. I got tricked into believing she was the nice lady I had watched on TV for years when I was a youngster.

I won't go into the whole story, but it didn't end well. In the middle of putting the production together, rumors were spreading that investors were backing out and dancers were being asked to wait another week for their checks. I started to worry about getting paid for the time I had put into the project. Luckily, I had not invested a great deal of time. I asked to be paid for the work I had done up to that point as well as my travel expenses.

I was given some song and dance about needing to wait a few days because the new investor's check hadn't cleared yet. I told them I couldn't work that way. My arrangement with Anita was to be the same as with Ronnie Milsap and Lee Greenwood: I was to be paid weekly. The next day, Anita and her husband called me to say they had decided to produce the show themselves and thanked me for what I had done. I was actually relieved since there was an air of doom and gloom over the project.

I had still not been paid when I left Pigeon Forge, but I was determined not to be stiffed. After a few threats and semi-nasty phone calls, a check came in the mail for almost what I was owed. I was lucky to get as much as I did considering some of the staff and dancers were totally stiffed.

The theatre did open but the show received terrible reviews and the lack of attendance forced a bankruptcy. I was very happy I wasn't there to go down with the ship.

CHAPTER 44—TRAVELING ACTING COACH

After teaching in Nashville, I figured out I could do the same in other cities. I started advertising and booking myself in cities like Miami, Orlando, Naples, Atlanta, Chattanooga, Indianapolis, Chicago, Memphis, Cincinnati, St. Louis, Champaign, Illinois and many others.

I was the mobile acting teacher. I kept a video camera, VCR, monitor, tripod, and three large boxes of scenes in my trunk at all times. I usually made money after expenses, but there were times when I lost my ass.

After two years of exhaustive travel, much of it on weekends, I decided to focus on Nashville and occasional classes in Chicago, Indianapolis and Champaign, Illinois. This allowed me to spend more time at home, but I was still usually away three to four days each week. It wasn't that I wanted to be away; I was the only one working and there was still a negative drain on the cash reserves. I knew no other way to make money with my skills. There was the occasional acting job out of Chicago, but not enough to allow me to stop my traveling acting coach business.

Then the lucrative live show producer gig for Ronnie Milsap came up and changed everything. After working with Ronnie for months on end, it became apparent that it was time to move the gang to Nashville.

I had trashed two new cars and traveled over 250,000 miles: It was time to stop. I felt very lucky I hadn't died on the highway after all that travel. It would have been insane to continue wearing out myself and cars going from Danville to Nashville and back each week. The trips from Nashville were particularly treacherous because I would leave Nashville around 10:00 P.M. after teaching an acting class. I would drive six hours in the dark of night, abusing coffee, and slapping myself in the face with the windows rolled down to keep from falling asleep. I never did fall asleep, but it was a concern.

It was time to leave Illinois. Although living near both sets of grandparents was a blessing for everyone, it was time to move back to Nashville. I was getting busier and busier and that meant longer stays away from the family. I needed to focus more energy and time on my music business. By not being in Nashville on the weekends, I was missing out on opportunities and events I desperately needed to take advantage of.

Ironically, after we moved to Nashville, I totaled a Hertz rental car when I hit a deer at 4:00 A.M. driving home from Danville to Nashville.

* * *

It was a sad day for my parents when we pulled away in the rental truck, but at least we would only be six hours away instead of two thousand miles away like we had been in Los Angeles.

I wasn't sure if I would be able to continue my prolific writing, since most of my best writing had been done while I was in one of my special creative trances: I only experienced those trances when driving long distances on uncrowded roads.

I hated ripping the kids away from their grandparents, but it came down to the grandparents or me. I knew the boys needed me to be there more than I had been while living in Illinois. The only way to do that was to move back to Nashville where I was working seventy-five percent of the time.

The quick sale of our house made the transition to Nashville as easy as a move can be. The boys were excited about moving where Dad worked, even though they would be leaving friends, grandparents, and all their cousins behind. We explained that friends and family were only six hours away and we would be going back on a very regular basis.

Cody was ten and Cooper was six when we made the move. It was a good time for the transition since Cooper would be starting first grade.

Our plan was to move into a nice apartment in the Franklin area and put the excess in storage until we found a house or built a new one. We wanted to live in Franklin because it was beautiful, had great public schools, and was twenty miles from downtown Nashville and Music Row.

We were very serious about buying a lot in a subdivision we liked. In fact, we were getting in the car, headed to pick out the building lot, when my phone rang. It was my friend Michael Spriggs, who had produced my album and all my song demos at his very cool home studio. He said, "I just bought a bigger house with the money from my newest #1 song. You always said you wished you owned a home with a studio like mine. You wanna buy it? I need to know today."

That was a game changer. I went back to the car and told Liz about the phone call. She was not happy and I think she may have even cried. She never liked Michael's house and she had her heart set on building a new house. I told her I really needed that recording studio, the boys would love the pool, we could move in within ninety days, and I promised her I would remodel the place to her liking. I may have begged a little before she gave in. We bought Michael's house and I had my studio. After all, I did move to Nashville for the music business.

The boys liked their new schools and made friends in the neighborhood quickly. In fact, Cooper is thirty-two-years-old now and his best friend today was his best friend from two houses down in our neighborhood.

Cody rode the bus to school, but I drove Cooper the few blocks to his school most days. Knowing Cooper would be riding the bus for thirty minutes while the driver picked up other kids, I decided to drive him and have some father and son time. We would always arrive early and play Tic Tac Toe in the parking lot.

It's funny what kids remember. Playing Tic Tac Toe with me is still something Cooper will talk about to this day. It's often the little things you do with your children that mean the most to them. It wasn't just that I saved him from riding the school bus; it was one of the rare times that it would be just the two of us. He could say or ask me anything without Cody or his mother chiming in. As a younger brother myself, I know what it's like to have an older brother always commenting or making fun of most anything you say or do. On those mornings it was a safe zone. I believe Cooper knew he was loved.

Those first few years back in Tennessee were rough for me professionally. It was very challenging trying to reinvent myself, raise children, and make a living at the same time.

Some of pressure I felt was because I wasn't working on my own career as a performer. I was doing big things on the production side for other performers, but nothing for myself. I wasn't acting and I wasn't singing. I kept saying to myself, "When this money gig is over, I will focus on my own career."

It seemed like the record companies were signing younger and younger artists. I realized that at my age, I wasn't going to be the next big thing, no matter what I did. I was writing but didn't have the time to pitch my songs. I was demoing my songs but doing nothing with them after that.

Chapter 45—Corporate Training: We Are All Acting

At one time I had two attorneys and two doctors in my class at the same time. One of the attorneys came to me because he felt he was terrible in the courtroom and desperately wanted to improve. I helped him create an alter ego which made him more comfortable. After that, he enjoyed going to court. He became very confident and was so respected for his abilities that he was later appointed as a federal judge by President Obama.

One doctor—let's call him call him Dr. P.—came to me for private instruction. He owned an upscale medical examination company that catered to large corporations and businesses that needed their busy executives working, not spending a day or two getting their yearly medical exams. His company made a big splash and he wanted that publicity. But he was asked to do television and radio interviews, which terrified him. He wanted me to help him with his on-camera interviews and his on-camera presence. In these interviews he was always asked to talk about his company and summarize what made his company special. He said he had so much anxiety about these on-camera moments that he was a terrible doctor for two to three days before each event.

I figured out his problem immediately: he was winging it all the time and had never figured out how to concisely describe his business and what differentiated it from other companies. His message was never clear, came out differently every time and was too long. The description and comparisons needed to be brief because the media wants sound bites, not long-winded answers. He knew it wasn't working so each time he would be scheduled to do another interview he psyched himself out.

The work I did for Dr. P. worked so well for him he wanted me to set up a program for his entire sales team. I taught them some basics of acting, body language, good personal communications, and then brought in a team of actors for mock sales calls.

* * *

This opened up a whole new niche for me as an acting teacher. Since the '90s, I have coached executives and key employees of many of the biggest companies in Nashville and the United States including Sprint, HCA, Community Health Systems (CHS), Dollar General, Dave Ramsey, AT&T, Merrill Lynch, Regions Bank, Indianapolis Colts, Cincinnati Bengals, LA Dodgers, LifeSigns, Caterpillar, Wells Fargo, SunTrust, Warner Bros. Records, Charter Communications, Capitol Records, Atlantic Records, Vanderbilt University, Vanderbilt Hospital, Baptist Hospital, Summit Hospital, DEA, United States Customs and MARS Petcare. And in 2018 I was asked to develop a training program for the United States Army.

I have also helped countless attorneys, doctors, pastors, politicians and judges become better communicators. Witness coaching and lawsuit films has been another one of my specialties.

My acting and music clients include major TV and music stars like Miley Cyrus, her brothers and mother, Chord Overstreet (*Glee*), Patrick Johnson (USA Networks *Necessary Roughness*), Rachel DiPillo (*Chicago MD*), Quinn Cooke (*Ozark, Chicago Fire, Brookmire*) Jay DeMarcus and Joe Don Rooney of the superstar group Rascal Flatts (country music's most successful band ever), 8-time Grammy Award winner Ronnie Milsap, country superstars Dierks Bentley and Trace Adkins, Trace's two daughters, Reese Witherspoon's mother and her niece, Jo Dee Messina, Lee Greenwood, pop idol Tiffany, Joe Diffie, Ketch Secor (lead singer of Old Crow Medicine Show), George Jones's grandson, and many others. I also coached two winners of the Miss USA pageant and one Playmate of the Year, Tiffany Fallon.

I'm proud to say my clients hold 9 Grammys and 15 CMA Awards.

Chapter 46—Let's Make A Movie Called *The Acting Teacher*

It really hit me that I hadn't done what I had planned to do when I switched my college curriculum to Film and Television: write and produce comedy movies.

I decided it would be impossible to create more bizarre and funny situations than the ones I had experienced as an ex-soap opera star teaching acting in, of all places, Nashville, Tennessee. So I wrote a lengthy treatment for *The Acting Teacher*, an over-the-top comedy loosely based on those experiences.

I ran the concept by Bobby C., a wealthy man I'd met when I emceed the Miss South Carolina pageant. I got to know him over the five days his two children and I were involved in that southern-fried fiasco. During a casual lunch, I mentioned to Bobby that I wanted to develop the movie. He thought the idea was very funny and said he might be interested in getting involved. After reading the treatment, he called me and asked what the next step would be. I told him the heavyweight entertainment attorneys I knew in Los Angeles would be a great place to start, since Liz had worked in the firm's accounting department at one time.

Bobby said, "Let's do it."

The law firm, Gipson Hoffman & Pancione, represented Sean Connery, Robert Redford, Carolco Films (*Rambo, Terminator 2, Total Recall, Basic Instinct*), Phil Collins and many others. They were very connected and had the ability to get to anyone in the entertainment business.

I called the law firm and told the receptionist my connection with the firm and asked who I should speak to about setting up a meeting. She said, "Well, Reg would be the best to talk with, but he's very busy right now. Oh, wait! He's off the phone. Let me see if he can talk."

I knew who Reg was, but I had never met him. I was shocked when he actually came on the line knowing he was the heaviest of the heavyweights in the firm: His was the first name on the door.

I reminded Reg that I was Liz's husband. He remembered Liz well and

189

that I was a soap opera actor. After a little small talk, he asked how he could help me. I told him I had a project I was developing. He asked me the title of the project and I said, *"The Acting Teacher."*

He immediately burst into laughter and said, "That is the funniest idea that's come into this office in years. We've all wondered how bizarre that world must be. Say no more. We will help." He asked when we could fly out and I told him I would check with my investor and call back.

I was floored. I didn't have to give him a short pitch or anything. The title alone was good enough for Reg. I called Bobby and told him the exciting news. Bobby said he wanted to be in on the meeting and would fund the trip, so I made plans for the trip and the meeting.

When we arrived in Los Angeles, we first met with an old friend of mine, Steve Callas, a business manager for some serious entertainment clients. When we mentioned the law firm meeting to Steve, he asked if he could go with us and pretend he was part of the team. Walking in with a team, including an investor and a business manager, sounded like a great idea to me. Steve was very aware of the firm's client list and hoped some future business might come from the connection. We all had our agendas.

The meeting went great. In the meeting, Reg and Randy, the other attorney I would be working with, highly recommended we hire an A-list comedy writer. Bobby asked, "What will that cost?"

They said, "$400,000 plus."

I was shocked but didn't react. Bobby came back with, "What do we get for our $400,000?"

Randy said, "A first draft and a rewrite."

Bobby said, "Okay." I couldn't read Bobby's poker face. After all, he was a businessman and sometimes gambler, so he knew how to play the game.

We wrapped up the meeting with everyone happy and planning to work together. We thanked Reg and Randy for taking the time to meet with us and give us their expert advice. I told them we would talk about everything and get back to them soon.

Outside, Steve said he was blown away by the reception we got and how eager they were to help out. He said, "I have never been in a meeting like that before in my entire career. They were kissing your ass to be involved with your movie."

After we said goodbye to Steve, Bobby suggested we not talk about what we had just learned at the meeting until dinner later at his hotel. He wanted to get checked in and make a few calls. I was fine with that because I was enjoying the high I was on from the meeting. I was staying with an old friend, so I went there to cool off and visit a little until time to meet Bobby.

It was a typical Southern business dinner, where you first talk about everything but the real reason you're meeting. After fifteen minutes of small talk, I asked Bobby what he thought. He said, "I'll tell you one thing, I'm not paying some a-hole $400,000 to write a script that we may not even like; and then all we get is one rewrite. I've read your treatment and a play you wrote and I would rather support you while you write it. Then if we don't like what we have, we can decide what to do."

I was in total agreement, so we proceeded to work out the details of our financial arrangement.

I wanted to write the script myself anyway after seeing how excited everyone was about the idea. I was very eager to get started on the script. I had a great head start since I had compiled at least thirty scenes I wanted in the film before the meeting at the law firm.

The next day I called Reg and Randy and told them what Bobby wanted to do. If it didn't work, we would ask them for names of A-list comedy writers. They offered another option, which was to hire a "script doctor" after I was finished to clean up my script if my draft was workable.

Back in Nashville, I started writing my ass off. I wasn't trying to follow any particular comedy screenwriting format. I hadn't read any of the many books on screenwriting and I didn't want to know what they said; I didn't want those ideas in my head. I wanted the script to be original and not derivative. I decided I would read the books before I did a rewrite.

I felt I had a very good sense of what was funny and, as an actor, I recognized good comedy dialogue. As someone who used to do stand-up, I knew how important timing was to a comedy piece. So, I went to my happy creative place and started cranking out funny scenes and then found ways to tie it all together. I let the script find its own way. I knew my script was going to be far too long, but I didn't care. I figured the attorneys were probably going to turn it over to a "real writer" anyway. But I wanted to have all my funny ideas on paper. Eighty percent of the scenes were roughly based on my experiences as an acting teacher/ex-soap star, so who better to write the first draft.

It took three months to get the script in shape to hand over to Randy, the attorney who would be guiding me on the journey. When I flew to Los Angeles, I wasn't expecting Randy to jump up and down and say it was the greatest comedy script he had ever read, because I hadn't sent it to him. I wanted to put my masterpiece in his hands myself.

I handed him the script and, without even opening to the first page, he said, "This script is way too long." He was holding the script with both hands, like he was a butcher weighing pork chops.

At the time, I didn't realize people who work with scripts all the time know the weight and thickness of an average script. A comedy script is generally shorter, so it's lighter and thinner. Randy could tell my script was at least twice as long as it should be. I told him it was long because I wanted to put all my ideas on paper to make sure anyone that read it would see the possibilities. Then, if another writer was brought in, they would have lots of great ideas to work with and my vision would not be lost.

Randy told me it might take him a month or so to read it since it was so long and he had a backlog of scripts he needed to address first. I knew that wasn't an exaggeration because there were piles and piles of scripts everywhere in his office. I told him I understood and appreciated the fact that he was going to take the time to read my script.

I was shocked when I got a call from Randy just five days later saying he had read my script. He said he thought he would take a quick look at the first few pages but was drawn in and read the entire script. He said, "OK, it's really funny. I like it a lot, but it's way too long. It has to be cut in half." I was very excited to hear that he thought it was funny. Then he said, "I don't think we need an A-list writer. What we need to do is bring in a script doctor to help you chop it down to something closer to 110 pages."

I loved this idea. Not that I wanted to get rid of half of my ideas, but I realized it had to be done.

Randy suggested a client of theirs, Rick Podell. I was aware of Rick as a known stand-up comedy guy and TV actor. I had not realized that he was an accomplished screenwriter having written the script for *Nothing in Common*, starring Tom Hanks, as well as several others. Bobby agreed this was a great way to go and it would end up costing less than 20% of what we had been quoted if we had an A-list writer start from scratch. After the financial details were worked out between Rick and Bobby, we were ready to get started.

The plan was for me to make three trips to Los Angeles to work with Rick. Each trip would be for a week. Rick and I would get together for several hours each day. Once we accomplished what we needed to do together each day, Rick would send me off to my hotel to rewrite and chop scenes. Rick's function was not to rewrite. He was there to help me do what, in the world of screenwriting, is crudely called "Killing Your Own Babies." Writers love all their ideas or they wouldn't have written them. It's very difficult to delete your own precious words and ideas; someone needs to make you do it. That was Rick's job as my script doctor.

We started hacking away from the very beginning of the script. Ouch!

Ouch!

It was painful at first, but I started to see how the script was getting tighter and better. Rick would take two scenes and say, "One of these scenes has to go." I would say, "I love both of those scenes. Let's keep both…and we'll get rid of something else later." Rick would repeat, "One of them has to go." I would say, "Ok. I'll cut this one…you cruel bastard."

Then Rick would say, "Now cut the keeper scene in half."

Rick was a real hatchet man, but that is the talent of a good script doctor. They are there to make the script better. There is something wrong with the patient/script initially, and the script doctor is there to heal the script. In this case, the script was far too long, so the doctor brought out the amputation equipment.

Although it was a painful process, Rick and I really gelled. We had a ball ripping my script apart. When we were finished, the script was exactly where it should be. I was very proud of the finished product and it was an incredible learning experience. I now had a salable comedy script to peddle. The history and journey of the script is a tale for another time. What is most important is that *The Acting Teacher* movie inadvertently led to my first executive producer credit on a feature film.

CHAPTER 47—BECOMING A FEATURE FILM
EXECUTIVE PRODUCER

I was driving through the beautiful Kentucky countryside to meet with a potential investor for *The Acting Teacher* when I got a call. The caller said, "Alan, my name is Brad Wilson and I was told, if a man wants to make a movie about country music, you're the guy to talk to."

What he didn't know at the time was I had tried to get in touch with him several times a few years before and he never returned my calls. It was obvious he didn't remember, and I decided not to mention that fact. I knew he was a movie producer who had worked with Robert Duvall for many years.

I said, "Brad, I'm actually the guy to produce a live multimedia show for country performers, not movies about them."

I told him, coincidentally, I was driving to meet with an investor about a comedy movie I was developing. He asked what my movie was about, so I gave him the short pitch. He laughed at my verbal synopsis and said he would like to read the script. He said, "Who knows, maybe we can help you get your movie made."

I FedEx'd the script the next day and heard back from Brad three days later.

He told me he and his partners had read my script and thought it was very funny. He asked if I could fly to LA to talk about the possibility of working on it together.

The next week I flew to Los Angeles and met with Brad and his partners, Ralph Portillo, and Jamie Elliott. Brad, Ralph and I went to lunch to talk about the project. They said if they were to produce the movie, they would like to keep the budget under two million. They said that amount and under was their sweet spot.

I had been thinking about a budget three times that amount. I wanted enough money to attract top comedy talent. I thanked them for their time and interest, but said I really wanted to find the capital to do the movie at the higher budget. They totally understood and we all agreed we should work on a project together somewhere down the line, even if it wasn't mine. I walked away from the meeting a little disappointed, but it was great to talk with two very nice and experienced filmmakers who actually saw the promise in my script. I also knew I could go back to them later if I wanted to do the project at a lower budget.

Two weeks later I got a call from Brad. He said they had lost an investor for a movie they were committed to start shooting in less than sixty days. That investor had been expected to come in with a third of the film's budget. They were in a pickle. Brad asked if I had any interest in trying to find investors to make up what had been lost. I asked him how I would be rewarded if I was successful. He told me that I would get a percentage of the money I brought in, plus I would get an executive producer credit on the project.

My first instinct had been to say no because I didn't want to cough up any potential investors that I might want to use on my project. But the money sounded good, and the executive producer credit was even more attractive than the money. I told him I would like to take a crack at it.

In the end, I did get the money together with the help of one of my students who later became a critical part of my life, Michele Ashton. We both ended up as executive producers on the project. It was a great learning experience in movie finance and low budget filmmaking. I learned more in two months of working on that film than I did from my college degree in film and television.

Since that time, I have served as an executive producer on six other films. Five of them were with Brad, Ralph, and Jamie. This is a professional relationship that has carried on for eighteen years. I consider them some of my closest friends and I'm sure we will work together again in the future.

I've also written, produced, and directed projects of my own since then. I would never have attempted those projects had it not been for the filmmaking knowledge and confidence I gained from those early films. I love the fact that everything started with a random call from Brad, who had been given the wrong information about my expertise.

Chapter 48—Dad Leaves The Planet

In March of 2000, Dad passed away. It was a shocker because he had been in the hospital, as he often was, for a persistent urinary tract infection. He was supposed to be released that morning, but instead he had a massive coronary about eight hours before he was to go home.

I got the call nobody wants to get about 1:00 A.M. It was Liz's mom, Francie, who called to give me the bad news. When the hospital called Mom in the middle of the night, Mom's first instinct was to call someone closer to the hospital that she could count on. Francie and Dale had become like family over the thirty years Terry and I had either been dating or married to the Dobbles girls. Terry had a long-term relationship with Liz's sister, Sally, before Liz and I started dating.

Somehow, Mom was able to keep it together enough to drive to the hospital by herself. She told me afterwards she was driving way too fast and almost wrecked more than once trying to get there. When the hospital had called her, they only told her to get to the hospital as fast as she could. When she arrived at the hospital, they told her Dad was gone. Unable to accept what they told her, she immediately ran into his room and started trying to bring him back to life by pushing on his chest. That image always brings tears to my eyes. Mom lost the love of her life, the man she had been married to since she was seventeen years old. That was so incredibly sad.

When I got the call, Liz could tell it was bad, since we had never had a phone call at 1:00 A.M. I knew it was bad as soon as I heard Francie's voice. I asked her how Mom was doing and she told me "not well." Mom would call me later. She was in no condition to talk.

I asked her for some details and then told her we would pack for the trip to Illinois in the morning. She told me she hadn't called Terry and his wife, Mindy, because Mom wanted me to do that. I immediately called them and gave them the bad news. I hate being the one who has to tell the bad news. Unfortunately, it seems I am the one who is always recruited.

I told Liz to go back to sleep, but I needed to stay up and wrap my head around what had just happened. I knew I wouldn't be able to go back to sleep anyway, so I did what I always do in terrible situations—I worked.

There were things I needed to take care of since I had no idea how long we were going to be out of town. I knew there were files I would need as well as electronics. Since I was wide awake and running on adrenaline, I started packing my suitcase and even snuck into the boys' rooms and started packing their things as well.

By the time the boys got up, we were pretty much ready to go. I told them that Grandpa had passed away and we were going to Illinois to take care of Grandma and be with our family for a few days for the visitation and funeral.

Dad passing was unexpected, even though he'd had health issues for thirty years. The fact that we could lose him at any time was always in the back of our minds. We were very lucky to have him as long as we did.

After Dad passed, Mom wouldn't eat and really didn't care if she starved to death. This lasted for a year and a half. I would call her and ask if she'd eaten anything and she would answer, "Yes, I had an egg and three saltines." Mom only weighed 127 pounds to begin with, so her losing weight wasn't healthy.

I witnessed my mother's intense grief and wondered if Liz would feel that level of pain when I passed.

Mom and I had to learn everything about the business because Dad hadn't shared anything with us. He always said we didn't have to worry because everything was written down in the large black book in the left bottom drawer of his desk.

None of us ever peeked to see what was in that book. But when he passed, we pulled it out to see if the guidance he had promised was there. It was all there. He had left detailed instructions: which suit, shirt, tie, shoes and socks to bury him in; who he wanted as pallbearers; where we would find all financial and insurance information; and who to call with any legal or tax questions. He had planned his exit extremely well. I have not planned as well.

Mom and I spent days going through every file, drawer, and cabinet in his office to make sure we knew how to handle the farm business, life insurance, Dad's will, and funeral proceedings. It was a daunting task, but we did it. It was a good distraction for Mom and it gave her a feeling of control, since she never really knew how things worked.

Dad had always handled the money, bills, banking, and other business tasks. Mom had her tasks of managing Dad's health and keeping the home running smoothly. It was an old style relationship that worked like a charm. They both wanted it that way. They had a beautiful life together.

After Dad was gone, Mom said, "I will never even have a cup of coffee with another man. I had the greatest husband any woman could want. I don't need another man in my life ever."

She kept that promise, and never did have a cup of coffee with another man.

Chapter 49—Alan And Liz: The Beginning Of The End

I was married to Liz for twenty-five years. People back home knew us as a couple that met as young teenagers, dated in high school, broke up in college, didn't care about each other for four or five years, got back together in San Francisco, married, had two children, and survived the entertainment business.

Liz's mom, Francie, picked me out in an elementary school basketball game. She admits that when she saw me play as an 8th grader, she decided her daughter was going to marry me. No one will deny that she orchestrated the relationship.

When we were in high school, Francie knew I was going to college in the afternoons and would be passing by their house around 3:30 P.M. She would make sure that Liz was sitting on the front steps of their home so she could wave at me as I went by on my way to Danville Community College. She knew I would eventually stop by. Her plan worked: I did stop by one day to say hello and hang out. That was the beginning of the relationship.

The timing was right. I wasn't in a relationship at the time, and neither was she. Liz went to Danville Schlarman High School, a Catholic high school that was always a sports powerhouse. Her high school never considered our school to be a rival, but we considered them as one of ours, since we had never beaten them in football.

It was an awkward situation for us at times. When we played their school in football, the chant was "Kill Dysert." Their student body didn't like the fact that their cheerleader/homecoming queen was dating the captain of the opposing team, especially since it was their school's Homecoming game.

Our team was the biggest and best our school had assembled in many years. I was a running back and had the best game of my high school career. Unfortunately, on one of my longer runs, I lowered my helmet and legally hit one of their players very hard in his back, causing him to be paralyzed for several hours.

We won! It was the first time Oakwood High School had ever beaten Schlarman. I made Liz listen to the replay of the game with me later that night because I'd never heard one of my games broadcast on the radio. I guess it was cruel, but it was a big deal for me and my school. She cried.

To make matters worse, she had been elected Homecoming Queen. At her school, the Homecoming Queen had always been escorted by her date, not a football player from their school. This meant the captain of the team that defeated them on their Homecoming was escorting their queen. This had never happened before. I was loving it as we walked down the aisle, but it was a nightmare for her. They booed. The only person that was really nice to me was the player who had been temporarily paralyzed. He was on crutches at the dance.

Liz was more of a rebel and I had always played by the book. I'm sure I was attracted to her rebellious side. She was often in trouble with the nuns at her school, while I was always doing what was expected of me. For some reason the odd combination worked very well until we went to different colleges.

We thought we could keep our relationship together while attending different colleges, but that was unrealistic. There were too many options for both of us, and we both took them. In the beginning, I would drive up to Chicago to see her on weekends when possible, but there were too many commitments at school and my fraternity. We were both very social people and there was just too darn much fun to be had.

The distance made it very difficult to be faithful. We got realistic and both admitted we were dating. I found out Liz was dating when she grabbed my hand to get on an elevator in her dormitory and said, "Come on, Kevin." Liz was dating the soon to be lead singer for REO Speedwagon, Kevin Cronin. I was dating a few coeds.

There was never a big breakup because we were both ready to play the field. We would still enjoy getting together two or three times a year for old time's sake.

I must give Liz credit for loosening me up a lot. In high school, I was probably one of the straightest guys on the planet. I had never tasted alcohol, never planned to, really didn't understand what marijuana was, or why anyone would want to smoke it and alter their mental state.

Earlier in this book I wrote about how we got back together in San

Francisco, due to the masterful manipulation of her mother, Francie. Her plan worked as we ended up getting married in 1977 and making our way to Los Angeles after two months in Europe.

The first three years in Los Angeles were exciting. We were two young kids from Small town, Illinois, trying to make a mark in Los Angeles, California. The odd thing was, I had never planned to pursue an acting career. I was shooting for a career in comedy. However, Liz had originally moved to San Francisco with the intention of exploring the world of acting. But she never did pursue acting once she arrived in California.

In 1978, at a hotel in San Diego, Liz took a bad fall, which changed her life forever. All the sidewalks around the property of this hotel were painted with high gloss paint to make hosing them off easier. It also made them slippery and hazardous.

One morning, as we started to go down three steps, Liz hit a very slick spot, causing her feet to fly out from under her and over her head. Even though I had been holding onto her arm, she came down hard and landed in a twisted position. She gashed her leg and tore her clothing.

I got her cleaned up and went to the office and asked for bandages. We told the woman at the hotel office what had happened and she said she was sorry. She wasn't surprised and admitted it happened a lot with the slick sidewalks. She gave me a business card and said to send them the bills for the ruined clothing and a doctor or chiropractor visit if needed.

At first, Liz tried to laugh it off. My parents had flown in for the weekend and had sprung for the hotel, so she didn't want to ruin everything by making a big deal out of how stupid the hotel was for painting the sidewalks with the high gloss paint.

When I contacted the hotel manager a few days after the accident to tell her about the chiropractor bill and the replacement costs for her clothing, they blew me off and said it wasn't their responsibility. In the end, this proved to be a big mistake on their part.

When we first got back to our home in Los Angeles, Liz started to feel more pain and stiffness from the fall. She saw our chiropractor a few times and thought everything was going to be fine. But two weeks later, as she was working in the garden, she felt a snap in her back and fell to the ground. I found her in very serious pain. I wasn't able to move her for about fifteen minutes. Once I got her in the house, I put her in bed and called the chiropractor.

Turned out she had herniated two discs in her back. Soon after this, she started having severe pain, numbness and weakness in her leg. When tested, she had lost seventy-five percent of her strength in that leg. She also started dragging her leg due to the weakness. This really affected her at work because she was a cocktail waitress in the international terminal at LAX airport and on her feet all the time.

At that point, it was necessary to get serious about her treatment. This was the beginning of many years of orthopedic doctors, physical therapists, and medications for inflammation and pain.

Her life changed drastically. Liz had always been a fun, active, bouncy, and physical person. She had been a cheerleader all four years of high school and one year at Loyola University in Chicago. She had to limit much of her physical activity from that point on. Many normal daily activities caused her a great deal of pain.

We did end up suing the hotel. It took five years and a jury trial in San Diego to resolve the case. The hotel lost. Our attorney found two former managers of the hotel who were willing to testify that many people had fallen on the slick sidewalks over the years. They testified that the owners didn't care, they just wanted it to look pretty. One of them testified that he had fallen several times himself.

Before these damning witnesses appeared, the judge was not helping our case at all. Her prejudice was obvious, but we couldn't figure out why. When I got on the witness stand, she told the jury that I was an actor and proceeded to read the definition of an actor from a dictionary, which basically says an actor is a person that is a trained liar. When Dad flew in to testify, she threatened to hold him in contempt if he mentioned the slick sidewalks one more time. She also threatened to call a mistrial more than once in the first two days of the trial.

In the end, we found out the hotel was owned by three prominent San Diego attorneys and they had chosen to self-insure the property rather than purchase a policy from an insurance company. We also found out the judge was a neighbor of one of those attorneys. This explained why she was so prejudiced against us, until our witnesses gave such damaging testimonies it would have been very dangerous for the owners to leave the decision up to the jury. We were claiming that not only would Liz be in constant pain for the rest of her life, but the accident was affecting her ability to have children.

They wisely decided to settle.

We were happy that Liz won in the end, but as she often said, she would give ten times that amount to be her old self.

This period coincided with our painful years of trying to conceive as I mentioned earlier in the book. Four years of fertility problems definitely put pressure on our marriage, but we ended up surviving all the in vitro failures and surgeries with our relationship intact. We resigned ourselves to the fact that it was not in the cards for us to have children. That was until some kind of miracle ended up giving us two children, even though the fertility specialist told us it looked like there was little to no chance of success in conceiving.

As any parent will tell you, having children changes everything. It's hard to understand if you have not been through it. The focus goes to the children, as it should. I do think the fact that Liz had been so convinced she was not going to be able to have children, she put 100% of her focus on them. There were times I felt like they were "her" children and I was there to help out. She was a very good mother, but she told me I needed to get used to the idea that I came in fourth.

Once we moved to Illinois from Connecticut, I was traveling a lot trying to figure out how to make a living in the entertainment business without raising the boys in LA or New York City. I'm sure all the travel put a strain on the relationship as well, although I don't think we were aware of it at the time. We were both too busy to realize it, let alone sit down and talk about it.

The move to Nashville five years later was good for the family once we got settled into the community and schools. I wasn't gone from the family for three to four days a week for the production work, songwriting, and the teaching of acting classes like I had been when we were living in Illinois.

We kept it together for six more years, a total of twenty-five, before we ended up divorcing. Divorces are never pretty, and ours was no exception.

The differences in us became more and more obvious. Fundamentally we were not the same. Our parents came from opposite worlds and we weren't raised the same way. In the early years, it all seemed to work despite those differences. But in those years, there were no responsibilities and no money concerns. We had our jobs and the rest of the time was all about finding ways to have fun.

Liz was casual and not a fan of dressing up or shopping. Dressing well was second nature to me.

It's true, compared to Liz, I was vain. But I didn't look at dressing like she did. I have a healthy ego and my attitude is we only live once. Why not try to look my best.

Sometimes, Liz would make fun of me for dressing up. I'm not talking about wearing a tuxedo or a suit and tie; I'm just talking about wearing dress slacks, starched shirts, and nice dress shoes or boots.

She also got to the point where she didn't like the entertainment business and the negative side of being married to a known TV actor. She hated it when fans would come up to me and want to talk or ask for an autograph. It drove her crazy and sometimes she would say nasty things to them. I wasn't good at blowing off fans, so she would take it upon herself to get rid of them, which would piss me off. I'm sure it's not easy being married to a "celebrity," but she knew what she was signing up for in the beginning.

I would often go to entertainment events in New York and Nashville by myself or take a friend because Liz didn't want to go. Sometimes I would go because I was expected to be there, and sometimes I would want to go for the networking possibilities. It was all part of the business I was in.

She didn't even care if I took a female friend, as long as she didn't have to go. Once she even said, "Don't you have a pretty student that would want to go with you?" I found that very odd.

Just to be clear, I never took a pretty student with me.

After 25 years together, we found ourselves with less and less in common. Two years before we split, I found the courage to suggest marriage counseling. She was offended so I never brought it up again.

I was not happy and I was not leading a healthy lifestyle; I was numbing myself. I had to admit to myself that it wasn't working for me. I tried to keep it going, but I was starting to have dark thoughts and I needed to try to find a way to be a happier person. I was tired of faking it.

Saying I wanted out was extremely difficult. I had known Liz and her family since I was fourteen. I also knew it was going to be tough on the boys, who were sixteen and twelve at the time. But I felt like I was no good to anyone in the state I was in. I had no reason to believe it was going to get better.

There was often confrontation and it seemed we were in disagreement on nearly everything. I was giving in way too much rather than fight for what I wanted. I said to myself, "If there is one more big blowup, I am out." The blowup came. While we never fought physically in 25 years, our verbal battle was terrible. Now, I can't even remember what triggered it. I started sleeping in the music studio.

More than once, Liz had said in the middle of an argument, "If you don't want to be here, you just let me know and we'll split everything down the middle and you can go on your merry way." That's not the way it went down.

I thought we could be civil and split amicably, but it got ugly. I may never know the full extent of the damage done to all of us, but it was the worst time of my life.

I wish I could say the split didn't do damage to the boys, but I'm sure it did. I'm sure there was a better way to handle it, but I don't have the answer for what that could have been. It troubles me to this day and probably will until the day I die.

I had no idea how mom would react when I told her that I wanted a divorce, but she was very supportive during this period. She was there for me as she had been all my life. She told me she had seen it coming and was surprised it hadn't happened before.

Liz and I have been friendly for many years now and I have even spent Thanksgiving twice with Liz, her fiancé, our sons, and our daughter-in-law, Brianna, when Michele was spending Thanksgiving with her family in Baltimore and Denver.

Chapter 50—My Boys

Cody and Cooper were very bright boys interested in computers, video games, skateboarding, BMX biking, and all things new. They played soccer, but I knew nothing about the sport and found it hard to follow due to my attention span issues. I also knew little about computers or video games.

My sons lived in a world where I didn't belong, and I really couldn't figure out how to participate. I couldn't start skateboarding or BMX bike riding at my age. I honestly didn't even know how to turn a computer on back then—and didn't really want to learn. They made fun of my lack of computer knowledge all the time. I was old school and didn't like what was happening in the new world.

I was a football, basketball, and baseball player, of which Cody had little interest. Cooper did like to toss the football around a little, shoot baskets, and play horse with me at times, but for the most part, I found it hard to engage with them in their world which was so different from mine.

I did finally give in and learn to use a computer, but by that time Cody had started his own computer business at age twelve. He was very computer savvy. He would buy each and every part for his computers online and build them without needing help or instruction. He offered a lifetime warranty on his computers. He was so far out of my league and Cooper was learning at a rapid pace by watching his older brother's example.

I couldn't relate to skateboards, cross country, video games and computers, and they weren't interested in my forms of exercise or entertainment. Sometimes I felt like I was just a guy who lived in the house that no one paid much attention to.

Hundreds of people (including country music stars, politicians, and corporate biggies) were paying a lot of money to learn from my experience, get my advice, tap into my creativity, entertain them, and hear my stories, but my sons weren't really interested. Maybe all young boys are like that. I'm sure I was wrapped up in my own little world as a young man too; but I would be a liar if I said it didn't hurt my feelings.

Maybe it was my fault. Maybe I could have tried harder. But to me, it seemed like it didn't make much difference to anyone if I was there or not.

It was not the boys' fault at all that Liz and I split and I hope they never feel like it was. It was our fault. We were too very different people whose differences got more magnified as the years went on. We often had different opinions on raising the boys, but I usually backed off because she had their attention. When she told me I was not first, but fourth, that summed up our relationship.

Telling the boys I was moving out was the hardest thing I ever had to get out of my mouth. That conversation around the kitchen table was forced by Liz. It did need to happen, but I wanted to tell them by myself; however, she insisted on being there. This meant I couldn't really say what I wanted to say to the boys.

Liz said she would never agree to splitting time with the boys. The only thing she would agree to was the boys living with her. I would get them on Wednesdays and every other weekend. Sometimes it seemed like Liz thought of the boys as "her children" since she went through so much to conceive them. But I was there all the way and went through everything with her as well as having a surgery myself. I felt like I got very little credit for hanging in there until we were able to have two beautiful children.

I'm sorry the boys had to go through that, but it had to happen. I was not happy and I can't imagine that she was. When the divorce was finalized, Liz looked me in the eyes and said, "Alan, if you had only changed." I think that says it all. She never really accepted me for who I was. I didn't think I needed to change.

Someday, I should sit down with each of the boys and a therapist and let them tell me anything they want to tell me about how they were negatively impacted by the split. I will gladly apologize to them for what they went through, but I can't apologize for leaving the marriage.

I have told them more than once over the years that I didn't leave them, I left the marriage with their mom. I think they understand that. They have never shown any hostility toward me and are always very friendly to my wife, Michele. I usually don't hear from them unless I contact them. But I'm not sure my Dad got a lot of attention from me when I was in my thirties either.

I would also like to find out what the boys were told during my split from their mother. Over the years, they have mentioned some things to me where the facts and timeline were totally wrong. I would like to make sure they hear my side of the story.

Cody and Cooper Dysert

CHAPTER 51—MOM JOINS DAD… AUGUST, 2018

Two years after Dad's passing, Mom started coming back to life. She wanted to live and be there for her sons and grandchildren. She started to enjoy shopping trips with her friends again and even played a little golf, which was not her strength by any means. She handled the farm business, bills, and banking very well, but she worried too much about getting everything done.

Mom had the issue, that she passed on to me, of wanting to get everything over with quickly. Sometimes small tasks would unnaturally weigh on her mind every minute until they were done. She would often call me, worried she couldn't get everything done she needed to do that day. I would try to tell her it would all work, and if she didn't get it all done, it would be okay. I would call her later in the morning and find out she had finished everything she was worried about by 9:30 A.M.

She started thinking of going to the post office, the bank, or picking up a couple things at the grocery store as a big deal. I know people tend to do that as they get older, but her worrying about the little things was not normal. I realized she had always been like that to some degree, and I had inherited the trait myself. I have learned to fight it, but I often catch myself worrying about the smallest of things or making a big deal out of a small task.

I worried about mom being out in the country all by herself. I didn't even like staying out there in the darkness myself. She didn't keep the outside security lights on. She was not worried about someone breaking in and robbing her or killing her. She said she was ready if it was her time to go. She believed she would see Dad if she died.

In 2012, Mom's life took a big negative turn. She was T-boned by an uninsured driver of an old minivan. She was admitted to the hospital with some bruising and abrasions. She was lucky she wasn't killed, but it caused some fractures in her spine that affected her posture and her movement. She visited a chiropractor on a regular basis but there wasn't much he could do because her bones were brittle due to her age and some osteoporosis.

She handled it well and didn't complain much but it was easy to see it was causing her pain. She remained active to a degree but started to resist traveling to see us in Nashville. She would, however, make trips to see her 100 plus year-old mother and her youngest sister, Donna, in Southern Indiana.

Two years later, she had a freak accident coming out of a floral shop that changed her life forever. On her way to the car, she walked on some wet grass and twisted her ankle. Her ankle bone snapped and severed a large artery. Luckily, there was a woman nearby who called 911. It was a miracle that an ambulance was only two blocks away. Mom lost a lot of blood.

They immediately rushed her to the larger hospital with a trauma center in Champaign about thirty miles away. Later, I was told she would have bled to death if it had taken five more minutes for the ambulance to arrive.

As soon as I was called with the horrifying news, I dropped everything and headed to Illinois. I was always called first because I was closer (325 miles) to Illinois than Terry. He was a nuclear engineer on a large nuclear project in Georgia and had very little flexibility in his schedule.

Mom had a complex surgery to rebuild her ankle and lower leg. A plastic surgeon was brought in to close the large wound caused by the bone tearing through her skin. The skin was so thin due to her age that it was impossible to close the wound completely; she was put on a wound VAC to help with the healing.

At that point, she needed in-home care due to the cumbersome wound VAC being attached to her leg at all times. I stayed for a few days to set up the in-home care. I headed back to Nashville after Mom told me she would be okay.

After two weeks at home, the wound was not healing as hoped, she wasn't feeling well, and she was losing weight. She was taken back to the hospital where they did bloodwork and the plastic surgeon examined her foot and leg. He told her there was nothing wrong with her. He said she needed to be patient and basically stop being a baby. He was not a nice man.

One week later, the in-home healthcare person found Mom barely conscious when she came to check on her. The woman immediately called her son to help her rush Mom to the hospital. She was so weak they had to carry her to the car and into the emergency room. When they arrived at the hospital, she was near death.

They called me and I rushed back to Illinois. Mom was in terrible shape when I arrived at the hospital. I asked the doctor on shift what was wrong with her. He said, "I just came on. Let me look on the computer and see what's going on with her."

After looking over her chart and the info on the computer, he said, "Well, she has MRSA. But you probably already knew that."

Knowing how deadly MRSA can be, I said, "There must be some mistake. She doesn't have MRSA. She just had her bloodwork done a week or so ago and the doctor said everything looked fine."

He said, "I'm sorry but here it is on the computer. You can see for yourself."

I saw he was right and asked, "Why didn't the plastic surgeon tell me that?"

"I wish I could answer that for you. You'll need to ask him that question." The doctor shook his head, which told me that someone had made a serious mistake. One of two things had happened: Either the plastic surgeon never read the report on her bloodwork or he did and foolishly failed to do anything about it.

It took Mom months to partially recover, but she never got back to the health she should have had. The MRSA blinded her in one eye and reduced the quality of her vision in the other. She had MRSA in her spine and other areas of her body. She remained on MRSA drugs for the rest of her life, almost six years. I'm sure you are wondering if there was a lawsuit.

Over those years, Mom bounced between the nursing home, assisted living, and a two-bedroom apartment at the Hawthorne Senior Living complex. Her quality of life was not great, but she rarely complained. I think she actually liked being around all the people in the assisted living wing and later in her two-bedroom apartment at the complex. They loved her there and she loved the people around her.

I think it was wonderful that she could spend the last years of her life around other people from her generation. She felt very safe there knowing she could get help at any time of the day. There were always healthcare workers close by and nurses next door at the nursing home section of the complex.

Mom's hearing was getting worse by the year, and we were worried it was affecting her ability to communicate with her doctors and healthcare workers. We wanted her to try hearing aids to make it easier to share conversations with family, friends, doctors, and healthcare workers. But she always resisted. Mom would say, "Maybe sometime in the future." She would often pretend she heard us when she really didn't. Occasionally, this caused big problems.

She was always very stubborn, but very sweet. If she didn't want to do something, good luck getting her to change her mind. One year at Christmastime, after a few days of frustrating conversations, I told her I needed to have a very serious conversation with her.

I looked her in the eyes and said, "It isn't fair to your family not to at least try hearing aids so we could have meaningful conversations with you without yelling."

She looked me in the eyes and said, "I understand."

Excited, I said, "So can we go to Costco and try out a hearing aid?" She smiled and said, "I can hear everything I need to hear."

And that was that. She died without ever having hearing aids at 91 years of age.

During the last year of her life, she was coughing a lot and often choking on her food. She ended up in the hospital diagnosed with pneumonia three times. They would treat the pneumonia for a few days and send her back to the senior residence. But the third time she went to the hospital with pneumonia, they did a video fluoroscopic swallowing exam (VFSE) to evaluate her ability to swallow safely and effectively. The test was to identify the thickness of liquids and foods that she could safely eat. The expert had to sign off on it before they would let her eat or drink anything.

The test didn't go well. It showed the muscles in her throat that facilitate the swallowing function were too weak to allow normal swallowing. The swallowing expert told me, "I'm very sorry but I can't allow your mother to eat or drink anything at this point. Not even water. She isn't swallowing properly and fluids are getting into her lungs and causing her to keep getting pneumonia. It will kill her eventually."

Mom's physician was called in to tell us her options: she could continue on like she was until she died from pneumonia, or they could surgically insert a feeding tube into her abdomen. He said there was a very small chance the muscles in her throat could get strong enough for swallowing, and she could be taken off the feeding tube after a period of time. He repeated that we should not count on that happening. With the feeding tube, she would not be allowed to eat or drink anything other than what she was getting through the feeding tube. This would very possibly be for the rest of her life.

The doctor pulled me aside and told me the atrophy of the throat muscles was actually the beginning of the dying process. He said Mom's quality of life would not be good with the feeding tube, but we could try it and see. I could tell what the doctor's decision would have been, but the decision had to be Mom's.

First, I explained to her what was going on since she couldn't hear much of the discussions about the swallow test and the feeding tube. She could tell the discussions were not good news because they weren't discharging her like she thought they would be.

I got very close to Mom, looked her in the eyes, and told her what I was going to tell her was very serious and I needed to make sure she could hear me and she understood what I was telling her. She said she understood. I told her we had to make a choice and it had to be her decision. I told her if she didn't do the feeding tube, she would probably die from pneumonia in the near future. Then, I explained to her that she would be able to live with the feeding tube without getting pneumonia, but if the muscles in her throat didn't get stronger, she would never be able to eat or drink anything for the rest of her life and there was only a very small chance she would ever get off the feeding tube.

Then I asked her the most painful and real question I have ever had to ask anyone, "Do you want to try to live, or do you want to let go?"

She looked at me with so much love in her eyes and said, "What would you do?" I couldn't say I would want to die. It's just not in me to say I would give up. I couldn't lie to her, so I told her what my choice would be. But I insisted it had to be her decision.

Still looking at me, she said, "I want to try."

Maybe in the end it wasn't the best decision, but we were both ready to try for a miraculous recovery and eventually get her back to eating food again. I just couldn't say, "I think you should die, Mom."

The surgery to put the feeding tube in was very quick and went very well. After a day, they sent Mom to the nursing home side of the senior living complex. She was stable and getting used to the new feeding process and the care of the tube insertion point. I never heard her complain. I found it all very sad because she wasn't even allowed to drink water. Everything had to go through the tube. They could only wet her lips with little foam brushes.

There really was no quality of life.

For the next three weeks, I was driving back and forth from Nashville to Danville to see Mom. That period is a little bit of a blur because it was one of the worst and saddest periods of my life. I felt guilty about not being able to stay with her all the time, but Mom would always tell me she was fine and well taken care of by the loving staff at the nursing home. They all said they loved her because she was their sweetest, most appreciative, and least complaining resident. I would call every day to try to talk to her, but she was starting to sleep a lot more and her speech was affected.

The next to last time I came up to see Mom, the head of nursing asked to have a meeting with me. She and the nursing home director were in the meeting. They told me they thought it was time for me to start talking to the hospice people. They said Mom's health was rapidly declining and from their experience it would make sense to start planning for what was inevitable. They made a point of saying she wouldn't be passing in the next couple of weeks. I agreed because I could see the decline and I wanted to make sure Mom was never in pain and her passing was peaceful. When I left later that day, Mom was resting as she held a teddy bear we had given her. She would never let go of that teddy bear. It was so sweet and sad at the same time.

On my last trip to see Mom, she was not doing well at all. She was sleeping a lot more and she was constantly grabbing her legs, even when she was sleeping. It was like her legs were falling asleep and she was trying to wake them up. I was told later this was all part of the body slowly dying.

She would sometimes look to the ceiling and talk to family members that had passed away: Dad, her mother, father, and both sisters. She had a smile on her face. She was also seeing angels. It was so believable. I had never experienced what I now realize was someone dying. I had always thought the talking to people that have passed away and feeling the presence of angels were just something that happens in movies. But after witnessing what I did with Mom, I believed these people/angels were guiding her from life on earth to life in another dimension.

The talk of angels was particularly strange because Mom had always denied the existence of angels and ghosts. Any talk about them freaked her out. She would turn off the TV or end a conversation if the subject came up. I always thought it had something to do with the psychic abilities she often displayed but totally resisted.

I started to leave on a Tuesday morning and Mom was resting. I thought I would just leave and not wake her. I said goodbye and kissed her and started to leave. As I reached the door, it hit me. "What if this is the last time I see my mother?"

I had to do better.

I went back and made sure she was awake and looking at me. It was so weird because for the first time in days she became completely aware and lucid and heard what I said. I looked her in the eyes and said, "You are the best mother a boy could ever want, Mom."

She said, "You are the best son any woman could want." I said, "I love you."

And she said, "I love you too."

That was the last time I saw my mother alive.

I got a call two days later from one of the nurses at the nursing home. She was crying so I knew what she was going to say. None of us really expected Mom's passing to come so quickly, so I was very surprised. At that moment, I was so thankful something had made me turn around and go back in her room and have those last beautiful moments with my mother that I will never forget.

I had taken care of her business and health needs for over ten years and I was happy to do it. She was the best mom a boy could ask for. She devoted her life to us. I'm so glad she knew I was there for her every time I got a call that she needed me.

I always dropped everything when I would get the calls. I never made an excuse because she would have done the same for me. We were a team those last few years. She was my greatest fan and my most loyal supporter. She never tried to tell me what to do as an adult but would give me great advice if I asked for it. She made me believe I could do anything or be anything I put my mind to.

I was glad that she didn't have to suffer any longer. She wanted to go and had no fear of it. I just hope I can go out the same way when it's my time.

Chapter 52—Michele, My Amazing Wife

I first met Michele when she came into my school as an acting student in February of 2002. She told me she had been so affected by 9/11 that she was compelled to try something she had always had an interest in pursuing. She said she had assumed there would always be time to do it later, but 9/11 had made her realize there are no guarantees in life and if there is something in life she always wanted to do, she should get to it now.

At that time, she was running a very successful business she had built over a ten-year period. She had put all her energy into building the business and raising her daughter, Amber, who was a young teen at the time. A modeling agent told her my school would be a good place to begin her journey into the world of performance. She called and registered for a six- week series of classes with me.

Being human, I couldn't help noticing she was very pretty, in great shape, and very well dressed; but she was a student, and that was all. She was regular in her attendance at first, but after several weeks of classes, the logistics of coming to a class from 7:00 P.M. to 9:00 P.M. and then making a 45-minute drive home wasn't perfect for her personal life. She decided afternoon private sessions would work much better for her.

In group classes it's not possible to know much about each student. Usually there would be ten to fifteen students in a class, so all I would know about any individual student would be what I could tell from their work in class, and what little they may have told me on the very first phone conversation I had with them before they started class.

With private sessions, I would learn a lot about a student's personal life, their fears, flaws, dreams, goals, and of course their talent. What I learned about Michele was that she was a very caring and compassionate person who went after what she wanted in her business and personal life. She was a hard worker and she brought that to the table in her training. She was also cautious, private, and a confessed introvert.

I never pried into a student's private life, but if they wanted to talk, I was there to listen. After all, actors are supposed to explore why their characters do what they do, why they do it, and what they want. Therefore, it's very important for the student actor to explore their own life: why they are where they are, and why they do what they do.

Some students would tell me they just needed someone to talk to and listen to them, because that was missing in their lives. Once, I was in a session with a woman and I started feeling bad that we weren't getting any acting done in her session. I said, "We need to stop talking and get to some acting before your session is over."

She sharply replied, "Don't you understand, I'm using you for therapy.

You're much cheaper than the therapist I've been seeing for years."

This was not Michele. She wasn't one to regurgitate all her hopes, dreams, and personal problems. She talked a little about her business, but her sessions were about learning the craft of acting and career opportunities. It was easy to see why she had been so successful in business when I saw her approach to an acting career. She was an excellent student and took direction very well. Unlike the majority of my students, Michele actually did the things I suggested would make her a better actor and speed up the possibilities of getting acting work. If I suggested a book, she bought it. She wanted it and she went after it.

A few months later, the opportunity for me to be an executive producer on a movie came up. To make this happen, I needed to find investors for a third of the budget of the film. The production company, Hemisphere Entertainment, was already in pre-production on the film and one of their bigger investors had backed out. They were desperate to replace that portion of the budget because production was scheduled to start shooting in ninety days.

At first, I wasn't interested because I wanted to use any possible investors I had for a comedy film I had written. But after thinking about it, I decided an executive producer credit might help me find more investors for my comedy film.

After reading the script, I asked the producers at Hemisphere if they had cast the part of the mother in the movie. It was a kid's movie, and the role of the mother was a good part for a woman in their thirties. They said they had not cast the mother role at that time.

"If I come up with a woman that would help finance the movie, could they have the role of the mother?"

They were reluctant until I told them my idea: I had three attractive students in their thirties who had access to funds or knew people that might be possible investors. I explained that any one of the three would do a great job with the role. I told the producers I would screen test all three of the women and send the tapes to them so they could pick which one I should approach about the project first. They agreed it was worth a shot.

I asked all three women if they would like to screen test for the role based on the idea of them helping find one third of the budget for the film. Not only would they get the part in the movie, they would receive an executive producer credit as well. As an extra incentive, they could set up a production company of their own, allowing them to get an "in association" credit for their production company and receive a percentage of the profits from the film.

One of the women was married to a catcher for the New York Yankees who had just retired: his best friend was Derek Jeter. Another woman, who was doing some work for me at the time, said she had access to Silicone Valley investors. The third was Michele, who had her own funds and knew many wealthy people from her business dealings.

After watching the tapes, they agreed that all three were very good and any one of the three would work. Since time was of the essence, I told all three that whoever could come up with the financing in thirty days, and set up their own production company, could have the part. The Yankee's wife panicked when I told her it would all need to happen in thirty days. She said she was going to be traveling too much and didn't think she could pull it off. The woman with the Silicone Valley connections balked at calling the entrepreneurs that she said she knew.

Michele said, "I'm doing it!"

I could tell at that moment that there was no question in her mind she was going to get it done. There was no "I'll try" or "I think I can do it." She was determined to be in the movie and have her own film production company as a financial partner in the movie.

Michele knew nothing about the movie business at the time, so we worked on everything together. She was picking up on how the business worked very quickly and soon realized it was a sales job, just like her own business. She needed to know the product she was selling (a percentage of a movie) and what the customer (the investor) should expect to receive from their purchase (profit and a little excitement).

She made a list of the people she planned to target. We sat together for many of the calls so I could be there to answer questions that she wasn't comfortable answering. Michele was fearless and didn't question herself at all. I had never witnessed a woman or a man with that kind of positive drive, confidence, and determination. I thought I had those qualities myself, but hers far surpassed mine.

Putting together that group of investors was a magical experience for both of us. We were a smooth running machine. It felt so good to work seamlessly with someone on a project with high stakes for both of us. Each time we brought in an investor, there was a sense of accomplishment like I had never felt before.

As we were working on our mission, I couldn't help noticing how much fun we were having working together on the difficult task of convincing people to invest in a movie. We never argued or had big disagreements. We were equal partners with equal say in all decisions.

We accomplished our goals and were soon headed to Chester, South Carolina to shoot the movie.

The movie, *The Ghost Club*, was my first experience working on an independent film. It was exciting and I loved the fact that, unlike the big studio films I had worked on, it was manageable and not like we were moving an army from location to location. There also weren't studio executives hanging around all the time suggesting changes and screaming about budget overruns.

What impressed me most on the shoot was Michele's ability to run her business from the hotel without affecting her work as an actress on the film. I was in awe of her ability to compartmentalize.

We had become great friends at that point. Michele was such a positive influence on my life at a time when I really needed it. I don't think she knows to this day that I felt that way at the time.

I was unhappy, and I have to admit I was self-medicating to try to make myself happy. I wasn't eating a healthy diet, drinking too much coffee, drinking Diet Coke in the afternoon, taking almost no supplements, and not drinking enough water. I was on a dangerous and self-destructive path. I wasn't sleeping well, so I would get up and go to the gym at 4:00 A.M.

I didn't like who I was at the time and I'd been feeling like that for too long. I really didn't know who I was or who I wanted to be anymore. People still treated me like a television star, but I felt like I was faking my way through life, pretending things were okay.

I watched Michele and saw what positive thinking and self-discipline was doing for her and I wanted that. I needed that. Somewhere along the way I had lost it. I used to feel like I could do anything I wanted to do, but I had stopped feeling that way.

I can't blame that on anyone but myself. I think I was disappointed in the way things ended with *All My Children* and I wasn't crazy with how things were going with my music. Everything in the music business had started to go very young, and I wasn't feeling young. I wanted to look forward to the future but I just couldn't figure out which path to take. I felt stuck and I needed to make some drastic changes.

What I didn't realize was that Michele wasn't happy either and things were not getting better in her personal life. She was also searching, even though she was very successful. But Michele is so much better at compartmentalizing than I am. If I have a problem, I have a hard time focusing on anything else. I tried to learn from her example.

* * *

After the smoke had cleared from my divorce and Michele's, we were free to explore our relationship. We've never had a fight. We have had disagreements but never have they become confrontational. We enjoy being with each other so much that we have only had two couples over for dinner in eighteen years, and we have never had a party. I guess it sounds like we're anti-social, but we think it's a testament to how much we love being together.

We love to travel together and we like doing the same things when we do. We like to just chill. I don't play golf and neither does she. We both work very hard but we've both structured our businesses so we are able to take time off whenever we wish. Before COVID-19, we were taking trips six to seven times a year.

We split all expenses. We've found this is the secret to happiness for two people. It would be impossible if we had kids together, but we started doing things this way because we each had children and the mixing of funds wouldn't have worked. We found it worked so well, we've kept doing everything that way. She buys her cars and I buy mine. She buys her clothing and

I buy mine. She pays for her food. It wouldn't be fair to split food since guys eat so much more.

Lots of people think it's weird but it really works for us. I can be excited when she buys new shoes or a car. She never goes, "It's my turn to buy a new laptop." We're both "car people" and appreciate nice things, but we don't go overboard. We're both great shoppers and love a bargain.

Michele is almost sixteen years younger, but our children are the same age; so we're at the same place in our lives family-wise. The kids are all "off the payroll" as we like to say.

We waited five years to be married because we were afraid it would change what was working so well. We decided to get married by ourselves in Cozumel in 2008 and make our marriage all about us. We were concerned the kids might be uncomfortable or feel weird about their parents remarrying. It made a lot of sense to us, but some people thought it was the wrong way to do it. But we wanted our wedding to be about us. We had a lovely wedding in a beautiful place, just Michele and me.

That was fifteen years ago, and we love each other even more than we did then, and have as much fun being together as we did in the beginning. I feel so blessed to have Michele as my partner in life.

Michele is the only person in my world that I like to hang out with on a regular basis. I swear I'm not saying that just because I know she will read this book. We like doing the same things and respect each other's opinions. Everything works so smoothly with our relationship; and it's never boring. I get just as excited about all aspects of our relationship today as I did in the beginning: never boring and always fun.

I like my alone time and so does she. We can actually achieve that in the same room together with the help of noise cancellation headphones. I'm definitely not an introvert. In fact, I've been accused of being an over-the-top extrovert at times. Michele claims to be an introvert. I believe she's just a private person who speaks when she feels the need or the desire to do so. She's a great listener.

One evening, after attending a gala, I asked Michele why she never said anything around our table with eight others that night. She replied, "I don't learn anything when I'm talking." I thought that was one of the most profound statements I'd ever heard. It made me realize I should shut up more often and listen. An actor's greatest skill is supposed to be their ability to listen. Sometimes I realize I'm not doing my job as an actor/person because I talk too much.

Michele and Alan at a Charity Event

Michele is the reason I'm alive today, even though none of my doctors expected me to be alive at this point. She read books every day to educate herself on cancer. She became a certified health coach, not to practice, but to help manage my health. She wanted the knowledge to make her a more informed advocate for my health, knowing most western trained doctors had very little training in areas of supplements and nutrition.

She has nursed me back from five major surgeries and makes sure I eat right and maintain a very healthy lifestyle. One of my heavyweight surgeons at Johns Hopkins asked me to ask Michele what supplements he should take and how he should change his diet.

222

Michele is determined to keep me alive, and if you know her, she will get the job done. If she really wants something, you had better get out of her way. If you bet against her, you *will* lose.

I am so lucky to be loved by such an amazing woman.

Chapter 53—Welcome To The Cancer Club

May 2, 2011 started out like most days with coffee and breakfast, followed by a trip to the gym: Michele and I usually work out six days each week. We had been members of that particular gym for about three years.

I was about to use the abdominal machine I had always used when my attention was drawn to the machine next to it that works the oblique muscle groups. Understand, this was not a new machine; it had been there for three years. Something was saying to me as I stared at the machine, "Why haven't you ever used that machine? You should try it."

It felt like that machine was reaching out to me.

I decided to switch my regular routine and tried the oblique machine for the first time ever. I didn't overdo it; I did three sets of ten reps for the right obliques and the same for the left. I felt good after the workout and decided I should definitely add this machine to my workout routine.

The next morning, I felt a stinging/burning near my belly button. It was an odd sort of sensation. I couldn't tell if what I felt was on the outside or the inside. I had never felt anything like it in my life as an athlete or a gym enthusiast. It wasn't bad enough to restrict my movement in any way, but it was a curiosity.

I decided the oblique machine had kicked my butt and the pain was simply from working out muscles that weren't involved in my normal routine. I decided to give those muscles a couple of days to recuperate, and then try that sneaky little oblique machine again.

I waited two days before I tried the machine again. By that time the stinging was gone. I did the same amount of sets and reps as I had done the first time. The next day, the stinging/burning was back, but it was a little stronger. This time I could tell it was definitely coming from the inside, just to the right of my belly button. I started poking around inside my belly button. When I pushed on the skin to the left, everything was soft, but when I pushed on the skin to the right, it was very firm. Since I never spent a lot of time poking around inside my belly button, I thought maybe it had always been that way.

I started driving myself crazy thinking about it. After a few days of

224

serious belly button poking, I decided to go to the Vanderbilt Walk-In Clinic. I was sure they would tell me it was not a big deal and very common in the belly button world. Then I could move on with my life, wasting no more time focusing on my belly button.

But that's not what happened.

The exam started with me telling the nurse practitioner, "I'm not that worried about the stinging and hardened area inside my belly button, but thought I should have it checked out, just to be safe."

Luckily, I had come to the right nurse practitioner, Amy Harden. After checking me out, she said, "That doesn't seem right. To be safe, we should do an ultrasound to see what's going on in there."

I had confidence in her judgment and believed the imaging would put an end to my constant thinking about it. She ordered the ultrasound, and I headed out to Cool Springs Imaging, a short ten minutes away. I called Michele and told her I was getting some imaging done but there was no reason to worry and I would call her after I was finished.

I was a little concerned, since I had never been told I should have an ultrasound before, but I wasn't expecting anything life threatening.

I was asked to wait in a small waiting room while they checked the results of the ultrasound. I will never forget hearing the technician, who must have thought I was deaf, say to another technician in the adjoining room, *"What is that?"*

I knew this was probably not a good sign. She came into the waiting room, where I was sitting by myself, and nervously said, "I don't mean to alarm you, Mr. Dysert, but there is something rather large in your abdominal cavity that shouldn't be there."

"What is it?" I asked.

She cautiously said, "I'm not saying it's cancer. I'm not overly concerned, but I would highly recommend you see your primary care physician to see what he thinks you should do." Then she said they needed to do a CT scan to get a better image of whatever "it" was.

After the CT scan, which gave an enhanced image of the "thing" growing inside me, I was a little shell-shocked. I was acting like I wasn't overly concerned, but it was hard to stop thinking about it, and I couldn't stop touching my abdomen.

I didn't want Michele to worry too much, so I put on my best *I'm not really worried act.* Michele and I talked about it and decided I definitely should see my primary care doctor, but not to overthink it since there was nothing we could do about it. The fact that I felt totally fine helped a lot.

My version of shell-shocked is basically being quieter than usual but having little to no physical or verbal expression of anxiety. It's not an out of body sort of thing, but I go into a "mode." I start moving and getting stuff done. I went into the same mode when I got the 1:00 A.M. call that Dad had died, and again when I got the call that Mom had died.

Unfortunately, it took a week to get the appointment with my primary care physician. I tried not to think that I was hosting an alien or some hideous abnormality in my abdominal cavity, but it was definitely on my mind. Anyone that tells you they're able to not dwell on something like this is lying to you.

I couldn't shake the memory of the concern I had heard in the voice and on the face of the sweet woman in the radiology department. After all, I was an actor and had been teaching acting for twenty years, so I could read a lot from her vocal tone and her facial expression. She was not a very good actor. I could sense her experience told her the images they had seen were very bad news. Little did I know I would end up having 28 more CT scans over the next twelve years.

Strange as it may seem, I met my primary care doctor when he registered to join my acting class. When he first told me he was a doctor, I was compelled to ask him if he would be my primary care doctor. I didn't have a doctor other than my allergy doctor and my dermatologist. It felt like it was meant to be.

I always called my doctor "Mike," instead of Dr. Beckham, because he was a student and it would've been weird to call my student Dr. Beckham all the time. When I met with Mike, he said he wasn't overly concerned, since I was healthy and my bloodwork was good, but he highly recommended I get an opinion from a surgeon. He referred me to a general surgeon in his medical group, whose name I can't recall.

The surgeon told me this "thing" was a very large, and rare, "urachal cyst." He said it could be malignant, but very possibly benign. He also explained how rare it was in an adult male my age, which was 60 years old at that time. He said urachal cysts are usually found in small children, and they would be tiny, not like my avocado-sized version.

Since it had been over a month since the first CT scan, the surgeon wanted to do another scan to see if there had been any growth. On my return visit to discuss the findings of the second scan, the surgeon told me the scan showed some possible growth. He said the urachal cyst should definitely be surgically removed. It would continue to grow, and if it wasn't malignant, it would most likely become malignant in the future.

He also explained, in great detail, the approach to this long and difficult surgery. He told me there would be surgeons from multiple departments in the operating room to assist him and consult as the operation proceeded. They would need to inflate my abdominal cavity with gas to make room for robotic equipment and cameras that would be inserted into my abdominal cavity. They needed to be prepared for anything once they started the surgery due to the many complications that might develop during the projected four- to five-hour surgery. They wouldn't know exactly what they were dealing with until they opened me up.

This is where things got weird and I really understood the rarity of my condition. I asked the surgeon how many of these surgeries he had performed. There was a long pause before he said, "None."

There was another long pause before he said, "And I don't know of a surgeon that has."

I said, "Oh."

He said, "I would understand if you would like to see if you can find another surgeon who has experience removing a very large urachal cyst."

I said, "OK," as my inner dialogue was screaming, "There is no effing way I'm going to have this guy do this surgery." I didn't know if he was an "A" student or a "D" student in medical school; I wanted a genius or at least a Harvard Med graduate.

* * *

I needed some serious research. Then came the revelation, "Kerry Hook would know how to find the right surgeon." Kerry was the mother of one of my teen students who was doing some part-time marketing for me.

Previously, she had done research in a major university psychology department for twenty years.

One might say, "What a coincidence that I would have a woman working with me that had these research skills in my time of need." I would say, "There are no coincidences." I would have to say it was another "God Thing." Some would say it was the Universe taking care of me. Either way, I will always be amazed that when I needed help, or an answer, it was there for me. I can't deny that.

No one is that *lucky*.

I called Kerry and explained what was going on. I asked her to keep it to herself until I told her otherwise. The last thing I wanted or needed was for the word to get out on Facebook or Instagram for several reasons; I didn't need 4,000 past students asking how I am; the story would turn from "Alan has a large cyst" to "Alan is dead" by the time the story got to the third level. Most of all, I wanted to keep it from my mother, who was in fragile health at the time. Mom was a world-class worrier, especially when it came to her sons and husband. It would have killed her for sure.

I asked Kerry to use her research skills to find a surgeon that had performed this very rare surgery. I didn't care what state or country they were in, I just wanted the best surgeon for this procedure. Luckily, I had great (*expensive*) health insurance with Blue Cross Blue Shield.

It took Kerry only two days to come up with what she felt was the closest thing to an expert she could find. She couldn't find a surgeon that had actually performed the surgery, but she did find a top urology surgeon at a prominent hospital in Nashville who had written a paper on the subject. I knew no other way to find a surgeon with experience in the surgery I needed, so I made an appointment with him. He had great reviews on the internet, so it was my best and only option.

This doctor was a very busy urologist/urology surgeon, so it took a month to get in to see him. In my four years of being one of his patients, the waiting room was always packed and many patients were forced to wait in the outer hallway and overflow seating. He was a very likable guy and exuded confidence. I could tell he was a good doctor by the time we were five minutes into that first consult. It was easy to tell he loved what he did and really cared about helping me. He also seemed pretty darn excited about the challenge that just walked into his clinic. After all, he had written a paper on the subject, even if he hadn't performed the surgery.

It took three months to get on the doctor's surgery schedule. I wasn't excited about waiting three months to get the "thing" out of my body and know if I had cancer. What was my option? If I started looking for another expert, it would probably take even longer.

The surgeon said there was a 75% chance the tumor wasn't malignant. He explained, as the first surgeon had, that it would be a very difficult and lengthy surgery, involving multiple surgeons from different departments. If it turned out the tumor was malignant, they would be prepared to deal with it.

It would be at least an hour into the surgery before the doctor would know if the tumor was malignant. If so, he would need to remove everything from my belly button down to my bladder. I tried to imagine what it would look and feel like to not have a belly button. The doctor told me not to worry: If it bothered me, he could build a new belly button for me later.

CHAPTER 54—JANUARY 29, 2012

I would be a liar if I said the surgery wasn't on my mind. It wasn't a fear thing: it was a desire to know one way or the other.

I definitely wasn't afraid of the surgery because I had experienced surgeries and hospital procedures before in my life. I was always intrigued by it all, and in a weird way, enjoyed the learning aspect of the experiences. Maybe that's why I started out in a pre-med curriculum when I went to college.

I'm one of those weird people that actually likes being in the hospital. I think it's totally based on the great experiences and care I had from the nurses I had as a child. I think nurses are angels. Strangely, I like the fact that I have to give up control in the hospital, which I never do in real life.

My surgery was scheduled for early in the morning on January 29th, 2012. We decided it would be less stressful to spend the night in a hotel close to the hospital. That way there would be no concerns with traffic or distracted driving, knowing the surgery would be on our minds. It also allowed us to get an extra hour of sleep, and Michele would be able to spend the night after my surgery close to the hospital, instead of driving home at night and driving back in the morning.

We both slept pretty well and we were relatively upbeat and positive, considering the circumstances. For me, the morning of a big surgery is always a little surreal. I know it's going to happen and I'm excited about getting the process started so we can get to the finish line. It's like, "Let's do this thing. Let's win—and move on."

I go into a similar mode when I'm getting ready to go on stage or on camera. It's the same mode I would go into right before a very important basketball game, football game, or track meet when I was an athlete.

I also know the surgery is totally out of my control, other than keeping a positive attitude. I know I can deal with whatever the outcome might be. I'm fine with giving up the control knowing I've done my best to find the right team. God has brought these people into my world for a reason, and we are about to find out why.

I have to admit, I love the whole anesthesia part of surgery where I start to count backward from 100 and try to get past 98. It's the perfect sleep.

Then I start to wake up thinking maybe I haven't had the surgery yet, until some gentle person says, "Alan. Your surgery is over. You are in the recovery room. Your wife is here." Then I usually fall back into a daze for a little while.

Michele was not fortunate enough to be sedated during my surgery: she had to be there in the surgery waiting room for every last minute of the five hours of surgery. She is a positive person but waiting to hear news about the surgery of a loved one is a horrible experience for anyone. Cooper and Cody arrived before the surgery started. They both lived only twenty miles away in Franklin, Tennessee.

After two hours, Michele and the boys were called into a consultation room. None of the other families had been directed to do that, so they knew something serious was going down. I'm sure it felt like one of those situations on a TV series where the family is called into a room and a very sad surgeon walks in and tells the family that something has gone horribly wrong in the OR and their loved one has died. I've been there before with my dad and mom. It ain't fun.

The doctor came into the consultation room, still in scrubs, looking very serious and a little disheveled. He gave them the bad news. The cyst was actually a malignant tumor: Urachal mucinous cystadenocarcinoma to be exact—one of the rarest cancers on the planet.

He told them he and his surgical team were removing the tumor, rebuilding my bladder, removing my belly button, removing the gelatinous material, and anything else that was part of the structure (urachus) between my belly button and my bladder. They would also need to remove a considerable amount of fascia: the sheet of connective tissue beneath the skin that attaches, stabilizes, encloses, and separates muscles and other internal organs. He told them it would take at least three more hours before the surgery would be completed.

When I came to, Michele was there with me in the tiniest of hospital rooms. They had already moved me to a hospital room. In my later surgeries, I was kept in recovery much longer before being moved to a hospital room.

Michele held my hand and talked to me, but I have no recollection of the conversation. I was told I appeared to comprehend what she was telling me, but later realized I wasn't with it enough to understand what she was telling me.

When Dr. X came into the room for the first time following surgery, the first thing I said was, "So, I guess I still have my belly button." Dr. X looked at Michele and she said, "I told him. I guess he doesn't remember."

He turned to me and said, "No, Alan. We had to take your belly button.

It was cancer."

I was still a little groggy, so there was a pause before I said anything. I said, "OK. I understand."

I had prepared myself for possible bad news, so I wasn't devastated. I asked, "So what do we do now? Chemo? Radiation?"

He said, "You had cancer. You don't have cancer now. There is nothing to do. We just have to wait and see if it comes back."

He explained they had infused warm chemotherapy into my open abdomen, towards the end of the surgical intervention, in an attempt to kill cancer cells that might have been left behind. He said that was a long shot, but it might have some positive effect. The insiders crudely call this procedure "Shake and Bake."

I spent the night in the hospital and, much to my surprise, they kicked me out the very next day around noon. I couldn't believe it. Damn insurance companies…

As the doctor said, though: *You don't want to be here anyway, Alan. There are sick people here.*

* * *

The morning after my surgery, one of the other surgeons involved in my surgery came in to check on me. The name on his badge looked very familiar. For some reason or other, it rang a bell.

I thought and thought, and then I remembered I had a student who had started my acting class two weeks before my surgery with the same last name.

When I got back to class three weeks later, I pulled her aside and quietly asked her if anyone in her family was a urology surgeon.

"As a matter of fact, my husband is," she answered.

I told her about my surgery. She said her husband had not mentioned recognizing my name. She asked him about it that night after acting class and he told her he had realized he was in surgery with her new acting coach, but due to privacy issues, he didn't mention it to her. She said he was always very strict on privacy issues. I was impressed he hadn't mentioned it to her considering the rarity of the surgery, and the amazing coincidence that his wife was a new student of the man on the operating table. How weird was that?

* * *

Thirty-six hours after I checked in for surgery, they kicked me out of the hospital. The insurance company guidelines said I had to leave the hospital. I was in serious pain from the multiple incisions and the major trauma to my abdominal cavity, even with all the pain medicine that was flowing through my veins.

They wheeled me out to valet parking and waited with me while Michele retrieved my Jeep. Thank God it was a Jeep Commander, which was the largest vehicle Jeep ever made. I was totally doped up on pain meds, but still, getting me in the Jeep was very painful. I was questioning their decision the whole way, but I really wasn't given a choice.

Once we arrived at our house, Michele got me out of the Jeep with what little help I could give her. I could walk but definitely needed to be stabilized. She didn't have to carry me, but I'm sure I was leaning heavily on her. Even at only 125 pounds, Michele was very strong from her demanding gym workouts. She was totally up to the task of getting her man out of the Jeep and into our bedroom. There is no stopping Michele; she will always find a way to get the job done.

It was such a relief to lay down in our bed and take more pain medication. The instructions were: take 1 to 2 tablets every 4 hours, or as needed. They were needed, but I didn't want to overdo it. It didn't take long to figure out the pain meds had unpleasant side effects.

I was allowed to take a short shower if I taped a plastic bag over the bandaged area, which was most of my torso. There was a large incision where they had removed my belly button; four holes where there had been drains and internal cameras; and a long incision across my pubic hairline where they had extracted all the bad stuff. I wanted to wash off the yellowish sterilizing antiseptic they always slap on heavily before surgery.

I just wanted to feel a little more human.

As I started to shower, I looked down and was horrified to see my penis had turned black. Something must have gone terribly wrong. I yelled to Michele and then showed her what I had discovered. She immediately put in an emergency call to the hospital. They told her to bring me back to the hospital immediately: they needed to do a CT scan to see what had gone wrong.

Oh, My God! Come on. You've got to be kidding?

No, they weren't kidding. Michele had to load me back into the Jeep and head back to the hospital. It wasn't easy and it was nighttime so they weren't staffed like they were in the daytime. The scan was completed and I was told my penis had turned black because all the excess blood from the surgery had drained to my groin and my penis. They said it was nothing that concerned them; it would go away on its own in a couple of days.

The recovery from surgery wasn't too bad compared to my later surgeries. I was instructed to be careful and not lift anything heavy or do anything strenuous for six weeks. I weaned myself off the pain medication after a few days because I didn't want to develop a dependency. It was easy to understand how people could get hooked on them. Also, they seriously messed up my digestive system.

After ten days, I started with very restricted workouts. I was instructed to be very careful as far as sexual activity went for several weeks. They didn't want me to develop a hernia.

I tried not to think about the whole rare incurable cancer that might come back, but that is easier said than done. There was nothing I could do myself, so I proceeded with little change in my life, other than some pain and what went on in my head.

After two weeks, I went back to teaching at my acting school. I used my mother's fragile health in Illinois as an excuse for my absence. I did that every time I had my four major cancer related surgeries over the next six years. I was only telling close family, a few friends, and the people who worked with me that I depended on.

I had a follow-up exam about a week after the surgery. The doctor said everything looked good with my incisions. He explained he had chosen not to use any mesh to put me back together. His decision was to pull everything together and hope I didn't develop a hernia later. He opted to wish for the best instead of using the sometimes problematic mesh. Now, after having three surgeries involving all kinds of mesh problems, his decision was a good one. Mesh sucks!

I asked what we should do next. He repeated what he had told us right after my surgery: there was nothing we could do. We just had to wait since there was no chemo regimen or cure for my very rare type of cancer. He said it would be a waste of time to see an oncologist. I would have regular CT scans for years. Every three months at first.

* * *

After leaving the clinic that day, we decided we didn't care what anyone thought; we wanted to talk with an oncologist to tell us more about this very rare cancer and what to expect. I knew the right person to call for a referral.

Nan Kelly, a wonderful person who had been a student of mine years before, was a cancer survivor, as was her husband, Charlie. Nan was the face of the Great American Country channel and the host of The Grand Ole Opry; and Charlie was a highly respected musician and producer. I called Nan and told her my situation and asked her if she liked her oncologist. She raved about Dr. Rafski at Tennessee Oncology. She and Charlie had both worked with him and found him to be a very knowledgeable and no BS doctor with a good heart. She offered to call his office for me.

In our consult, Dr. Rafski told us there was nothing they could do if the cancer came back. I will never forget his very straightforward statement, "You have two years for sure, five maybe, and if you're very, very lucky… ten years."

Wanting to know if there was any hope out there if the cancer came back, I asked him if there was any hospital or oncology group in the world that had some kind of treatment for urachal cancer. He said Sugarbaker Oncology Associates in Washington D.C. had a very aggressive and invasive regimen that might slow the process.

From what I understand, the Sugarbaker procedure involves going into the abdominal cavity and removing any organ, gland, fascia, muscle etc. that can be removed without killing the patient. The procedure is not meant to "save the life" of the patient, it is meant to "extend the life" of the patient. It's a last ditch effort if the cancer spreads to other areas or organs in the abdominal cavity.

We walked out of Tennessee Oncology not feeling uplifted by any means. But at least we knew the deal. No matter what, we were talking about "life extension, not life saving."

As a side note: I found out a few years ago that Dr. Rafski was killed by a drunk driver just three years after my consultation with him. I find it tragically ironic that the man who gave me, "Two years for sure, five maybe, and if you're very, very lucky…10 years" is dead.

* * *

Wait and see if the cancer comes back. That was my option. I would be doing CT scans every three months for the first year; every six months the second year; and then every year. My surgeon also said, "Alan, every time you have a pain…don't think it's cancer." That was very good advice because I'm sure there is a natural tendency for the mind to go there when experiencing any new sensation. Parts of my body had been seriously altered, so of course there would be weird sensations.

* * *

Anyone who has had cancer will tell you the realization that you are truly mortal and may not have as long to live as you had thought completely rewires your brain. It changes pretty much everything: the way you look at time, nature, people, your past, your work, money, you name it.

I particularly became aware of time. I felt like I needed to make the most of every day, but that seemed to just make the days go faster. As I would get in bed each night, I would think, "There goes another one. I wonder how many I have left." I felt like I was on the last day of a great vacation: the day you have to start packing to go back home.

My grandmother lived to be almost 109 years old, so I thought I would at least beat Grandma. Vegas would bet heavily against that at this point.

Money and owning stuff was no longer a priority. I didn't worry as much about what other people thought about me or what I was doing. I also knew I wasn't in a position to just stop everything and take off on a trip around the world, even if I wanted to.

There was also a sense of vulnerability and not wanting to get too far away from my support system and my doctors.

I noticed some of the people close to me, who knew about my situation, disappeared. Some people can't take it, or they don't want to feel bad, so they just divorce themselves from the situation and focus on themselves. I believe some people decide not to see you again until your funeral.

There were days when I would feel like it was some kind of dream. Did all that really happen? Did I really have a rare type of cancer with a tumor the size of an avocado growing in my body for my entire life?

Why did I decide to use that specific abdominal machine at the gym that day—that saved my life?

How did I have a woman working for me part-time that had twenty years of experience in research?

Should I stop everything and just travel and see the wonders of the world?

How did I get so lucky to have the unconditional love and strength of a woman like Michele at my side?

I did realize it was going to be very important not to let my brain be in control of the narrative. I needed to control my brain rather than have my brain control me. I had to make sure it was working for me instead of against me. I needed to believe I was going to be okay and proceed on with my life with a new way of looking at the world. I had to develop ways to stop any negative self-talk. I found it necessary to deal with the negative self-talk on a regular basis. I got better and better at stopping myself from going in negative directions.

It seemed like anytime I would start to drift to the negative, magically someone would be put in front of me to remind me just how lucky I was to be alive; to be somewhat healthy again; have all my limbs; have a wonderful relationship with a beautiful and amazing woman; be financially sound; and have two healthy and very smart sons who had never been in any trouble.

CHAPTER 55—CANCER AND THE MIND

There is a certain amount of anxiety that goes with the regular CT scans. At first you don't expect any surprises because it's only been three months since the surgery or the last scan, but it's still a relief when they tell you they don't see any signs of new tumor growth or signs of cancer anywhere else.

When the scans get to be six months apart, there's a little more anxiety because you know there's a greater chance something could have popped up. But when they say you don't have to come back for a year, two things go through your mind: they don't need to test for a whole year and a year is plenty of time for a new tumor to grow.

* * *

For the next two years I did a good job of believing I was going to be fine. I would do my occasional CT scan, eat healthy, work out six days a week, and be grateful that I discovered the tumor before it had metastasized. It was a gift. But why was I saved?

My three-year CT scan was the first scan where a full year had passed since the last scan. I was a little anxious but positive. My bloodwork was good, so I had convinced myself everything was going to be fine. Still, there was a feeling of relief when the results showed there was no recurrence. It was definitely a "Thank You, God" moment.

* * *

One month before I was to have my four-year CT scan on October 12th of 2015, I felt a little knot very close to where I had discovered the first tumor. It wasn't visible but was easy to feel when I put a little pressure on my abdomen. I wasn't too worried about it but felt it necessary to mention it to my doctor.

The normal routine was to have the CT scan and then see my surgeon in the urology clinic to get a preliminary verbal summary of the scan. The doctor said he was a little surprised...but very happy no sign of cancer had shown up after four years. Surprised because most patients with urachal cancer don't live more than five years, or at least have a recurrence.

I told him about the knot and asked him to feel it. He could feel what I was talking about but said it was probably just post-surgical scarring and nothing to worry about. He said he would take another look at the scan and ask the radiologist to do the same, then would let me know if they saw anything that concerned them. I never heard back, so I assumed all was well.

I had a bad feeling about that knot. After five months of thinking about it, I knew my body was telling me something important: something was not right. I decided to schedule another scan on my own, without telling my doctor.

Two days after the new scan, as Michele and I were getting in my car after a workout, a call came in from my primary care physician, Dr. Margaret Sanders. She had very bad news. There was a tumor the size of a small lemon buried in my abdominal wall. Somebody had made a huge mistake on the scan reading just months before.

Within ten minutes a call came in from my surgeon. I hadn't realized the imaging center where I had my "secret scan" was owned by the hospital where I had my surgery. This meant my scan report was also sent to him. The nervousness in his voice alarmed me. I knew it was bad news, but his voice made it feel even worse.

I asked how a tumor could grow so large in the short time between the two scans. He wouldn't admit they had missed the tumor in their scan. He deflected by saying, "These cancers are unpredictable and are capable of multiplying rapidly."

He said I needed surgery right away to remove the new tumor, but the hospital wouldn't allow him to perform the new surgery. He explained he performed the first surgery because it was considered a "urology surgery" until the surgery revealed the tumor was malignant. The new surgery was classified as a "cancer surgery" and had to be performed by one of their "cancer surgeons." I could tell he wanted to do the surgery and thought the protocol was stupid. After all, he knew more about urachal cancer and my case than any cancer surgeon at the hospital. He was not happy.

* * *

In the meantime, Michele had been reading a lot about integrative cancer treatment and thought we should approach the subject with the cancer surgeon. Integrative oncology is an approach to cancer care that uses complementary therapies to support the whole patient, not just chemotherapy.

This usually includes supplements, diet, and therapies for the mind, body and spirit.

The cancer surgeon had a condescending attitude in general and didn't really want to hear what our thoughts and concerns were. He wanted to remove my tumor and move on to the next patient. When we asked him about integrative cancer treatment approaches, he said, "If that worked, we would all be doing it."

At the end of the short consultation, he asked me what I did for a living. I told him I had worked as an actor for many years, owned an acting school, wrote music, and had served as an executive producer on several films. He said, "I just told my wife last night that if I could dance, sing, or act…I wouldn't be doing what I'm doing now."

And then he walked out.

Wow! It was obvious he hated being a cancer surgeon. No way was I going to have him operate on me. The last thing I needed in the operating room was an unhappy camper

Chapter 56—Act Of God 3: My Student Stephanie Schreiner, And Dr. B

Whether you call it an act of God, an intervention by the Universe, or fate, Stephanie Schreiner was mysteriously and miraculously placed in my path.

Stephanie was a former acting student of mine and a pathologist by profession. Her eight-year-old daughter, Gracie, was a current student. Stephanie knew about my first cancer surgery because I had confided in her and had asked her questions about tumors.

She was a pathologist for a few hospitals and did most of her pathology work from her home office. When I told her about the cancer recurrence and how the radiologist and surgeon had missed the large tumor in my scan, she told me she needed to get me away from both that surgeon and hospital. Stephanie's pathology residency was at Johns Hopkins University in Baltimore. She told me Johns Hopkins was one of the top five centers for cancer surgery and treatment in the world. After getting the details from me, she offered to contact her former professor, a world-renowned pathologist, and ask him for a referral to a cancer surgeon at Johns Hopkins.

Her pathology professor said his first choice would be Dr. B, a superstar cancer surgeon highly sought after by urology cancer patients. He offered to make the referral for me, but made no guarantees, since Dr. B's global reputation meant it could be difficult to get on his schedule.

Luckily, since the referral came from the Johns Hopkins pathology professor, a consultation was set up with Dr. B about a month out.

Michele and I flew to Baltimore on July 11th, 2016 for the consultation with Dr. B on the 12th. Michele spent the first twelve years of her life in Baltimore and her two sisters still lived there, so it made the trip seem a little more comfortable.

Dr. B was a confident, high energy, and intense man in his forties. After talking with him, Michele and I both felt there was no question he was the surgeon for the job. However, he suggested chemotherapy first to try to shrink the tumor, since the tumor was so large.

The size of the tumor was a huge problem in that it was buried in my abdominal wall. Removing the tumor as it was would require the removal of a large part of my abdominal wall and abdominal muscles; I would need major abdominal reconstruction using synthetic mesh and the dermis of a fetal pig.

He explained, as we already knew, there was no cure for urachal cancer: not chemo…not radiation. He said there had been some good results with shrinking, but not eliminating, tumors with a specific chemotherapy, FOLFOX (5-FU).

My first question was, "What percentage of the cases had some success?"

I was not excited when he said 20-25 percent. I asked, "If it were you or one of your children, would you do it?"

"Yes," he answered. "I would try it before the surgery."

Chapter 57—The Block Center For Integrative Cancer Treatment

Due to research conducted by Michele, we knew exactly where we would go for the chemotherapy treatments. In Michele's search for healthier ways to treat cancer, she discovered The Block Center for Integrative Cancer Treatment in Skokie, Illinois, a suburb of Chicago. She had actually booked the appointment at The Block Center before we went to Johns Hopkins to meet with Dr. B. Dr. Block was heavily booked so we took the first appointment we could get, which was July 28, 2016, just two weeks after the consult at Johns Hopkins.

We really didn't know what to expect from our visit to The Block Center. The information we had was from their website and some information they had sent us. We knew the visit would include a consult with Dr. Block as well as sessions with their dietician, clinical professional counselor, and a patient advocate.

We knew the Block approach was not going to be cheap. I had turned 65 in June, so I did have Medicare and a Blue Cross Blue Shield supplemental policy, but this is not your average treatment center: Many of the more exotic infusions wouldn't be covered as well as the $650 I paid just to walk in the door. There were also specialized treatments to minimize neuropathy and other side effects from the chemo. Each of these treatments--infrared, massage, and acupressure--had their own price tag.

We flew in on the 27th and booked the Residence Inn across the street from The Block Center for two nights. The Residence Inn had a special rate for Block patients, so all the out-of-town patients, from all over America, stayed there. It was extremely convenient and comforting to know you never had to go more than 100 yards to get back to your room. This became a second home to us during our bi-weekly trips to Chicago for the months I did chemo treatments. You would think a hotel full of cancer patients would be depressing, but it wasn't at all. It made me realize I was battling my disease along with millions of other people around the world.

We took the tour of The Block Center and found it to be modern, bright, airy, and non-threatening. The windows started about two feet from the floor and then curved over the top of the infusion area. There had been a lot of effort put into the design and layout of the facility to make it look and feel unlike other chemo infusion centers I had seen in photos or in movies. There were only twelve infusion stations, six on each side.

Each station was set up like a private room with a recliner for the patient and a chair for a visitor. There were dividers on each side, but all the stations were open to a large center aisle where there was a calm flow of nurses and Dr. Block moving from station to station. There was a curtain that could be drawn if you didn't want to be seen, but usually everyone left their curtains open.

At one end of the aisle was the very active nurses' station. At the other end, there was a small open kitchen area where you could make tea or heat soup, a relaxation area, stretching area, and a small gym. At the very end of this large open area was Dr. Block's office, which was all glass. There were other offices on this floor that could not be seen from the infusion area. On other floors there was a pharmacy, business office, and the room where the different chemotherapy cocktails were mixed.

It was a very expensive adventure with flights for both of us every other week, three nights at the hotel each trip, transportation to and from the airports, airport parking in Nashville, meals, and all the extra expenses of going a big step further than your average cancer treatment approach. But when you're trying to save your life—or at least extend it—you do whatever it takes.

The Block Center, as one would expect with their holistic approach, insisted on an aggressive supplement regimen. We had always taken lots of supplements because Michele had been in the supplement business for ten years at one point in her life. But The Block Center regimen was different, and very expensive. One of the supplements cost $250 per month. When I totaled the cost, I was paying around $600 per month for their supplements. They said their supplements were more expensive because their sources were different from what we could get at Whole Foods or anywhere else. Part of me wanted to call BS on this, but I decided to trust them and go all in. However, after my treatments were completed, I decided I would take my chances on the supplements from Whole Foods and Vitacost at one third the cost.

Chemotherapy medications target cancer cells and basically poison them. Since the chemicals work within the entire system, chemotherapy can attack and destroy healthy cells throughout the body, not just the cancer cells. However, healthy cells are able to repair themselves and recover during the time between treatments. Since the cancer cells have faulty DNA, they are not able to repair and recover. Eventually, the repetition of exposure to the toxic effects of the chemo drugs will kill the cancer cells.

At least that's the hope.

The Block Center's research had shown that the time of day, the chemo delivery rate, and the style of the infusion curve can reduce the drug's toxicity and maximize the benefits of the treatments. They developed specialized infusion pumps that deliver the chemicals at the optimal circadian times (sleep/wake cycle) and infusion rates to maximize effectiveness and minimize toxicity to the rest of the body.

This enhanced methodology is called "chronomodulated therapy." The goal is to improve treatment response, reduce the side effects, and increase the patient's chances of survival.

* * *

Before my treatments could start at The Block Center, I needed to have a chemo port implanted in my chest. The port would be the permanent connection for the IV lines and the chemo pack.

On August 29, 2016, I was sent to Saint Francis Hospital to have the permanent "PowerPort" surgically implanted under the skin on top of my right pectoral muscle. They put me under for this surgical procedure so the process was painless. The port had a lead that went directly into a vein right below my neck. The chemo, vitamins, and other medications would be delivered into my bloodstream by way of the port and the lead.

* * *

The first treatment at the Block Center started on August 30th with some basic blood tests, etc. The first IV I received was a bag of high potency Vitamin C. They also administered anti-nausea drugs and other concoctions through the IV line that they connected to my PowerPort.

At the end of this several hour-long session, they introduced me to and connected my chemo pack. This pack looked like a very large fanny pack, but inside, there was a computerized infusion pump with tubes that connected to the port in my chest. The chemo mixture was also in the pump. The chemo type was 5-FU (FOLFOX). The pack had a strap so I could carry it on my shoulder or strap it around my waist. The tubes were long and visible, but I could put my shirt on over the tubes if I didn't want it to be so obvious when we were in a restaurant or walking around town. A person could easily mistake it for a camera bag.

The chemo was programmed to kick in around 10:00 P.M. The computer of the infusion pump controlled the amount administered depending on how they had set the infusion curve. That all happened while I was sleeping. The program would finish around 10:00 A.M.

That first night, I was so curious about the whole process that I stayed awake to see what it felt like when the chemo started to flow into my body. I was lying in bed and Michele was asleep when I saw the infusion pump and its function indicators go on. I was actually excited about it. There had been so much build-up to this event, and after years of hearing about other people going through it, I was going to know what it was really like. I was glad that Michele was asleep because I needed to quietly go through it by myself in the dark of night. I wanted to believe I was feeling the chemo killing cancer cells.

Shortly after the program kicked in, I swear I could feel a surge from the chemicals. It's hard to explain what it felt like and what went through my head, but I felt like there was a warmth to it all. I was totally at peace with the process and decided it was time to rest my body after an intense and exciting 24 hours.

I felt good the next morning and went down to see what the hotel offered at their free breakfast. I was surprised to see they had several items labeled Block Center Diet, since so many of the guests were patients at the center. Most were attempting to eat healthier than what one usually finds at a free hotel breakfast. Michele brought along a large stash of organic food for us since it's always difficult to find organic foods when traveling. Michele is very good about resisting the free hotel breakfasts.

After breakfast, I did a little catching up on my computer, then decided to work out in the hotel gym. Working out every day was something I forced myself to do each time I was in Chicago for treatments. I worked out all through my years of treatment, surgeries and recoveries, except when I was extremely ill or too weak from surgery. I believed working out, along with eating right and taking all my supplements, would seriously increase my chances of success and survival.

So there I was, in the gym with my chemo pack/infusion pump. I didn't care what anyone thought. In fact, I was proud of myself for not letting all the cancer stuff get me down. I wanted to dominate and be in control as much as I could.

We went back to the Block Center for more treatments that day after the infusion pump turned off. Each time I visited The Block Center, the infusion would be administered over two sequential nights. Each day would be filled with tests and IVs of vitamins and other substances to decrease the toxicity to the healthy cells. After they would release me later in the afternoon, we would try to go somewhere to make it seem a little bit like a vacation, instead of a sad cancer treatment story.

Sometimes we would go out for dinner or a movie. It depended on how I felt, but usually I felt like getting out. I knew Chicago pretty well since I grew up in Illinois and made many trips there in my younger life, and still did at times for business.

One evening, my old college fraternity brother and former roommate, Steve Stratton, and his wife, Sarah, stopped by the hotel for a visit. It was nice to see an old friend even though I knew it had to be very weird for them. I didn't look sick, but the infusion pack probably freaked them out. They hid any negative thoughts well and were very supportive. Not long after this, we found out Steve was going through his own battle with prostate cancer.

The third day was always more vitamins, anti-nausea medicine, and Neulasta. Neulasta stimulates the growth of neutrophils, a type of white blood cell important in the body's fight against infection. It's used to reduce the incidence of fever and infection in patients with certain types of cancer who are receiving chemotherapy that affects the bone marrow. Neulasta costs between $6,000 and $8,600 per single dose (cancer is expensive) administered once per chemotherapy cycle. The most common side effects are bone and muscle pain, but as with most medicines, there can be some dangerous side effects as well. I was lucky in that I had very little problem with the Neulasta.

We often saw the same people at the hotel that were at The Block Center for treatments. They were from all over the country. Some of them stayed for several weeks at a time because it made more sense than flying back and forth all the time. Some were very ill and wanted to be close to The Block Center and great hospitals in case they became even sicker. Mostly the patients were older adults, but sometimes there would be a patient in their late twenties or thirties. I always felt worse for them because they hadn't had a chance to live a full life yet. The rest of us really couldn't complain since we'd been on the planet much longer.

For some, this was their last-ditch effort. A couple of the patients expressed to me they were ready to stop, but their families wouldn't let them. There was always one more treatment they wanted them to try. They were tired of the pain, the fatigue, the restricted diets, lack of independence, constipation, hair loss and on and on. I understood where they were coming from, but I was not in the same place: I was not in pain, I still had good energy, and a strong belief that I could beat my cancer. Yes, I had another large malignant tumor, but it appeared it hadn't spread. Of course, there was always concern that it would metastasize or spread if the tumor weren't removed soon. It's not possible to ignore these possibilities 100% of the time; but I had my ways to turn around the negative thoughts and negative self-talk.

Chemo Infusion at The Block Center

It was a little bit like ten people of different ages, different backgrounds, and from different places, all on a boat in the middle of a huge storm just hoping to find land soon. We could express things to the other patients that we couldn't to anyone else. I felt a kinship with these people because we were all trying to save or extend our lives. If you've never been in this position, you could never know what it's like.

I assume it's something like being in a war together: You can tell some-one about it, but that would only describe about 10% of what it's really like. There's an insane amount of emotions and sensations that are beyond words. I hope that you never have to know them.

After the third day of treatments, we would always make our way to the airport for the flight back to Nashville. I was usually very tired at that point. They hadn't told me they had added an extra booster called a "bolus" to my chemotherapy. Their goal was to kickstart the poisoning of the can-cer cells. Unfortunately, this backfired and I had terrible experiences with my digestive system (I'll spare you the details). It was such a horrible experience that I remember thinking death would be better. That's saying a lot because I never feel like that. My reaction was so bad and extended that we had to postpone my second round of chemo for a week.

The next three rounds went without any big problems. I was still able to work out even though I was weaker. I was starting to notice a little thin-ning of my hair; but at times like that you convince yourself that life is much more important. I was lucky on the hair loss side of things. I don't think it was enough to be noticeable to anyone other than myself and Michele. I'm not sure if that had to do with all the supplements, the diet, the infusions of high dose Vitamin-C, or the type of chemo I was getting, 5-FU.

After coming back home each time, I would rest but still get my work done. I would generally go back to teaching the very next week with none the wiser. I don't think my students noticed. I became aware that most people are so focused on themselves, they don't pay that much attention to others. They look, but they don't see. They hear, but they don't listen. Maybe they would have noticed if I had an extra nose or gained a quick 50 pounds, but not a little thinning of the hair or a ten-pound weight loss.

I kept my chemo treatments secret. There were times when I wanted to scream my situation out to everyone that I knew, as well as the 4,000 stu-dents that had taken classes at my acting school. But I had a total of almost 7,000 "friends" on three different Facebook accounts and I definitely didn't need a few thousand people checking on me or spreading the word. Knowing how communication changes as it goes down the line, it would end up that Alan is dead!, not *Alan is battling a rare cancer.*

Once again, I only told my sons, brother Terry, his wife Mindy, my nephew Ethan, the key people I worked with and a few friends that I knew would be furious with me if they found out later that they hadn't been included in the small group of "insiders" who were told.

* * *

Alan Working Out at the Hotel Gym Wearing His Chemo Pack

After the first four rounds of chemo, I had another CT scan to see if the chemo regimen was shrinking the tumor. Dr. B, at Johns Hopkins Hospital, had originally suggested I try four rounds, even though the success rate for urachal cancer was low. He said, if there was no significant shrinkage after four rounds, we should schedule the surgery.

There was no clear evidence the tumor was smaller. Dr. Block said the chemo may, however, be keeping the tumor from getting larger. He felt very strongly four rounds was not enough to give the chemo a real chance to work on the tumor. I agreed to do three or four more rounds, and then check again.

By the fifth round I was starting to have some signs of the very negative side effects of the chemo. I was having issues with neuropathy in my fingers and feet. Whenever I hear others speak of their neuropathy, they seem to always mention burning in their feet and hands from the peripheral nerve damage. I never described my neuropathy as burning pain. My neuropathy was more numbness, tingling, and a feeling that my feet were made of hardened clay. When I moved my toes or walked, it felt like they were cracking and crunchy. I still have these symptoms even though it's been four years since I stopped the chemo treatments. My hands and fingers are pretty much back to normal.

I believe another side effect of the chemo, or perhaps from the chemo and the anesthesia from five major surgeries, is the slowing down of my brain. I find it harder to pull up information that is stored on my hard drive. My brain used to be quicker. I could pull names out of my memory very quickly before, but now I have to let my brain grind longer to pull up information that I know is in there. It's very frustrating, especially when it happens when I'm talking to a group or in the middle of an important conversation. It doesn't happen all the time, but often enough to be annoying.

I know I should write it off as one of the prices I pay for being alive, but I liked the way my brain worked before. Some will say, "Alan, you're getting older and your brain is changing," but I don't think that's what it is. I've had too many strange chemicals introduced to my brain. Besides the five major surgeries in the past eight years, there were four in my younger years. My grandmother, who lived to be almost 109, could recite poems, sing songs from her childhood, and remember everything that ever happened to her until she was blind and deaf in her early 100s. I want my brain to work like hers did.

After the 7th round of chemo, they ordered another CT scan to see if the tumor was shrinking. The results were inconclusive. Dr. Block said there may have been a slight reduction in size, but depending on the angle, there may not have been any real change.

Dr. Block wanted me to do even more chemo treatments. He said there was a chance we were at the point where the chemo would start making a difference. I wasn't feeling it. My gut was telling me it wasn't working and I had already done three more rounds than I had originally agreed to do.

I realized there was nothing for The Block Center to lose if I kept doing more chemo, and there was a lot of money to be made by my continuing. I'm not saying money was his reason for wanting me to continue, but it is a business, and businesses need to make money, as well as save lives.

I told Dr. Block I would think about it, but I knew what I was going to do as soon as we got back to Nashville.

CHAPTER 58—CUT THE CHEMO PLEASE

Having decided I wasn't going to make any more chemo trips to Chicago, I called Johns Hopkins Hospital and scheduled my surgery with Dr. B. I had tried the chemo they originally suggested and more. As far as I was concerned, it hadn't worked. I never liked the odds of 20-25% possibility of shrinking the tumor in the first place. I had only decided to try the chemo experiment because Dr. B had said he would do it if it were him or his children in my position. I wanted to stop the chemo treatments before more good cells were killed and the neuropathy got worse. I wanted to be as strong and healthy as possible before I had another major cancer surgery.

They wouldn't perform the surgery until I'd been off chemo for two months, so surgery was set up for February 20th. The surgery would include the removal of a large malignant urachal tumor (cystectomy), a small bowel resection, abdominal wall mass lesion excision, and lymph node removal. The section of the small bowel had to be removed because the tumor had invaded a small area of the bowel. This didn't mean the cancer had spread to the bowel; it was pressed so tightly against the bowel, there was no way to remove the tumor without taking a section of the bowel.

* * *

Since I had to wait two months for the surgery, we decided to head to Cancun for eight days starting on January 21, 2017. After my first cancer surgery in 2012, I had decided I would travel as much as possible. Having cancer made me hyperaware that one day traveling would become too difficult or even impossible.

YOLO (You Only Live Once) became a term that meant so much more to me than it had in the past.

We have been to Cancun sixteen times over the past twelve years to cool down and reboot. We love the weather, the beautiful color of the Caribbean water, the magnificent resorts, and their friendly and happy staffs. Every time we think of going somewhere else, we worry we won't have the same wonderful experience we've always had in Cancun. We were actually

253

married in Cozumel, just a short boat ride from Cancun, on January 2, 2008, after having lived together for five years.

I was able to relax, not worry about the surgery, and have a great time in Cancun. It was a relief to know I was done with chemo, and that I had the best surgical team possible ready to fix my current cancer problem. I've said it before: I don't mind having surgery and I never have. I guess that makes me a freak, but I was ready for the next step.

* * *

On February 16, 2017, I flew into Baltimore by myself because they needed to see me in the clinic and do several tests in preparation for my February 20th surgery. The consultations with my two surgeons had to be done on a Thursday, even though the surgery wasn't until Monday. I saw no reason to fly back to Nashville for just two days, so I decided to stay in Baltimore, relax, and enjoy myself. It made no sense for Michele to come in that early since there were many work details she needed to take care of, not knowing how long she would be in Baltimore after my surgery.

On Friday I got a call from my ex-wife, Liz, saying my sons, Cody and Cooper, were on their way to Baltimore. Earlier, I had told them it wasn't necessary for them to come since Michele would have her sisters, who lived in the Baltimore area, to be with her; there was little they could do. I also knew it would be expensive for them to travel, stay in a hotel, and miss work for a few days. I didn't see any reason to put them through the whole cancer surgery thing for a second time.

They had driven through the night to get there and had made reservations at a nice hotel in the Inner Harbor. I met them at their hotel, and we went across the street to an Irish pub for a nice lunch. I was very happy to see them but felt bad they had driven all night to get there.

Later that day, they called to tell me they were going to head back to Nashville the next morning. I was shocked. I had thought they were coming to be there for the surgery, but Cody thought they were just coming for a short visit before my surgery. I guess they thought they should come in case I didn't make it through the surgery. I have never asked them why they didn't stay.

Later the next day, Saturday, Michele arrived and joined me at the hotel. We went out for a nice dinner, knowing it might be a long time before we would be able to experience that again. We had a great evening and didn't talk about the upcoming surgery. We had been through it before and we both felt very positive about Johns Hopkins Hospital and my surgical team. We were both a little baffled by the abrupt departure of Cody and Cooper but didn't dwell on it.

Sunday the 19th, the day before surgery, was an unusually beautiful and warm day for February in Baltimore. It was in the upper 60s which was great for walking and exploring the Mt. Vernon area near our hotel. I had a restricted diet that day and a pre-op regimen to clear my digestive system. Since our regular diet was vegetarian, Michele brought along healthy food choices from Nashville so she wouldn't need to run right out to Whole Foods in downtown Baltimore. We also took a little time to work out at the downtown Planet Fitness.

My scheduled surgery was early in the morning, so I got up around 4:00 A.M. to get to the hospital by 5:30. Always no food or drink on the morning of surgery.

Once ready, we ordered an Uber and were soon on our way to The Weinberg Surgery Center at Johns Hopkins Hospital. We had never used Uber before all the chemo trips to Chicago, but we found the service to be invaluable on all the medical journeys.

It has always amazed me how many people are at a hospital so early in the morning waiting to help those of us who need medical care. If it weren't for all these wonderful people, we would all be in big trouble. Our hospitals couldn't function without all these caring, giving, and hardworking individuals. They aren't paid nearly enough, or given enough credit, for the difficult and often very dangerous work they do. I have always been treated so incredibly well by all the staff and employees at Johns Hopkins.

After signing in, there was a short wait before they called Michele and me to follow a staff member, and three other surgery patients, to the pre-op/recovery area. Once there, I was asked to take off my clothing and shoes, put everything in a plastic bag, and don a surgical gown and non-slip socks. Drawing blood samples and other tests began pretty quickly once I was suited up for battle. The mood was upbeat as we met some of the team members I had not previously met: the anesthesiologist, nurses, and a few others that would be in the operating room.

After all the prep was completed, Dr. Justin Sacks, the director of oncological reconstruction and plastic surgery, came in to say hello and wish me luck. He would be reconstructing my abdominal wall: a very large hole would need to be filled after the removal of the tumor and a large part of my abdominal wall. Each time I had met with Doctor Sacks, he was always very nice and never rushed our conversation. I felt like I was in the right hands from the first time I met him. I would rank him as one of the best doctors I have known, and I've known a lot. He has rebuilt my abdominal wall a total of three times. We actually text as friends now.

Doctor Sacks loved the fact that I was a former soap star. He would call nurses into his office, pull up my *People* Magazine cover on his computer, and tell them I was famous. It was funny and a little embarrassing.

Doctor Sacks was one of the most respected in his field and having him perform my abdominal wall reconstruction gave me the best chance of having a somewhat normal life post-surgery. He explained he would be using two different types of mesh to put me back together: one mesh would be from the dermis of a fetal pig (pretty freaky) and the other would be a synthetic mesh.

A large percentage of my abdominal musculature had to be removed and replaced with the two meshes. This meant I would never have a six pack or do a sit up again. You can't build stronger mesh. It is what it is— not human. The mesh would be stapled to my oblique muscles on the sides, my uppermost abdominal muscles on top, and then one inch below my pubic hairline. This meant I would have an 6-inch by 4-inch section of mesh instead of muscle tissue. It also meant certain movements would always be difficult, since the core is so important for movement and balance.

The last to rush in was Dr. B, who would be doing all the serious cancer related surgery. As I mentioned earlier, he is a very talented, high energy, and highly sought-after cancer surgeon. To say he is confident would be an understatement, but that's not a bad thing when you want a surgeon to save your life. He also doesn't have the greatest filter, so you have to be prepared for his sometimes condescending attitude. He listens to very hard rock while operating and comes out of surgery pretty jacked up. This is who he is; but he gets the job done, and if that's what it takes, so be it.

The surgery went as planned and both surgeons felt good about the outcome. Dr. B told me he took wide margins, unlike what was done with my first cancer surgery in 2012. He had originally believed the new tumor may have grown from cancer cells that were missed in the earlier surgery. He said he believed this could very well be the end of my urachal cancer problem. I was counting on that to be true.

* * *

This was a very big surgery. The incision was about nine inches in length. There was a catheter, IV, oxygen, and several surgical drains coming out of my abdominal cavity that were draining post-operative fluids. I definitely looked like I had been hit by a truck full of surgical supplies, but I didn't care because I was on several pain medications. They were giving me fentanyl, gabapentin, oxycodone, and some morphine, all at the same time. Some were given orally by the nurses and one I could administer myself with the press of a button.

I was trying not to hit the pain medication button too much, thinking it would be better to gut it out. But I was in a lot of pain and not resting well, so it was highly recommended that I use the button more when I was in pain.

One doctor actually said, "Alan, you can't heal if you're fighting pain. You just had a huge surgery and there will be a lot of pain from it. Hit the button!"

I took the suggestion after realizing no one was impressed with my warrior approach. I relaxed into it and decided I should take the advice of the people who knew a lot more about healing than I did.

Michele was staying at the Indigo Hotel and usually came to the hospital between 7:30 and 8:00 each morning. She would try to get there before the doctors made their rounds so she would be there to hear their evaluation of my progress and any other information I would never remember since I was under the influence.

The second day after surgery, I was feeling pretty good, probably due to all the pain medications. Early that morning, a woman from the nutrition department came in, before Michele arrived, and asked me what I wanted to eat. I was surprised at what was on the list of foods she said I was allowed to order. Feeling good, and under the influence, I decided to celebrate and ordered some foods I wouldn't normally eat like ice cream, mac 'n cheese, and cream of tomato soup. I can't remember what else I ordered, but I do know it was a mistake. I think the woman made a huge mistake and gave me a menu I wasn't supposed to have after my particular surgery. Michele would have caught this and not allowed me to eat the crap I ordered, but I was high on pain meds and really living it up. I had eaten much of it by the time Michele came in. She was horrified at what I'd been allowed to eat.

It was a huge cluster#%^k… One that nearly killed me.

CHAPTER 59—THE WORST NIGHT OF MY LIFE

Around 2:00 A.M. that night, long after Michele had gone back to the hotel, I started to feel weird and the upper part of my abdomen was starting to swell up. I called for a nurse to come into my room. She said she would check back but let her know if I started feeling worse.

Not long after that, I started vomiting uncontrollably.

The liquid was reddish in color. I was in big trouble. I was hitting the call button and it was taking too long for a response. When the woman finally answered, I was having a hard time talking because I couldn't stop puking. All I could do was scream, "HELP! HELP!"

A nurse came running in. I will never forget the look of terror on her face. Knowing she had probably seen everything before, I knew it was as bad as it felt. She called for backup. Soon there were several people in the room just as horrified as the nurse had been.

There was a lot of frantic talk between them and then two of the nurses came close and one of them looked me in the eyes and said, "Alan, listen to me closely because your life is at risk at this very moment. This is an emergency situation. We have to insert something called an NG tube. The NG tube will go up through your nose, down your throat and esophagus, and then into your stomach to drain this toxic liquid from your stomach and digestive system. But we need your help to do this. We need you to listen to our instructions on when and how to move to help us get the tube in properly. It's going to be very unpleasant because we can't give you any pain medication. Your gag reflex is going to kick in the whole time we're doing it."

I was vomiting the entire time they were inserting the tube. I can't even begin to explain how horrible this experience was. Maybe having your fingernails pulled out with pliers would be worse, but I'm not sure. Ask any nurse or doctor that has inserted an NG tube and they'll tell you that it's a horrible procedure to perform, let alone endure. When the tube was finally set, the vomiting stopped and there was a sense of relief in the room. The reddish fluid was now coming up through the tube from my stomach, out my nose, and into a large plastic bottle on the floor. More than two liters of this toxic fluid was drained from me.

Michele didn't know this had all gone on through the night, so she was very shocked when she came into the room and saw me with a large tube coming out of my nose that was taped to my face. I was hideous. I can't remember who explained to Michele what had happened during the night and what was going on with the NG tube. She was told I wasn't to have any fluids or food whatsoever until further notice. We knew they were serious when they wouldn't even let me have ice chips.

This went on for days. Each day they would assess my progress and say, "No food or water today."

This is how I understand what happened: when they operated, they had to remove a section of my small bowel. To do that, they had to put my digestive system to sleep. They didn't realize my digestive system was still shut down on the second day. When I ate, my body couldn't process what I had put in my body, so it staged a violent rebellion. At that point, they needed to wait until my system was functioning properly before introducing water or food again.

I was hungry and thirsty at first, but by the third day of no food or water, I had given in to the situation and wasn't feeling the need to eat or drink. I was very weak from not eating or drinking, which made it difficult to take the short walks they insisted I take three or four times each day.

At first, these walks were humiliating because I had all nine tubes and multiple gadgets attached to me as I hung onto the rolling IV tower like it was a life preserver. The urine bag that was attached to a catheter and the NG tube apparatus went along for the ride as well. I was wearing the ever- unpopular hospital gown. Michele would hang onto my other arm to make sure I didn't fall from weakness. I have never felt weakness like that before—and hope never to again. I really didn't want to get out of my bed. Even taking a few steps was exhausting. When I did take a short walk, my hospital bed looked like an oasis in the desert to me. My other recoveries were not like this, but the lack of food and vitamins was devastating to my normal energy. I was having trouble seeing the light at the end of the tunnel for several days.

* * *

On February 25th, in the midst of all this drama at the hospital, the Indigo Hotel, where Michele was staying, had a multiple alarm fire in the middle of the night. Alarms went off and emergency lighting came on in her room as a recorded message said, "This is not a false alarm. Proceed to the nearest fire exit and exit the building."

Everyone had to quickly flee the building at 3:35 A.M. All the guests were outside in the brutal February cold wearing whatever clothing they were able to quickly grab.

All Michele grabbed was her purse, but she said some of the silly people came out ten to fifteen minutes later with all their luggage. Shortly after most guests were outside, multiple fire trucks arrived with lights flashing and sirens blazing. They were finally allowed to re-enter the hotel after two hours of standing in the street.

Understandably, Michele was not able to get back to a restful sleep after the hotel fire drama. She arrived later that morning feeling a little ragged, but she still looked beautiful and well put together as always. I'm sure that was all she needed after a rough day at the hospital, but she was always a trooper and never really let it get her down, or if it did, she didn't let it show.

Last year I told Michele I was surprised she had never been driven to tears during any of the horrible experiences we went through on my cancer journey. She said, "I did cry. I just made sure you never saw me cry." She did that for me.

People were always very nice when we passed by on those little walks, but I will never forget the looks of concern and pity for the poor man trying to take a few slow and cautious steps down the hospital hallway. It was a huge ego buster. Maybe I needed that. I feel it's good for me to remember how lucky I am to have lived through that, and especially to have someone as wonderful as Michele to be there for me all the way.

Each day we would ask if I would be able to have at least some water. The nurse would always answer with, "We will have to wait and see what the doctor says when he comes in."

And each day the doctor would say, "Sorry, not today. Maybe tomorrow."

Finally, after the fifth day of no food and water, the doctor said, "Let's see how you're doing this afternoon."

Michele let loose on the doctor and told him he needed to stop the madness right then and start feeding me and letting me have some liquids. The toxic fluids had stopped draining two days before this. She was tired of seeing me getting weaker and weaker and losing so much weight. I looked terrible. I'm sure it was a horrifying experience for Michele to watch me wasting away day by day. It was like Groundhog Day. Every day they would come in at the same time and say the same thing. Michele decided to end that cycle. Enough was enough.

The doctor backed off and said they could start me out slowly with some ice chips. Later they would try some water and clear liquids and see how I handled it. You can't imagine how excited I was to have those ice chips.

I know they had good reasons for all they did. They weren't trying to starve me to death, but it started looking like someone had made a huge mistake by letting me eat too soon after the surgery and now they were trying to cover their asses and make sure that it didn't happen again. They were being overly cautious.

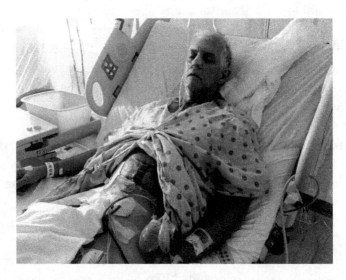

A Very Ill Alan Following His Second Cancer Surgery at Johns Hopkins

The transition went more smoothly as my digestive system became fully operational. They were cautious about my diet, so they had to approve the food Michele brought from Whole Foods. Even though the food was better at Johns Hopkins than any other hospital I had experienced, I was used to eating mostly fresh, organic foods at home. This would be the worst time to change my eating habits.

* * *

In 2012, after my cancer surgery, Michele wanted to find alternative, healthy ways to fight my cancer. Western medicine is basically chemo, surgery, and radiation. She wanted to learn about other ways to fight cancer and hopefully keep mine from coming back. She enrolled in a health coaching program at The Institute of Integrative Nutrition. She was a voracious reader of books and articles about cancer, nutrition and supplements. She had been in the supplements business for many years earlier in her life, so she already had great knowledge about supplements; but she wanted to know more. Michele was on a mission and she would not be stopped. She is a fighter with warrior mentality and she was determined to keep me alive. That was her focus.

She finished the program and was certified as a health coach. She never had any intention of practicing as a health coach. She did this to keep me alive. She truly loves learning about how the amazing human body works and what can be done to keep it running smoothly for as long as possible. She continues to study to this day simply for the knowledge.

By the time the doctors felt comfortable enough to let me fly back to Nashville, I had been in Baltimore for nineteen days. Fifteen of those days were in the hospital. I was originally expected to be in the hospital for three or four days. Our flights were expensive since we had no advance notice, but at that point we didn't care. Even as weak and skinny as I was, we desperately wanted to get back to our home as long as the doctors felt I was in good enough condition to do so.

On March 5th, I was wheeled out of Johns Hopkins Hospital to a waiting Uber and on to BWI (Baltimore/Washington International) Airport, where they loaded me into another wheelchair. I felt vulnerable in that wheelchair with so many wounds, stitches, bandages, and a drain coming out of my abdomen. I was very weak and on pain meds.

Thank God for Michele. She took total control of all the travel issues and made me feel safe. As an independent person with a strong ego, this was not easy for me. I felt like a very old man being wheeled through the airport by my beautiful, healthy, younger wife. I could see people looking at us, wondering what the relationship was. Through all of this, I learned a lot about myself and gained greater understanding and compassion for those with serious health conditions and disabilities.

* * *

It was a tough recovery. I needed to gain back some of the twenty-two pounds I had lost from the scary fifteen-day hospital stay, start very light workouts, and become more mobile. I also wanted to get back to work and start bringing in some income; I had been out of commission since I had left for Baltimore. I felt it was important to get back in the studio as soon as I could.

The doctors wouldn't let me drive for ten days, but I was eager to get back behind the wheel. It wasn't easy to drive, but as someone who had grown up in a rural culture where driving meant freedom and independence, I desperately needed to know I could transport myself. Something as trivial as being able to drive to Starbucks meant a lot.

I was back in the studio within ten days of my return. I was in bad shape, but I figured if I could move around the house and talk, I could do the same at the studio. I attribute my success in faking out my students to my acting training and experience. I acted like I was OK. If they could tell, they didn't let on. I thought surely someone would say something about the extreme weight loss and slow movement, but no one did. Maybe they were just being nice, but I think most people are just not very observant.

Slowly but surely, I started to put on weight and gain strength. It wasn't easy. I had to force myself to eat more and push myself as hard as I could in the gym without doing any damage to the surgical area. It was a delicate balance. It was weird pushing a maximum of ten pounds on a weight machine that I would normally have pushed many times that weight; but I had to set my ego aside and realize it was recovery and rehab time—not ego time.

After six weeks, I was allowed to slowly ramp up my weight workout. Caution was necessary because my artificial abdominal wall was stapled into the muscles that were left intact. It takes time for enough scar tissue to form around the staples to ensure stability of the reconstruction. The last thing I wanted to do was negatively impact the integrity of the meticulous work performed by my amazing reconstructive/plastic surgeon, Dr. Sacks.

CHAPTER 60—IT'S NOT OVER YET

By April 18, 2017, I felt my recovery was going extremely well and I was allowing myself to believe I'd seen the end to my surgical nightmares. It had been almost two months since my near-death experience at Johns Hopkins Hospital. I was gaining back some of the weight I had lost and getting stronger from my daily workouts.

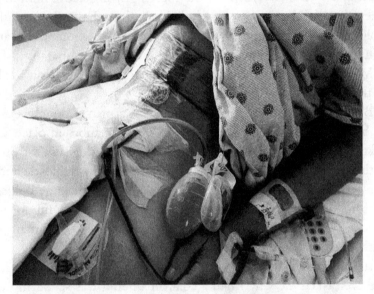

Alan's 9-Inch Incision and 9 Tubes Coming Out Of His Body

But on April 19th, I looked down at my stomach as I was drying off from my morning shower, and there was this giant pimple-like "thing" in the middle of my stomach where my belly button used to be. It wasn't there even fifteen minutes before my shower. I immediately took photos with my iPhone and sent them, along with a "WTF IS THIS" to my primary care physician, Dr. Sanders, and my oncological reconstruction/plastic surgeon, Dr. Sacks.

Dr. Sacks texted me back within five minutes saying, "Go to the hospital immediately to have a surgical drain inserted." Dr. Sanders agreed and set up the appointment for the procedure and yet another CT scan at Saint Thomas Hospital.

Dr. Sanders explained this pimple-like thing was called a "seroma." It was probably a result of serous fluid that sometimes builds up after surgery. Serous fluid is composed of blood plasma from ruptured blood vessels and inflammatory fluid produced by the injured and dying cells. These fluids try to exit the body by finding a channel to the surface. There were multiple possibilities that could have caused the fluid to be created, but a likely source was the mesh. But they were focused on resolving the issue not what caused it.

At Saint Thomas Hospital, the radiologist injected a numbing agent and then threaded a large needle-guided tube into the area where the fluid was collected. Once that was in place, a negative suction pump was attached. Unfortunately, this was not a tiny pump and collection apparatus.

My first thought as I walked out of the hospital was, "How the hell can I hide this damn thing?"

But it didn't take long to come up with a plan: I bought three large elastic bands to wrap around my torso to hold the tubes in place and then tucked the suction pump under the elastic bands, making sure the pump was lower than the insertion point. I kept the pump on my right side and would keep my right arm in front of the pump to disguise the large bulge. It was uncomfortable, but it was my best option. I had to be careful not to move too quickly or the needle in my abdomen would stick me. I wore my shirttail out with a heavy coat over everything.

It was late April, so the coat made no sense at all, but believe it or not, no one ever asked me why I had a coat on when it was so warm outside. I guess people just don't pay attention. This went on for several awkward days filled with meetings and teaching acting classes.

The radiologist said the pump would need to stay in place until the drainage stopped.

The drainage stopped seven days later, so I was sent back to Saint Thomas to have the drain removed. I was very excited about getting rid of that restrictive contraption. The radiologist needed to do some imaging first to make sure there was no sign of collected fluid.

Unfortunately, there was a new collection of fluid in an area close to the pocket that had just been drained.

"I'm very sorry," he said, "but I need to take out the drain and insert another drain into the new pocket of fluid. I know this isn't what you wanted to hear."

I was not a happy camper when I walked out of the hospital. Back to wrapping myself up again.

After a few days, the new drain stopped collecting fluid. I told my doctor I wanted it taken out since it wasn't doing anything and it was seriously restricting my activities. I had already rebelled and clamped off the tube and disconnected the pump myself. I figured if no fluid was being collected, why do I need the suction pump? It was such a relief to get rid of that pump and not have to wrap myself up like a mummy to hide the bulge made by the contraption.

The next day, Dr. Sanders scheduled the removal of the drain. It was decided I should try keeping the area sterile and letting any fluids drain into large bandages rather than have a surgical drain. If that didn't work, the only other option was to go back to Baltimore for another surgery at Johns Hopkins.

After a month of changing the large bandages on my abdomen several times each day, I decided the issue needed to be addressed in a more aggressive way. This could only be achieved by the surgery Dr. Sacks suggested as the last resort. I had no problem with another surgery; I just wanted them to find the source and fix it.

Getting consultations with both surgeons on the same day was tricky. Since my surgery wouldn't be considered an emergency cancer surgery, it took almost a month to get the appointments with Dr. Sacks and Dr. B. Both surgeons are generally only in the clinic for appointments two days a week since they are in such high demand for surgeries. June 29th was booked for consults along with yet another CT scan and bloodwork.

Chapter 61—The Senator Comedy Or Mr. Alan Goes To Washington

After my first cancer surgery, I had written, directed, produced, and starred in an over-the-top political comedy called *The Senator*. At that time, I thought I might not have long to live, so I wanted to do a short comedy film I could leave behind after my death to remind people I never started out to be a serious actor. I wanted to write, produce, and act in my own comedy projects because ultimately, I wanted to make people laugh.

I used the funniest actors I had worked with at my school over the many years I had been teaching. I was having so much fun I kept writing and filming. The project kept getting longer, and funnier, as time went on. We filmed whenever I was healthy, not too skinny, could get the right actors, had extra cash, and my studio was quiet enough to film.

That wasn't always easy. My studio was big and beautiful, but it had a metal roof and shared a wall with a Jazzercise studio. We could hear and feel the bass from their music when they held classes. This meant I had to schedule filming around Jazzercise classes as well as the classes in my studio. After three years of intermittent filming, the project had expanded to an unplanned 55 minutes in length: too long for a short film, but too short for a feature. I didn't really care. I was doing it mostly for myself and it was a great distraction from all the cancer and surgery stuff.

I thought that since Baltimore was so close to Washington D.C., I should shoot some extra material for the film at the nation's capital. All I needed to do was to fly into D.C. instead of Baltimore the day before my appointments with my camera equipment, find an actor to do a few scenes and operate the camera when I was doing my shtick, and sneak around filming comedy scenes guerrilla-style (without permits).

The second part was easy to accomplish since a recent acting student, Ramsey Zeitouneh, had just finished law school at Vanderbilt and moved back to Baltimore. Ramsey was all in for being in the movie and helping out and, lucky for me, his sister lived in D.C., so Ramsey knew the city well.

268

Ramsey drove down from Baltimore, picked me up at the airport, and we set out to do some filming. We filmed the guerrilla filmmaker's way because I didn't have time to get permits from the city to film. We worked quickly and acted like tourists. My wardrobe for my character, Senator Albert Lincoln Endicott, was a Hawaiian shirt, so I definitely looked like a tourist.

We shot the biggest scenes with the Capitol Building in the background. We also shot scenes in front of the Dirksen Senate Office Building and the Lincoln Memorial.

We worked very fast and ended up doing way too much walking considering I still wasn't strong from my last surgery. I also had fluids draining from my body into large bandages. But I was a man on a mission who had only eight hours to film, drive to Baltimore, check into my hotel, and get some rest for the tests and consultations the next day.

Unfortunately, I forgot to drink water. Actually, I didn't forget, I had left a large bottle of water in Ramsey's car, but it was parked far from where we were filming; and the Capitol Building vicinity isn't exactly the place you find a 7-Eleven. I kept thinking we would be done soon and I would be back at the car, but we still needed to go to the Lincoln Memorial, where I wanted to shoot a goofy bit.

It was rush hour and not one available taxi in sight, so we decided to walk to the Lincoln Memorial. That was a huge mistake; it was much farther than we thought. At a certain point, there was no turning back.

But my bandages needed to be changed and it was extremely hot, with no water in sight.

I didn't tell Ramsey I was almost in crisis mode because I wanted to finish what I came to do. But he knew why I was headed to Johns Hopkins so he was concerned when he saw me dragging and getting short of breath.

I started having serious problems. My heart rate shot up to 160-180 beats per minute, when my normal walking heart rate would be around 100. I knew exactly what was happening and I had beta blockers to control it, but the medicine was in the car. This problem pops up if I get dehydrated. It had happened several times before, so I knew what to expect. Even with the medicine it would take two to four hours for my heart rate to come down. I didn't tell Ramsey about this because his parents are doctors and I knew he would probably call for help. That would end my mission.

We got the shots I wanted at the Lincoln Memorial and were very lucky to catch a cab as I was getting weaker and weaker. It would have been a big mistake to try to walk it.

Ramsey couldn't remember exactly where we were parked, but thought we were very close when he had the driver drop us off. Then we realized we were not close at all. My body was in crisis mode from dehydration; then suddenly, like a mirage in the distance, I saw a sketchy looking corner market two blocks away. I had just enough strength left to reach the market, dart in, and buy two large bottles of water. I downed one bottle quickly to combat my dehydration, but I was still in drastic need of my medicine. My heart rate had been very high for about an hour-and-a-half.

We stumbled around for about ten minutes before we found Ramsey's car. Once in the car, I grabbed my meds from my bag and downed it with the water I should have taken with me in the first place. Normally, I would have taken the water with me, but I had no way to carry it and all the camera gear. I had mistakenly thought there would be an abundance of places to buy water.

I felt good just knowing I was in a car, had hydrated, and taken my medication. Now, the question was how long it would be before my heart rate would go down. I felt safe in Ramsey's hands, even though he admitted he was not the best with directions. We had multiple GPS apps and went with Ramsey's gut feeling as to which app we should follow considering it was rush hour.

Google maps said a little over an hour, but for some reason it took us almost two hours to get to the Indigo Hotel in the Mount Vernon neighborhood of Baltimore. I felt like I was home since Michele and I had both spent many nights there when we were in town for tests and my last surgery. I paid Ramsey for his acting and insisted he take some money for driving down from Baltimore and taking me back to my hotel in Baltimore. He was great about everything and really didn't want to take any money for driving, but I insisted.

Once in the hotel, I took another half of a beta blocker since my heart was still racing. I rested on the bed for an hour before I did anything other than call Michele to let her know the shoot went well and I had made it safely back to the hotel. I didn't tell her I'd made a dangerous and stupid mistake by not carrying water. I was hoping I hadn't screwed up anything for my tests the next morning. By the time I was ready to sleep, my heart rate was better and I was able to get a fairly good rest.

Before the consultations with both surgeons the next morning, I had another CT scan, bloodwork, and the rest of the ritual I had become so accustomed to. The consults were pretty routine since they expected it to be a fairly simple surgery to close the channel that was carrying fluid to the surface. The appointment with Dr. B, my cancer surgeon, was a follow-up appointment for my previous surgery; he wouldn't be involved with the new surgery unless there was an unexpected problem. Dr. Sacks would perform the surgery since the drainage issue was related to the mesh he had used for my abdominal reconstruction.

Dr. Sacks said the surgery would be nothing like the other surgeries and the incision would probably only be two inches in length. That was nothing compared to the long incisions I had from the cancer surgeries. He was sure the surgery would resolve the issue. The surgery was schedule for August 10th, forty days away.

By the time August 10th rolled around, I was more than ready to have the surgery and stop wearing the large bandages. There was also the constant concern about possible infection in the open wound.

Michele and I flew into Baltimore-Washington International on the 9th and took an Uber as usual to The Indigo Hotel. We had a relaxing evening as I did my required pre-operative regimen. I was only allowed clear liquids that had no red or purple coloring the day before surgery. The goal is to clear the digestive system. I usually start eating very lightly a few days prior to surgery to make the prep work more efficient.

I was up at 4:00 A.M. to start getting ready to be at the hospital by 5:30. Not knowing exactly what condition I would be in after the surgery, I made sure I was caught up on email, texts, banking, and online bill payments before we left. I always make sure I have everything in order at home as well, just in case there is an unexpected negative outcome. Michele was up at 4:30 and ready by 5:15 to jump in the livery car we had reserved to take us to The Weinberg Building, the surgery center at Johns Hopkins Hospital, where I had my previous cancer surgery.

Check in was simple and they followed the same procedure as my previous surgery, where they quietly took us back to the pre-op area along with three other nervous patients and their family members. The tone was lighter this time since it wasn't a cancer surgery; but anything can happen, so they take all surgeries very seriously.

The next several steps were exactly the same as I described for my last surgery at Hopkins. Dr. B didn't come around since he wasn't expected to be involved in the surgery. As expected, my pre-op conversation with Dr. Sacks was fun and gave me confidence the outcome would be very good. Shortly after, I was given my first drowsy medication, I kissed Michele, and then I was rolled down the hallway to the OR.

I know I'm repeating my weirdness, but I love the time in the pre-op and especially the drowsy trip to the OR. I feel great, partially due to the medication, and also my love for hospitals and all the wonderful, caring people that work there. I'm very chatty. I feel incredibly safe. It's totally out of my control at that point: nothing to think about; no list of tasks to perform; no planning; no watching the clock; and nothing to worry about. I'm not worried about anything, and the possibility of dying doesn't really seem to bother me; maybe because I have so much confidence I will be OK.

In my heart, I believe I will know when it's really my time to go.

Chapter 62—Surprise! The Mesh Is A Mess

Waking up after the surgery felt very much like every other time: *La La Land*. It's my second favorite time when it comes to surgery, and very high up on the list for life as well. A nurse/angel gently whispers, "Alan, your surgery is over. How are you feeling? Your wife is waiting outside and we'll bring her back in just a few minutes."

When I was finally coherent, I was told the surgery ended up being very different and more complex than expected. Dr. Sacks had expected to go in with a small incision and close a channel that he believed was allowing the fluid to drain from my body. But once he opened me up, there was a big ugly surprise: he discovered the mesh used for my abdominal wall reconstruction was seriously infected. The infected mesh was the cause of the fluid production. It was necessary to make a much larger incision and remove all the infected mesh. I was left with virtually no abdominal support, just a large cavity covered by my sutured skin. It was not good news.

When I was told the bad news, I was still in my happy state from the anesthesia. I don't remember being overly upset about the turn of events. I also didn't realize the problems that would come along with this different outcome. I found out the next morning when two members of the surgical team came to see me.

They explained what had been revealed during my surgery and how the problem was addressed. I had only been told the basics in the recovery room. Basically, my artificial abdominal wall was an infected mess that had to be cut out. They had to deal with the infection right away before it got out of hand and spread throughout my body. That meant removing 90% of the mesh that had been holding me together.

Dr. Sacks was very surprised I hadn't developed a fever or serious abdominal pain considering the amount of infection that was present. He said my body had done an amazing job of protecting me from the infection. He wasn't willing to put the blame on the synthetic mesh or the pig dermis mesh but admitted one of the meshes may have caused the infection. We will never know.

The surgical procedure is technically called a torso debridement. Debridement is the removal of necrotic (dead) or infected skin tissue to help a wound heal. It's also done to remove foreign material from tissue. The procedure is essential for wounds that aren't getting better. Usually, these wounds are trapped in the first stage of healing.

They told me I would need to wear heavy six-inch wide elastic hernia bands around my waist and pelvic area to support my internal organs, except when I was sleeping and showering. I asked for how long.

"Forever," they said. "Or until you have a surgery to replace the infected mesh."

I was told I would be on antibiotics for weeks to rid my body of the infection. Replacing the mesh was not an option until the infection was gone for months. They said most people wouldn't have the mesh replaced since it would mean another major surgery; they would choose to live with the elastic bands and a large hernia bulge in the abdominal wall. I didn't want to live that way if I didn't have to. But I had some healing to do.

My energy was surprisingly good after this surgery even though I had another nine-inch incision over the top of the old one. I was allowed to eat real food pretty quickly and I was walking a lot on my own the morning after surgery, even before Michele arrived early in the morning. The nurses commented that they were surprised at how much energy I had and how much walking I was willing to do. I was on a mission to recover as fast as possible this time. The memories of the last recovery were fresh in my mind, and I refused to have an experience anywhere close to that one.

I also realized the sudden heart rate spiking issues I had been having for three months may have been caused by the infected mesh. My heart doctor never suggested that was a possible cause: he told me it was common and sometimes people just start having the issue. I will never be convinced that my body wasn't signaling me that there was trouble brewing in my abdominal cavity.

On day four, the surgical team decided I was doing so well it wouldn't be a risk for me to travel back to Nashville. We happily gathered my things at the hospital, packed up Michele at the hotel, booked last minute flights (expensive), ordered an Uber, and headed to the airport, knowing it wouldn't be my last trip to Johns Hopkins Hospital. I was so happy to be headed home with my lovely and super supportive wife.

I went back to Baltimore two weeks later for a follow-up exam. Dr.

Sacks said everything looked good, so I flew home a happy camper wrapped up tight with my elastic bands. While I was there, appointments were made for my next CT scan to make sure there were no new signs of cancer.

On September 28th, I did a "fly in and fly out" on the same day, managing to do my CT scan, my bloodwork, and even have a short, unscheduled meeting with Dr. Sacks. I texted him and told him I was at JHH for my CT scan and asked him if I could say hello. He said if I came to the family waiting room at the surgery center, he would come out of surgery to see me.

After a short wait, he came out with a very big smile on his face and pulled me into a consultation room to see how my incision was healing. He was very pleased with my progress and the results of his fine work. There was no sign of a hernia, but he wanted me to understand a hernia might develop from the lack of support. If a hernia developed, we would talk about options. I was so lucky to have had Dr. Sacks as my reconstructive/plastic surgeon.

Dr. Sacks even pulled strings to allow me to recover from my last two surgeries in the little-known Marburg Pavilion that is located in the historic Marburg Building of The Johns Hopkins Hospital. The Pavilion is more like a five-star luxury hotel than a hospital. There are only fourteen rooms at The Pavilion.

Two nurses at the hospital told me they had heard stories about it but didn't even know where it was. I think this is the way they wanted it. When they transported me to Marburg on a gurney, it seemed like we went a mile through multiple hallways and elevators. I had no idea what to expect at the end of the journey.

The first thing I noticed was the private and tastefully decorated elevator with ornate hardwood flooring and an Oriental rug. When the elevator door opened, it felt more like I was entering a mansion from the early 19th century than a floor in a hospital. The walls were adorned with tasteful artwork and the floors were artisan hardwood with Oriental rug runners.

My room was set up like a suite and was tastefully decorated with a small mahogany table and two Chippendale chairs for dining. The floors, cabinetry and entertainment center were all made from fine woods. The room had a fax machine and a DVD player.

The sheets and other bedding were not typical hotel sheets; they were high thread count and there was also a duvet. The only water I was ever given was FIJI water. Never did they bring water in a cup or a plastic container—always FIJI.

In the hallway there were always fresh-cut flowers, and the guest lounge served only Starbucks coffee, imported teas, fresh fruit, yogurt and healthy snacks at all times of the day and night.

Marburg is where the royalty from The United Arab Emirates reside when they come for specialized treatment. After all, they have invested billions in Johns Hopkins. They take the entire floor, the hallway is turned into a very long dining room, and the entourage and security stay on the floor as well. I found it intriguing to think of this as I strolled down the hallway with my IV tower, wearing my upgraded Marburg hospital gown and robe.

When I was there, only six of the fourteen rooms were occupied. I noticed in one of the rooms they were serving the patient dinner at the table with white linen and silver service. It was crazy.

There were no techs or LPNs at Marburg. Everyone was a registered nurse. Nurses did everything at Marburg.

It was a unique and special environment, and I found it very conducive to healing.

I will always remember the special care and attention Dr. Sacks gave me. We are still in touch to this day. How many extremely busy and talented surgeons would do what he did for me?

Chapter 63—My Stomach Is Growing A Head; Time For More Surgery

Two weeks after I returned from Baltimore, I noticed I was developing a large "bump" to the left of where my belly button used to be. It looked like a small grapefruit was starting to push up under my skin. It wasn't that noticeable at first but it increased in size pretty quickly.

I texted Dr. Sacks and he instructed me to take photos with my phone and send them to him. After seeing the photos, he told me it would get bigger, but it was not dangerous to my health. He said most people choose to live with it; but knowing I was an actor who wouldn't want to "just live with it," he said he would be willing to rebuild my abdominal wall again using different mesh, if I reached a point where I didn't want to deal with it. I reached that point very quickly. I was eager to fix the large hernia, but also didn't want to mess up our annual January anniversary trip to Cancun that we had taken every year since we were married. We also considered the possibility of bad winter weather conditions in the Baltimore area. After a consultation with Dr. Sacks, April 27th was picked as the magic day to repair my abdominal wall for hopefully the last time.

We flew in on April 26th for a pre-surgery consult with Sacks, another CT scan, bloodwork, etc. Everything looked good, so we were a go for surgery early the next morning.

I also had a consult with Dr. B the day before the surgery. It didn't go well. He tried to talk me out of the surgery, saying it was a ridiculous and dangerous thing to do. He said I should live with the hernia like so many of his patients had in the past. He was way out of line and too aggressive in his negativism.

I told him I felt positive about the surgery, had great confidence in Dr. Sacks, and I was not like any of his other patients. I was having the surgery no matter what he thought. He really had no power over the situation since it wasn't a cancer surgery. I wanted to say, "Shut up! This isn't your surgery, you egomaniac." Instead, I remained calm, but I didn't back off an inch. It never should have happened, but I didn't let him get in my head at all.

A surgeon should never try to undermine the confidence of a patient right before surgery, especially when they won't be the surgeon performing the surgery. He was only supposed to be available if something cancer- related popped up. I was told later that Dr. Sacks had a firm discussion with him and told him never to do it again.

I could almost cut and paste the routine from the last surgery at Johns Hopkins. Technically, the surgery was a "ventral hernia repair and flap revision/reconstruction." The surgery went well and I woke up in my happy place.

Three days later we were headed back to Nashville.

I was back in the gym within a week, starting the process of getting my strength back and putting on weight. It was a slow process and it forced me to have patience, which was never my greatest attribute. However, having done this four times, I was getting pretty good at it.

Chapter 64—What Now? Four Years Since My Last Surgery

I've had no problems with the mesh or my abdominal reconstruction in the four years since my last surgery at Johns Hopkins Hospital. I've had eight more CT scans (that makes a total of 29), two PET scans, an MRI of my brain, and too many blood workups.

I believe I had the greatest team I could have assembled to get me through my long and complex medical ordeal. I learned some great lessons about taking the time to find the right people for the job.

I give credit to Michele and a few medical professionals for helping me put together my all-star team of doctors, surgeons, and hospitals. During this process, I learned it's okay to say no to surgeons and hospitals that don't feel like the right fit for me. I have trusted my gut and it has paid off with years being added to my life.

I would also like to thank Michele's 7.5-pound silky terrier, Ali, for comforting me every time I was sick, down, or recovering. Ali would lay her little head on my leg or snuggle me whenever I was down physically or emotionally. I had never witnessed how dogs are sensitive to changes in their people and can often sense an illness before the person knows they're sick. If a person is infected with a virus or bacteria, chemicals are released that a dog can sense because they have fifty times the number of olfactory receptors in their noses than humans have. I believe she knew my mesh was infected before my surgery revealed the infection. Now, when Ali starts spending time beside me, I know something is brewing, because she doesn't do this unless there's something negative going on in my body.

I know I'm very lucky to be alive. I try to squeeze as much pleasure as I possibly can out of each day, knowing tomorrow is not guaranteed. I'm good for now.

I have TODAY…and all indications are that I will have tomorrow.

I'm a better and wiser person thanks to all I've been through. Cancer completely rewired my approach to life. I needed a slap in the face to realize just how lucky I've been all my life. I needed to show more appreciation and gratitude. And now I do.

Cancer was an awakening I desperately needed. As painful as it was, I am so grateful to have learned how truly valuable life is before I leave the planet.

I have become a much better listener to the voice in my head and The Universe. Is God the voice in my head?

Someday I will know, but for now I would have to say the answer is Yes.

THE END

Acknowledgements

Thanks to my friend and award-winning mystery writer, Steven Womack, for convincing me that what started out as a 660-page memoir written for my current and future family members would be a book that would help other cancer patients and survivors.

Steven, a member of the "Cancer Club" himself, consulted me all along the way in the difficult and painful task of removing 300 pages from my original manuscript. Steve's scalpel was precise yet gentle. I can't thank Steven enough for his guidance and friendship.

I would also like to thank Steven's brilliant wife, Shalynn, for coming up with the title for my book. She nailed it.

I would highly recommend you read Steven's Edgar award-winning Harry James Denton Music City Murders Series.

I need to thank all the brilliant surgeons, doctors, nurses, radiologists, anesthesiologists, phlebotomists, medical techs, hospital cleaning staffs, physical therapists, and my chiropractor for giving me the very best treatment and care possible.

I would like to single out Dr. Justin Sacks at Johns Hopkins Hospital. Justin is the oncological plastic & reconstructive surgeon who rebuilt my abdominal wall three different times. The man is a genius as well as a great guy who will answer my texts, even when he's getting ready for surgery. Without his surgical skills I would not be walking in a straight line or able to lead a normal life. I consider him a friend for life.

Dr. Margaret Sanders, my primary care doctor, has been with me for my full eleven year cancer journey. She has always been there to give me the best care and advice, pray for me, worry about me, remove stitches and other gross stuff, call an ambulance, hug me when I needed it, and be my health advocate when it was necessary. I am so grateful to you, my doctor and friend, Peggy Sanders.

Two nurses, Maria and Teresa, saved my life at 2:00 AM on February 23, 2017 at Johns Hopkins Hospital, when I had a major medical crisis. At one point, I thought, and I believe they thought the same, that they might be the last two faces I ever saw. It was a nightmare, but they kept their heads

281

and made all the right moves. I hope to find them someday and tell them that I will never forget that night and what they did to allow me to be here today.

I want to thank Dr. Keith Block and his caring staff at the Block Center for Integrative Cancer Treatment in Chicago for making my chemotherapy treatments more bearable and less toxic to my body. Comparing the chemotherapy treatments at the Block Center to most infusion facilities is like comparing a Ritz-Carlton to a Holiday Inn. I was not just a number at The Block Center.

Who would think I would have a student who was a very busy pathologist trained at Johns Hopkins in Baltimore. I have Stephanie Schreiner to thank for connecting me with the world-renowned surgical team at Johns Hopkins.

My entire family and close friends back in Illinois helped me keep my cancer surgeries and treatments a secret from my dear mother for seven years. In fragile health at the time, she would have worried herself to death had she known before her passing in 2018. Everyone deserves a Best Actor Award for their many years of keeping my secret.

I must thank Joshua and Denise Johnson, who came in as students but became indispensable team members over the last fourteen years. They helped me continue my teaching mission even during my many surgical recoveries and chemo treatments. They were always there to pick up the slack and help me disguise my limited strength and mobility in front of my students. I think we did a great job of faking everyone out, even when I was wearing a surgical drain and pump under my clothing. I so appreciate their caring and their friendship.

Over 4,000 students have passed through my classes over the last thirty years. They changed me and my life for the better. Even though I never planned to teach, it has been the most rewarding part of my professional life. Thank you to one and all for allowing me the great privilege of knowing, growing, and working with you.

Many teachers, agents, casting directors, managers, directors and producers have graced the classrooms of my school. Thanks to all for being participants in this amazing thirty year experiment of building a school for actors, singers, voice-over artists, speakers, preachers, politicians, executives, and people who just want to be a little braver.

My producing partners, Brad Wilson, Jamie Elliott, and Ralph Portillo made me a filmmaker. Over the past twenty years we have experienced so many wonderful times creating something from nothing. We have also experienced the extreme difficulties of getting a movie made. They have been there for me during my worst family and health crises, as I have been there for theirs. Friends to the end.

Finally, I would like to thank my entire family for their support and prayers. I love you all.